T0314174

MEASURING SOCIAL CHANGE

MEASURING SOCIAL CHANGE

Performance and Accountability in a Complex World

Alnoor Ebrahim

STANFORD BUSINESS BOOKS, AN IMPRINT OF STANFORD UNIVERSITY PRESS

Stanford, California

Stanford University Press

Stanford, California

© 2019 by the Board of Trustees of the Leland Stanford Junior University. All rights reserved.

Special discounts for bulk quantities of Stanford Business Books are available to corporations, professional associations, and other organizations. For details and discount information, contact the special sales department of Stanford University Press. Tel: (650) 725-0820, Fax: (650) 725-3457

Printed in the United States of America on acid-free, archival-quality paper

Library of Congress Cataloging-in-Publication Data

Names: Ebrahim, Alnoor, author.
Title: Measuring social change : performance and accountability in a
    complex world / Alnoor Ebrahim.
Description: Stanford, California : Stanford University Press, 2019. |
    Includes bibliographical references and index.
Identifiers: LCCN 2018060866 (print) | LCCN 2019001436 (ebook) |
    ISBN 9781503609211 (e-book) | ISBN 9781503601406 (cloth : alk. paper)
Subjects: LCSH: Nonprofit organizations—Evaluation. | Social entrepreneurship—
    Evaluation. | Organizational effectiveness—Measurement. | Social change—
    Evaluation.
Classification: LCC HD62.6 (ebook) | LCC HD62.6 .E277 2019 (print) |
    DDC 361.7068/4—dc23
LC record available athttps://lccn.loc.gov/2018060866

Cover design: Michel Vrana

Cover illustration: Plate XIV–1 from *Interaction of Color*, 50th Anniversary Edition, by Josef Albers, courtesy of Yale University Press.

Typeset by Newgen in 11.25/15 Baskerville

for Shirin and Sadrudin
beyond measure

CONTENTS

ACKNOWLEDGMENTS

For their inspiration and relentless pursuit of social change, I am indebted to the many leaders and staff of the organizations profiled in this book, particularly Marty Chen, Naresh Jain, Niraj Joshi, Ravi Krishna, Shaffi Mather, Apoorva Oza, Naveen Patidar, Vasim Qureshi, Adam Rocap, Scott Schenkelberg, and Joann Vanek. Thank you for sharing your experiences in the interest of advancing the sector, and for your time and patience with me as I shaped this project over many years.

Three extraordinary colleagues have been sparring partners on key ideas: Kash Rangan at Harvard University, Gerhard Speckbacher at the Vienna University of Economics and Business, and Paul Brest at Stanford University. A special thanks to David Gergen and Jeff Walker for encouraging this project and its vision.

Several excellent research assistants helped during different stages of this book. Vidhya Muthuram was indispensable with interviews, data collection, and early drafts of the case studies in India, going above and beyond the call of duty to track down quotes and materials. David Forte assisted with the US interviews and cases, Nashwa Khalid with graphics, and Floor de Ruijter van Steveninck with the resource appendix.

Harvard Business School supported my field research, and the Fletcher School of Law and Diplomacy gave me the space and time to write.

For their intellectual engagement and insights, I am grateful to Lehn Benjamin, Dave Brown, Julia Coffman, Peter Frumkin, Joe Galaskiewicz, Mary Kay Gugerty, Sherine Jayawickrama, Matt Lee,

David Lewis, Johanna Mair, Chris Marquis, Mark Moore, Alex Nicholls, Len Ortolano, Woody Powell, Patricia Rogers, Christian Seelos, Steven Rathgeb Smith, Melissa Stone, Peter Uvin, and Julie Boatright Wilson.

I also wish to thank many leaders in the social sector whose work has been a constant source of motivation: Tom Adams, Clara Barby, Jonathan Bloom, David Bonbright, Jeff Bradach, Sir Ronald Cohen, Sasha Dichter, Sarah Gelfand, Lisa Jordan, Kelly McCarthy, Katherine Milligan, Mario Morino, Jeremy Nicholls, Luther Ragin, Khalil Shariff, Nan Stone, Tom Tierney, Brian Trelstad, Michael Weinstein, and Peter Wuffli.

At both the Fletcher School and the Tisch College of Civic Life at Tufts University, I am grateful to have many colleagues committed to research on social change, and to imparting our students with the global outlook and skills to be active agents of change. For their support, I thank Steven Block, Bhaskar Chakravorti, Peter Levine, and both of my deans, Admiral James Stavridis and Ambassador Alan Solomont.

A spot in my heart is reserved for my wonderful students at Fletcher, whose engagement with a draft version of this book was everything a teacher could want: incisive, constructive, and fresh. You brought joy to the classroom and to the arduous work of scholarship, and you inspire hope for the future of our precious world.

In bringing this book to fruition, I have been fortunate to work with two fantastic editors at Stanford University Press—Margo Beth Fleming, with whom I started this book, and Steve Catalano, with whom I completed it—with the able editorial assistance of Olivia Bartz, Nora Spiegel, and Sunna Juhn, project management by Charlie Clark, copyediting by Kristine Hunt, and the immensely helpful feedback from reviewers.

In the end, none of this would have been possible, or even worthwhile, without the trinity of poetry, friendship, and family. The works of Seamus Heaney and Tomas Tranströmer have been anchors. To Michel Anteby, Julie Battilana, Lakshmi Ramarajan, Marion Fremont-Smith, Jane Nelson, E. M. Shashidharan, and to your families, I am forever grateful. To Edward and Lisabeth Weisband, from you I have learned what it means to put love into one's teaching and art, that is, to merge the hidden and the visible in our lives. I think often about my first teacher, my late aunt Zarin, who taught my siblings and me to embrace the English language as our own, and who understood the long-term impact of early childhood education before it was formally measured. And to my siblings—Ezmina, Yasmin, Amin, and your families—thank you for always being there, rock solid and wonderful.

The word *gratitude* feels so inadequate for describing the all given by Maria, my wife and dearest friend. Chef extraordinaire, intellectual partner, and editorial eagle-eye are better descriptors but still don't hold a candle to you. All I can say is I promise to be your sous chef for life.

And finally, my parents Shirin and Sadrudin, who embody the spirit of social change in their daily lives, and who traversed continents, risking everything, to give their children better lives—this book is dedicated to you.

MEASURING SOCIAL CHANGE

INTRODUCTION

THE IDEA FOR THIS BOOK crystallized on an icy winter day in Ottawa. I was attending a meeting with representatives of the bilateral aid agencies from six countries—Canada, Denmark, The Netherlands, Norway, Sweden, and the United Kingdom—all of whom were under pressure from their governments to demonstrate value for taxpayer money allocated to international development. Collectively, they had funded hundreds, if not thousands, of civil society organizations around the world on social issues as diverse as poverty alleviation, the environment, education, health care, and agricultural development.

I had been invited to suggest a methodology for assessing how much social benefit their investments had produced. But as the discussions with these senior managers progressed, it became increasingly clear that existing tools for measuring social performance fell far short of addressing their complex needs and constraints. It was at this meeting that I first probed a new approach to measurement that would eventually become this book.

Leaders across the social sector—in nonprofit and nongovernmental organizations, social enterprises, international aid agencies, philanthropic foundations, and impact investors—have long struggled with how to measure social change. Unlike assessing the performance of a business, there is no common currency of measurement. Money is typically a means rather than an end. Results are not easily comparable across organizations with diverse social goals such as fighting poverty, improving public health, reducing climate change, or advancing human rights. And time horizons are long, sometimes taking years or even a generation to bear results.

The significance of this challenge has only grown as the sector has burgeoned in revenue and size. In the United States alone, there are over 1.5 million registered nonprofit organizations accounting for over $2 trillion in annual revenues.[1] In addition, the rapidly emerging global impact investing industry represents a market of several hundred billion dollars.[2] And for a new generation of donors and investors, allocating money to a worthy cause is no longer sufficient—measurable results are essential.

Over the past decade, I have had the good fortune of engaging with hundreds of leaders in the sector on these challenges through executive education at the Harvard Business School, Harvard Kennedy School, and the Fletcher School of Law and Diplomacy. I have also worked closely with practitioners on a working group established by the G8 to create global guidelines on measuring social impact, and through advisory roles with impact investors and industry associations such as the Global Impact Investing Network. These experiences have shaped my thinking and the research in this book.

In the pages that follow, I tackle three main challenges of performance common across the social sector: *what to measure*, what kinds of *performance measurement and management systems* to build, and how to align multiple demands for *accountability*. Over the past ten years, the sector has become consumed by the mantras of "impact" and "accountability"—an expectation that organizations must be held to account for their performance in solving difficult social problems. A growing body of literature has emerged to help managers to clarify their models of cause and effect (theory of change), to develop indicators along that causal path (logic models), and to conduct rigorous assessments of their interventions (impact evaluation). This work has no doubt advanced the field.

But the push for impact is also underpinned by unquestioned assumptions: that long-term outcomes are more valuable than short-term outputs, that clarity about cause and effect is a precondition to good strategy, and that everyone can agree on what constitutes good performance. On the face of it, these are rational expectations about performance fueled by an increasingly competitive funding environment. After all, who could object to payment based on solid evidence of performance? Yet, in a world of messy problems that lack straightforward solutions, there remains a substantial gap between expectations and reality.

Unambiguous evidence of cause and effect turns out to be rare in the arena of social change, and most managers have neither the expertise nor the resources to parse the social science research (about which scientists themselves often disagree). They are busy building their organizations in resource-constrained environments, and need information to help them with decisions today, not years down the road. Moreover, rarely can a single organization address a social problem by itself, as it typically lacks control over the various factors affecting an outcome. Yet, if it collaborates with others, it runs into the problem of how to isolate, measure, and claim credit for the impacts of its own work, especially when trying to convince potential funders to invest in it.

To unpack these challenges, I take a "contingency" approach to measurement—in which *what one measures* depends on a set of practical conditions or constraints experienced by the organization. What are the conditions under which it might make more sense to focus on short-term results, and others where the long-term is essential? What results can an organization reasonably measure, and legitimately take credit for, when it operates in an ecosystem of many other actors? These questions bear the mark of contingency. To address them, I untangle a pair of constraints widely experienced by social sector organizations: *uncertainty* about cause-effect knowledge for addressing a social problem and limited *control* over the activities and conditions necessary for producing long-term outcomes. Based on these contingencies,

I develop a framework for guiding managers in deciding what they should measure.

Building on this framing, I then identify the types of *performance measurement and management systems* (henceforth referred to as *performance systems*) best suited to different types of organizations. Put simply, different organizations need different types of performance systems. For instance, a provider of emergency medical services needs a performance system focused on quality control and standardization, whereas an advocacy organization needs a system that enables constant adaptation to changes in its policy environment. Drawing on a series of in-depth case studies, I identify four key types of performance systems, and I provide a basis for managers to decide what type of system might best fit their needs.

This book also unpacks a third closely related challenge: the dilemma of *multiple accountabilities*. Even when organizations have reliable measures of their social performance, those measures are unlikely to satisfy key stakeholders when their interests are divergent or in conflict. Such stakeholders may include various funders, regulators, and even different types of clients or beneficiaries. Social sector leaders often speak with exasperation about the many demands for accountability they face, as though caught in a web, struggling in many directions but getting nowhere. Their key task, however, is not to be more accountable to everyone for everything but rather to align and prioritize among competing accountability demands. The structural problem is that "upward" accountability to funders tends to be well developed for the simple reason that funders control resources, whereas means of "downward" accountability that give voice and influence to clients or beneficiaries are typically weak. It thus falls upon social sector leaders to be clear about their accountability priorities and to design their performance systems accordingly. They are not simply on the receiving end of accountability, but have agency in shaping its terms.

These broad themes at the heart of this book—what to measure, what kinds of performance systems to build, and how to set the terms of accountability—point to a couple of fundamentally different views on the purpose of performance measurement. The first is to enable better organizational decision making. In serving this purpose, measurement is seen as a rational-technical process that develops objective metrics and procedures for achieving organizational goals. It enables midcourse corrections (monitoring) while also assessing progress (evaluation), through instruments such as logic models, scorecards, and randomized control trials. This function of measurement appeals to the agent of change in each of us who wishes to use information to make better decisions and, consequently, to deliver better results for society. This approach to performance measurement is consistent with the predominant literature on strategy and outcome management, and it is the primary perspective adopted in this book.

But at the same time, as anthropologists and sociologists have shown, measurement is hardly a purely rational endeavor. It is an act of social construction, where metrics are imbued with the values of actors, signaling what is important and what is not.[3] The challenge of multiple accountabilities arises from this aspect of measurement, where stakeholders apply varying yardsticks to judging the performance of an organization, often perceiving its worth differently. It is thus not uncommon for organizations to tailor their metrics and communications to their stakeholders in an effort to secure not just funding but social legitimacy. Accountability, as such, is a relationship of power; it does not stand objectively apart from the expectations and demands of external actors. Social sector leaders must understand both of these roles of measurement, rational and social, in building their performance systems.

Structure of this Book

The first chapter provides the conceptual foundation for the book, introducing a framework based on the two contingent factors that managers must understand in developing their performance systems: uncertainty about cause-effect, and control over outcomes. These two factors provide a basis for differentiating among four types of social change strategies: niche, integrated, emergent, and ecosystem strategies. The key managerial implication is that each type of strategy requires a distinct type of performance system.

The ensuing four chapters use case studies to illustrate and develop each of these strategy types and their attendant performance systems. Chapter 2 examines a *niche strategy* in an emergency medical response service, where the relationship between cause and effect is relatively well understood, but there is low control over long-term outcomes. This strategy requires a performance system based on *standardization* to produce outputs of reliable quality. The broader value of this case lies in its illumination of the key features of a performance system needed by any organization with a niche strategy. Following a similar logic, Chapter 3 considers an *integrated strategy* in rural agricultural development, where the relationships between cause and effect are relatively well understood but where multiple interventions must be combined in order to produce long-term outcomes. This strategy requires a performance system based on *coordination* to produce, prioritize, and sequence outputs that generate interdependent outcomes.

Chapters 4 and 5 move on to organizational contexts where relationships about cause and effect are poorly understood or complex, typically involving many moving parts and players. The first of these chapters examines an *emergent strategy* in global policy advocacy work, where an organization's ability to control policy outcomes is severely constrained. This strategy requires a performance system based on *adaptation* that allows the organization to recognize and take advantage of new opportunities to influence key actors within its system. Chapter 5 turns to an *ecosystem strategy* in addressing urban homelessness where, although cause-effect relationships are complex, it is possible to increase control over outcomes by aligning the work of many interdependent actors. This strategy requires a performance system based on *orchestration* that restructures relationships among key players in a system in order to generate joint outcomes.

Chapter 6 brings together the key insights, synthesizing the learning from the case studies and revisiting key questions in the book:

What should an organization measure? What kinds of performance systems best fit its needs? What should be its accountability priorities? I provide a side-by-side comparison of the performance systems used in each of the cases, identifying not only what they have in common, but also how they differ in fundamental ways. This analysis leads to a typology of distinct performance systems, each suited to supporting one of the four strategies noted above.

Finally, in Chapter 7, I turn to the roles of funders in supporting performance measurement and management. Funders, be they grant makers or investors, have the potential to help or hinder the organizations they support. Leaders of nonprofits and social enterprises often complain that their funders expect rigorous monitoring and evaluation of performance but are rarely willing to support it. There are exceptions, of course, and I draw on the experiences of three innovators—an impact investor, a grant-making foundation, and a bilateral aid agency—to illustrate the critical roles that funders can play in enabling better performance measurement, not only within their own portfolios but also in raising the bar among their peers. I distinguish between different stages of funder decision making—search, diligence, improvement, and evaluation—to show that each stage requires a different toolkit for performance measurement. The experiences of these pioneering funders also demonstrate how measurement can help to close the gap between upward accountability to funders and downward accountability to clients or beneficiaries.

This concluding chapter also highlights the measurement challenges that funders face, not only in comparing the performance of one grantee or investee to another, but also in assessing their aggregate performance as a portfolio. I argue that funders are much better positioned than their investees to achieving social impacts at a system level. Because they support and oversee many, sometimes hundreds, of nonprofits and social enterprises that typically act independently of one another, funders are poised to connect and leverage the combined impact of that work. Few funders have risen to this strategic challenge, but they are uniquely situated in the organizational ecosystem to do so.

In a world beset by enormous social challenges, there is an urgent need to measure and improve the social performance of organizations, be they public, private, or nonprofit. Pressures on managers to be clear about results, and on investors to allocate capital based on social performance, will only increase. This book articulates a pluralistic rather than a singular model of performance measurement. I hope it will enable social sector leaders to be clear about what they aim to achieve, to be realistic about the constraints they face, and ultimately to have the courage to set their own terms of accountability.

Chapter 1

CONCEPTUALIZING SOCIAL PERFORMANCE IN A COMPLEX WORLD

> We will need to give up childish fantasies that we can have total guarantees of others' performance. We will need to free professionals and the public service to serve the public. We will need to work towards more intelligent forms of accountability.
>
> ONORA O'NEILL (2002)

IN A SERIES OF LECTURES on BBC radio, the Cambridge philosopher Onora O'Neill offered a provocative take on accountability in public service. She argued that efforts to improve the performance of public service providers, be they doctors or teachers or police officers, had a dark side: they were leading to a compliance-driven culture focused on rule-following behavior and quantitative targets rather than actually improving performance (O'Neill 2002). Her apprehensions can be extended to the social sector more broadly, including nonprofit organizations and social enterprises, where the mantras of "accountability" and "impact" have been ascendant for over a decade. Yet, despite the proliferation of reporting requirements, measurement procedures, and auditing rituals, there is limited evidence that performance in the sector has substantially improved (Ebrahim and Weisband 2007; Espeland and Stevens 2008; Hwang and Powell 2009; Lewis and Madon 2003; Power 1999).

What then might meaningful performance measurement based on "intelligent forms of accountability" look like? The purpose of this chapter is to provide a way of thinking about performance and accountability that is strategy driven rather than compliance driven. I develop a pair of frameworks that enables social sector leaders to clarify what they realistically can and cannot achieve through their organizations, while simultaneously providing a basis for holding their own feet to the fire. In other words, the frameworks are devices that managers can use to specify their own terms of accountability.

This chapter is divided into two main parts. First, I provide a brief introduction to the foundations of organizational performance assessment, drawing from the literatures in business and nonprofit management, program evaluation, and development studies. I also take a closer look at the approaches to performance and impact measurement used in two practitioner communities: philanthropic foundations, impact investors, and nonprofit organizations (NPOs) based primarily in the United States; and organizations working in the field of international development such as bilateral aid agencies and nongovernmental organizations (NGOs). These two communities are in the midst of starkly parallel dilemmas about impact measurement and accountability, although they operate almost independently. I identify the ongoing concerns about performance measurement in both communities, devoting special attention to the uses and limitations of "logic models" that have been foundational to both.

In the second half of the chapter, I build on this analysis to develop two frameworks for measuring and improving social performance. The first is a general model of social sector performance comprising three core components: an organization's value proposition, its model of social change, and its accountability priorities. All organizations need to be clear about these components if they are to make systematic and measurable progress in addressing social problems.

I then build on this general model to develop a more nuanced "contingency framework" for social performance. I argue that what an organization should measure, and consequently should be held accountable for, depends on two key factors that vary from organization to organization: *uncertainty* about cause and effect, and *control* over outcomes. The framework offers a strategic basis for deciding what to measure, while recognizing the difficult constraints facing managers in impacting social problems. This contingency approach suggests that—given the varied work, aims, and environments of social sector organizations—some organizations should be measuring long-term outcomes while others would be better off focusing on short-term outputs. More importantly, I offer a logic for determining which kinds of measures are appropriate, given not only the organization's goals but also its position within a larger ecosystem of actors.

My normative argument, embedded in this contingency framework, is that it is not feasible or even desirable for all organizations to develop metrics that run the full gamut from outputs to societal outcomes. The more important challenge is one of aligning measurement with goals and strategy, especially the goals that an organization can reasonably control or influence. I contend that organizational efforts extending beyond this scope are a misallocation of scarce resources. For many social sector leaders, there is a temptation to overreach, to claim credit for social changes that may be beyond their actual control, in order to secure funding and social legitimacy. The challenge for managers is to be more realistic and grounded in framing the performance of their organizations, and thus to better achieve goals within their control.

Some readers will no doubt be troubled by my argument that not all social sector organizations should be measuring long-term outcomes and impacts. After all, if they don't measure outcomes, how will we ever know if they are making a difference? This reasoning fails to recognize that social change is contingent on many factors—that organizations vary in their goals, their knowledge about cause and effect, and in their interdependence with other actors in their ecosystems. The purpose of a contingency framing of social performance is to unpack these differentiating features, so that managers can be realistic about what they aim to achieve and then measure and improve performance accordingly.

Conceptual Foundations

Much of the current writing on the performance of organizations is rooted in the vast literature on organizational effectiveness, which has long identified three basic types of indicators for judging organizational performance: outcomes, processes, and structures (Goodman and Pennings 1977; Scott 1977; Suchman 1967). Outcomes are forward-looking measures in that they are the results predicted from a set of outputs such as goods or services; processes are measures of effort that focus on inputs and activities carried out by organizations; and structural indicators assess the capacity of an organization to perform work. Of these three types of indicators, organizational sociologists have noted that outcomes are often considered "the quintessential indicators of effectiveness, but they also may present serious problems of interpretation" such as inadequate knowledge of cause and effect, the time periods required to observe results, and environmental characteristics beyond the control of the organization such as market conditions or receptivity of external stakeholders (Scott 1992, 354).

The vast literature on organizational performance and effectiveness appears to converge on one key insight: there are rarely any singular and unambiguous measures of success in organizations. Even in for-profit firms, where it is tempting to assume that outcome metrics are unambiguous because of the profit motive, this turns out rarely to be the case. Meyer (2002; Meyer and Gupta 1994) identifies four broad types of measures common in profit-making businesses: valuation of the firm in capital markets, accounting measures, nonfinancial measures, and cost measures. Not only is there no single measure that is adequate for measuring firm performance, but some metrics can even point in opposite directions.

For example, key accounting measures (such as return on investment, return on assets, cash flows, and other measures of sales and profit) are not necessarily correlated with market measures (such as market value, return on equity, and change in share prices). It is not uncommon for a firm that fails to turn a profit to nonetheless see an uptick in its share price, or for a firm that makes considerable short-term profit to lose the confidence of long-term investors. In short, firms tend to use multiple performance measures simultaneously, with the value of these different measures resting in the fact that they don't correlate with one another—a characteristic that Meyer (2002; Meyer and Gupta 1994) has called the "performance paradox"—for if the measures did correlate, it would be possible to rely on a single roll-up metric. The main point here is that even in a sector where there is general convergence around profit, there is a need for multiple simultaneous measures in order to judge performance.

These challenges are even more pronounced and complex in the social sector (Ebrahim and Rangan 2014; Stone and Cutcher-Gershenfeld 2001). Financial measures are generally treated as an input rather than an outcome, and there is wide variation across industries on what constitutes a valuable outcome (Anthony and Young 2004; Oster 1995). Nonprofit ratings agencies that have traditionally relied on efficiency ratios such as program-to-administration expenses for rating performance are now widely criticized even by their advocates for being too narrow and misleading (Philanthropy Action 2009). A primary metrics challenge remains in establishing reliable and comparable nonfinancial measures. While there appears to be a growing convergence around the notion of "impact" as the ultimate nonfinancial measure of performance, there remains considerable ambiguity around how to operationalize it and whether it helps or hinders organizations in managing performance.

Moreover, because ownership is generally less clear in nonprofits and hybrid social enterprises than it is in for-profit firms, this can lead to demands for accountability and reporting from multiple funders (such as foundations, private investors, government agencies, and individual donors) and varying expectations about performance from clients, communities, regulators, taxpayers, and their own staff and boards (Edwards and Hulme 1996b; Kearns 1996; Lindenberg and Bryant 2001; Najam 1996a; Oster 1995). Some scholars have suggested that there are as many types of accountability as there are distinct relationships among people and organizations (Lerner and Tetlock 1999), characterizing the pronounced nature of this condition in social sector organizations as "multiple accountabilities disorder" (Koppell 2005).

Despite these many challenges, there have been important advances in the social sciences on the measurement of social performance. To anchor our discussion of these developments, I draw on a long tradition of research in program evaluation that offers a body of theory and methods for the design and assessment of social programs (e.g., Bickman 1987; McLaughlin and Jordan 1999; Rogers 2007; Weiss 1972). A foundational body of work in evaluation research is "program theory," which provides a basis for conceptualizing, designing, and explicating social programs; for understanding the causal linkages (if-then relationships) between program processes and outcomes; and for diagnosing the causes of trouble or success (Blalock 1999; Funnell 1997; Rogers 2008; Rogers et al. 2000). Program theory may be seen as a method of applied social science research (Lindgren 2001) that allows for empirical testing of hypotheses embedded in any social program and thereby for advancing knowledge on the validity of program hypotheses in real-life environments (Chen 1990; Greene 1999; Weiss 1995).

A specific manifestation of program theory, the so-called logic model or "results chain," has emerged as a dominant instrument through which organizations in the social sector identify their social performance metrics. Figure 1.1 depicts the key components of the logic model—inputs, activities, outputs, individual outcomes, and societal outcomes—including examples of the types of measures under each step. The direction of arrows in the figure, from left to right, emphasize the predictive, or propositional, aspect of the model and the measurement of performance as far down the chain as possible, in order not only to capture the causes (inputs and activities) and immediate goods or services delivered by an organization (outputs) but also to assess their long-term effects on the lives of individuals and communities or societies (outcomes).

The term *impact* has become part of the everyday lexicon of social sector funders in recent years, with frequent references to "high-

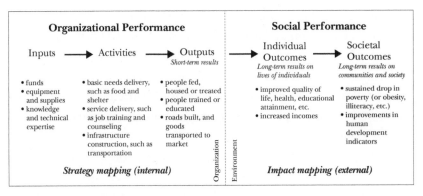

FIGURE 1.1 Logic Model and Results Mapping

impact nonprofits" or "impact philanthropy" and "impact on steroids" (Brest, Harvey, and Low 2009; Morino 2011; Tierney and Fleishman 2011). But the term has not been consistently defined. An established literature in international development and evaluation often uses the term to refer to "significant or lasting changes in people's lives, brought about by a given action or series of actions" (Roche 1999, 21) or results that target the "root causes" of a social problem (Crutchfield and Grant 2008, 24). A widely used, if expansive, definition adopted by many international aid agencies explains impact as "the positive and negative, primary and secondary long-term effects produced by a development intervention, directly or indirectly, intended or unintended" (Leeuw and Vaessen 2009, ix).

What most of these definitions share is an emphasis on causality—changes *brought about by* actions or effects *produced by* an intervention—suggesting that it is not sufficient to simply assess what happened after an intervention, but rather to assess whether those effects or changes can be causally linked to it (Brest and Harvey 2018; Jones 2009; White 2006). As such, an impact is the "difference made" by an intervention, be it short term or long term, and it may arise at individual, community, or societal levels. Many definitions, however, use the term *impact* to refer only to long-term societal changes. For example, a number of manuals on logic models describe impacts as occurring at the level of organizations, communities, or systems after a period of many years (e.g., Knowlton and Phillips 2013, 38; W. K. Kellogg Foundation 2004, 2). In this book I opt for the former usage, reserving the term *impact* to mean the changes produced, or difference made, by an intervention or set of interventions. It is up to the organization to specify the nature of that impact—short term or long term, on individuals or society—and then to measure accordingly.[1]

In order to identify their intended impacts, both short and long term, social sector organizations have increasingly turned to logic models and their variations such as logical framework analysis (LFA). The use of these instruments is often required by funders, and they have been diffused by a global industry of international development professionals, particularly professional evaluators employed by bilateral aid agencies and multilateral development banks (Roche 1999, 18–20), as well as by private philanthropic foundations seeking to measure the impacts of their grantmaking and to be more strategic about their giving (Brest 2012; Frumkin 2006; Morino 2011; Porter and Kramer 1999; Tierney and Fleishman 2011).

Although the logic model has emerged as a dominant instrument for clarifying metrics of social performance, using it as a planning tool is far from straightforward. Its utility is constrained by the complex and often poorly understood nature of cause-effect relationships for achieving social results. A major challenge in using the logic model for measuring performance is that it implicitly contains two causal chains, with the dividing line being at outputs or the organizational boundary, as represented by the dotted vertical line in Figure 1.1. On the left-hand side of the figure (inputs, activities, outputs), results are largely within the organization's control, and the causal logic is determined by strategic decisions on how to produce products or services. In elaborating this part of the results chain—organizational performance— the task facing social sector organizations is largely similar to that facing for-profit organizations. However, social sector organizations confront the additional challenge of establishing cause-effect relationships that occur *outside* their organizational boundaries—social performance—where organizational level activities and outputs (causes) are expected to lead to outcomes on the lives of beneficiaries and society (effects).

The mapping of cause-effect relationships is, of course, also important to profit-seeking firms.[2] In particular, cause-effect relationships are integral to "balanced scorecards" that map causal relationships between the objectives and activities necessary for executing a strategy (Kaplan and Norton 1996, 2004). However, the cause-effect relations mapped by these concepts and tools are primarily internal to the organization (the left half of Figure 1.1) for establishing a pathway from activities to organizational-level results (Nørreklit 2000, 2003; Speckbacher, Bischof, and Pfeiffer 2003) rather than societal-level results. And although the concept of the balanced scorecard has been extended to social sector activities (Kaplan 2001), it has not been adapted to include the more complex cause-effect relations between outputs and outcomes that typically arise outside of organizational boundaries.[3]

In short, social sector organizations require attention to two cause-effect chains subsumed within the logic model: (1) a "strategy map" that links inputs and activities to outputs within the organization, comparable to those used by for-profit businesses; and (2) an "impact map" that links outputs to outcomes for assessing social performance. It is these complex causal logics of how organizational level results (outputs) transform into social change (outcomes) that are at the heart of the vexing challenges for performance measurement and accountability in the social sector.

Before elaborating a measurement framework that begins to address this challenge, it is useful to take stock of the current state of measurement practice. The experience of practitioner communities offers important insights for developing conceptual frameworks relevant to managerial decision making.

The Current State of Measurement Practice

Variations of the logic model and outcome management have become increasingly common in two practitioner communities that I discuss here: philanthropic foundations and impact investors seeking to allocate their resources effectively, and international development organizations such as bilateral government agencies and nongovernmental organizations seeking to improve accountability and "value for money" in development aid. These two practitioner communities are at the epicenter of current debates and innovations in social performance. The academic literature in management, nonprofit studies, and philanthropy lags behind in providing theoretical and analytical insights to this growing field of practice. Because of the vastness and diversity of the social sector, I focus the discussion below on organizations working mostly in the field of poverty alleviation. This field is wide but well established, with an increasingly coherent set of debates on performance measurement.

Impact measurement debates have taken center stage in the world of American private philanthropy as foundations have placed renewed emphasis on measuring the impacts of their grantmaking and thinking more strategically about their giving (Frumkin 2006; Porter and Kramer 1999). This spirit of "smart philanthropy" was captured by Paul Brest and Hal Harvey during their tenure as presidents, respectively, of the Hewlett Foundation and the ClimateWorks Foundation:

> [A]ccomplishing philanthropic goals requires having great clarity about what those goals are and specifying indicators of success before beginning a philanthropic project. . . . This, in turn, requires an empirical, evidence-based understanding of the external world in which the plan will operate. And it requires attending carefully to milestones to determine whether you are on the path to success with a keen eye for signals that call for midcourse corrections. These factors are the necessary parts of what we regard as the essential core of strategic philanthropy—the concern with *impact.* (Brest and Harvey 2008, 7, emphasis in the original)

This concern with impact has fueled efforts to quantify it in order to allocate funding among competing possibilities—what Brest and Harvey have called "impact on steroids." And it has attracted considerable attention in the burgeoning field of impact investing, characterized by investors that intentionally target social and financial objectives and seek to measure the achievement of both (OECD 2015; Social Impact Investment Taskforce 2014).

But this attention from a growing set of foundations and investors is not the only driver of the attention to outcomes and impacts. Over the past two decades, nonprofits have come under increasing governmental scrutiny to demonstrate results and to improve accountability to the public, particularly when they are involved in public sector contracting (Krauskopf and Chen 2010; Smith 1999; Smith and Lipsky 1993). The Government Performance and Results Act of 1993 led many state agencies to develop milestones and adopt performance-based contracts with service providers, including nonprofit agencies, as part of broader efforts to "reinvent government" (Behn 2001; Poister 2003, xv). In a report to the U.S. Congress, and motivated by concerns raised by the U.S. Senate Finance Committee in the wake of the Sarbanes-Oxley legislation, the independent Panel on the Nonprofit Sector recommended that every charitable organization should "provide more detailed information about its operations, including methods it uses to evaluate the outcomes of its programs, to the public through its annual report, website, and other means" (Panel on the Nonprofit Sector 2005, 5, 37).

The most recent manifestation of this movement towards performance-based public funding is known as pay-for-success (PFS), an umbrella term for a wide range of mechanisms that typically involve partnerships between governments and private investors to finance social service providers based on performance. Among the mechanisms that have attracted the most attention are social impact bonds (SIBs) and development impact bonds (DIBs), in which private investors provide upfront capital for a social program, nonprofit organizations deliver it, and the government repays the investors with a rate of return only if the program meets prespecified performance targets.[4] Early research suggests that SIBs are best suited to a fairly limited set of circumstances—where there is clear evidence of performance, coupled with a potential for substantial savings to public agencies—with much of the upfront capital coming from philanthropy rather than private investors (Berlin 2016; Chamberlin 2018; Rangan and Chase 2015). Better evidence on the effectiveness and suitability of these mechanisms will become available over the next decade; as of early 2018, over one hundred impact bonds had been launched worldwide in sectors as diverse as health care, employment, agriculture, education, and social welfare, with results expected in over the next several years (Dear et al. 2016; Gustafsson-Wright et al. 2017; Shumway, Segal, and Etzel 2018). What is clear, however, is that the future of PFS will hinge on robust performance measurement—on setting metrics that accurately capture desired social outputs or outcomes, and in negotiating performance benchmarks among the contracting parties.

Performance measurement has a considerably longer history in the field of international development, where it is generally divided into impact evaluation (IE), and monitoring and evaluation (M&E). The former, as the nomenclature suggests, typically refers to the assessment of end results or impacts, while the latter is oriented towards informing midcourse correction by tracking the progress of a project or program. Since the 1950s, the international development field has seen various approaches to IE and M&E come in and out of fashion, with logic models and frameworks having become ubiquitous in the past forty years (Roche 1999, 18–20), diffused by a global industry of international development professionals, particularly consultants and evaluators employed by bilateral aid agencies and multilateral development institutions.

The use of logic models in particular, and program and project evaluation more broadly, has been spread in part by national governments and their development arms. These actors include bilateral aid agencies such as the United States Agency for International Development (USAID) or the United Kingdom's Department for International Development (DfID) and their counterparts elsewhere, as well as by multilateral institutions such as the World Bank and various agencies of United Nations. A more elaborate variant of the logic model, known as "logical framework analysis" (LFA), grew in popularity among bilateral government agencies through the 1980s and 1990s, having been originally developed for USAID in 1969 (e.g., AusAID 2005; Commission of the European Communities 1993), more than a decade before its widespread adoption by nonprofits and their funders in the United States. The performance discourse in international development is often cast in terms of "results-based management" or "development effectiveness," with a focus on setting clear goals and targets, identifying a causal logic model or results chain, and measuring results as a basis for continuous improvement (Morgan and Qualman 1996; Roduner, Schläppi, and Egli 2008).

More recently, bilateral aid agencies have sought to find ways of aggregating or assessing the sum total of results from their support to thousands of projects, programs, and civil society organizations worldwide. Their interests in doing so are twofold: to respond to accountability demands from their own finance ministries and taxpayers who want to know the "value for money" of their aid, and to increase development effectiveness towards global targets such as the Millennium Development Goals and the now more ambitious and ambiguous Sustainable Development Goals. These motivations were originally codified in the Paris Declaration on Aid Effectiveness, an international agreement signed in 2005, and the Accra Agenda for Action in 2008, both of which emphasized the need not only to measure results but to do so in a way that reflects national priorities and helps build country systems for managing development.[5]

The spread of logic models and impact measurement cannot, however, be attributed to foundations and government agencies alone. In the mid-1990s in the United States, for example, a number of national-level nonprofit organizations, particularly industry support groups, began to advocate for outcome and impact measurement while also developing tools for nonprofit managers. Among the most visible proponents was the United Way of America, which was one of the first national agencies to ask members of its network to distinguish between outputs and outcomes, supported by a series of resources designed to assist agencies in outcome measurement. The United Way's rationale for doing so was twofold: "To see if programs really make a difference in the lives of people" and "To help programs improve services" (United Way of America 1996). Over the following decade, the Urban Institute developed a common outcome framework and a series of indicators for over a dozen categories of nonprofits, later launching a web portal in collaboration with a software provider to house survey instruments and other tools for performance management (Urban Institute 2006, 2016).

The evidence on whether outcome measurement has led to improved performance is mixed. A study of thirty leading US nonprofits found that measurement was useful to the organizations for improving outcomes, particularly when they set measurable goals linked to mission (rather than trying to measure mission directly), kept measures simple and easy to communicate, and selected measures that created a culture of accountability and common purpose in the organization, thus helping to align the work of disparate units and chapters (Sawhill and Williamson 2001). The United Way of America showed gains in effectiveness among 391 agencies that it surveyed in 2000. It reported that over three-quarters of its partner organizations found outcome measurement useful for communicating results and identifying effective practices, as well as for helping to improve service delivery of programs. But the results were not all positive, with about half of the responding agencies reporting that implementing outcome measurement had led to a focus on measurable outcomes at the expense of other important results and an overloading of the organization's record-keeping capacity, and that there remained uncertainty about how to make program changes based on identified strengths and weaknesses (United Way of America 2000).

Funders, too, have a mixed record of using impact assessments and evaluation in their decision making. In an analysis of evaluation methods used by philanthropic foundations over a period of three decades, the late nonprofit historian Peter Dobkin Hall argued that such evaluations lacked rigor and that key decision makers were often indifferent to the findings (Hall 2005, 33). Others have suggested that philanthropic giving is often motivated by "expressive" interests of donors and not necessarily by evidence of what works and what doesn't (Frumkin 2006; Knutsen and Brower 2010; Mason 1996). Many foundations continue to struggle with how to integrate a range of measurement approaches into their decision making. And some skeptical practitioners have suggested that while outcome measurement appears to be "a good tool to help funders see what bang they're getting for their buck" (Glasrud 2001: 35), it runs the risk of being counterproductive when it draws precious resources away from services and reflects more of an obsession with expectations of funders than an interest in actually improving services and results (Benjamin 2008; Edwards and Hulme 1996a).

The practice of measurement is similarly mixed in the arena of impact investing. A survey of 146 impact investors conducted by J. P. Morgan and the Global Impact Investing Network found that while most investors lamented the lack of quality data, capacity, and methods for assessing the social performance of their investments, they were nonetheless satisfied with the social performance of their portfolios, as measured primarily by outputs rather than outcomes (J. P. Morgan and GIIN 2015). A more detailed follow-up survey found numerous improvements: 77 percent of 169 respondents claimed to be measuring outcomes rather than just outputs (although what outcomes were actually measured was not reported), and about one-quarter reported that the industry had made significant progress in improving investor understanding of impact measurement practice and in greater sophistication of tools and frameworks. Investors also identified a number of key challenges facing the industry, with about half expressing concern with a fragmentation of approaches to impact measurement and management, and one-third noting significant challenges to integrating social and financial management decisions, as well as on transparency about impact performance (Mudaliar et al. 2017).

These experiences of practitioner communities suggest that while social performance measurement remains at an early stage of development, it is developing rapidly and perhaps even beginning to converge on common practices. Three broad convergent trends are particularly notable over the past decade. The first is a spurt of innovation in methods and tools for making measurement more useful and timely for decision making. This shift is captured by one of the pioneers in the impact investing field:

> Metrics and evaluation are to development programs as autopsies are to health care: too late to help, intrusive, and often inconclusive. . . . [W]e set out to build a performance management process that would allow us to refine our thinking, change course, and diagnose problems before they became too significant. (Trelstad 2008, 107)

In the language of international development, this trend emphasizes the "monitoring" in "monitoring and evaluation" efforts. Nearly every large international development NGO has sought to reshape its M&E department to focus less on postprogram evaluation and more on midcourse correction and learning. And, there has been a flurry of efforts among impact investors and development evaluators to create "client-centric," "lean," and "right-fit" measurement approaches suitable for early stage and midstage enterprises with limited resources and capacity (Acumen 2015; Dichter, Adams, and Ebrahim 2016; IPA 2016; McCreless 2015). Ideally, of course, organizations need both—measures that help them refine and improve what they do on a day-to-day basis, and measures that help them keep sight of their long-term goals.

The second and closely related trend has been among providers of capital. One survey of approaches to evaluation in philanthropy pointed to a "shift from the use of evaluation to measure the impact of past grants and toward a more timely and pragmatic process of gathering forward-looking information that will enable both grantors and grantees to make ongoing improvements in their work" (Kramer et al. 2007, 5). Since then, many large funders have built up strong evaluation departments and measurement methodologies as part of a deeper commitment to strategic and outcome-oriented philanthropy (Brest 2012; Twersky, Buchanan, and Threlfall 2013; Weinstein 2009).

Over the past decade, the emerging impact investing industry has begun to build a measurement infrastructure characterized by standardized metrics, mapping and categorization initiatives, and third-party analytics and ratings systems (Mudaliar et al. 2017; Social Impact Investment Taskforce 2014). And the public sector, which has long used performance-based contracting, is showing renewed interest in its latest variation, pay-for-success contracts.

The third and deeper trend is a growing rationalization and marketization of the sector as a whole (Eikenberry and Kluver 2004; Hwang and Powell 2009; Mair and Hehenberger 2014; Powell, Gammal, and Simard 2005; Smith and Lipsky 1993). This rationalization is apparent in the hiring of professional managers and the widespread adoption of formalized practices typically associated with business such as strategic planning and independent auditing. Nonprofits and social enterprises are increasingly recruiting graduates of MBA programs while also seeking the services of strategy consulting firms. As part of this rationalization of the sector, they are also increasingly seeking to measure and even quantify their performance (Brest 2012; Bromley and Meyer 2014; Ebrahim 2003b; Frumkin 2002; Tuckman and Chang 2006; Young and Salamon 2002).

These three broad trends—a spurt in innovation around real-time feedback and midcourse correction, growing capital markets for social performance, and a steady rationalization of the sector—all point to the increasing institutionalization of performance measurement in the social sector. They also portend a growing need for managers to be more deliberate about what they seek to achieve and how to measure progress towards it. These are challenges of both measurement and strategy.

Linking Measurement to Strategy

I turn now to the core practical challenges that emerge from the above discussion. How can leaders of social sector organizations be more deliberate about performance measurement and management? This is a question of strategy. I use the term *strategy* to mean *how an organization seeks to achieve long-term performance.*[6] The role of performance measurement and management is *to support the design and execution of strategy, as well as its improvement over time.* The key strategic challenges of performance can thus be captured in terms of three foundational questions facing every organization:

1. What does my organization seek to achieve?
2. How will we bring about that change?
3. How will we hold our feet to the fire?

The first question captures the organization's value proposition, the second its operational or social change model, and the third its own terms of accountability. Figure 1.2 depicts these components of social sector performance, which I discuss briefly below. The concepts and terms discussed here will be familiar to many; my intent is to get all readers on the same page as quickly as possible before proceeding to a more complex and nuanced examination of performance measurement. For those less familiar with the concepts described below, I provide further resources in the appendix to this book.

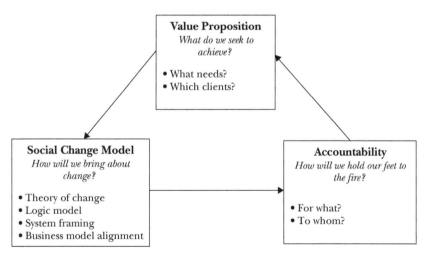

FIGURE 1.2   Core Components of Social Performance

Value Proposition

At the heart of any strategy lies a value proposition (Moore 2000; Porter 1980; Rangan 2004). It answers a fundamental question: *What do we seek to achieve?* It is outward looking, specifying the value to society that the organization seeks to create in terms of two questions:

- What problem or needs will be addressed?
- Which clients or population will benefit?

A good social value proposition provides clear answers to the above questions and is thus ultimately measurable. While most social sector organizations have mission statements, many are too broad to qualify as a value proposition. Consider an organization serving the homeless. In this book, we will examine the case of Miriam's Kitchen, which changed its mission from a vague statement—"to provide individualized services that address the causes and consequences of homelessness in an atmosphere of dignity and respect both directly and through facilitating connections in the Washington, DC community"—to a more concise and measurable value proposition—"to end chronic homelessness in Washington, DC." This much simpler statement clearly identifies both the social problem and a well-defined target population. The organization targeted an especially difficult subset of the homeless population: the chronically homeless, defined as individuals who have been continuously homeless for at least one year and have experienced four or more episodes of homelessness in the prior three years. The clarity of this value proposition provides a starting point for designing an operational model to address the problem.

Social Change Model

While a value proposition looks outward to the value created for a segment of society, a social change model looks inward to the organization's operations, posing the question: *How will we bring about change?* Any model of social change is made up of multiple parts:

- theory of change

- logic model or results chain

- system framing

- business model alignment

A *theory of change* (or causal logic) explicitly articulates how an organization's interventions will address the social problem specified in its value proposition. Put another way, it specifies the cause-effect relationships or pathway through which actions are expected to generate results (Center for Theory of Change 2014; Keystone 2009; Weiss 1995). A good theory of change can be stated as a series of hypotheses or "if-then" statements—*If* we do a, b, and c, *then* we expect results x and y to occur. For example, an organization serving the homeless may engage in many activities including providing meals, overnight shelter, substance abuse counseling, health services, or even lobbying city hall to allocate resources for permanent housing. Its theory of change must articulate the pathway through which these activities can be expected to reduce homelessness in the city. The cases in the next four chapters of this book illustrate a variety of theories of change, ranging from fairly straightforward pathways supported by substantial scientific evidence to complex ones for which research remains sparse. A challenge facing many social sector organizations is to surface their unquestioned assumptions about cause and effect in order to develop an explicit and testable theory of change. The appendix to this book provides several resources to help organizations develop their theories of change.

A theory of change is further operationalized with the help of another tool—a *logic model* or *results chain*—that specifies the key inputs and activities required to generate the desired outputs and outcomes (see Figure 1.1 above). The primary value of a logic model lies in its role as a disciplining mechanism, forcing managers and staff to articulate the steps in their interventions and the measurable results they expect to see along the way. Each arrow in a logic model can thus be understood as a hypothesis amenable to testing: Do the activities produce the expected outputs? Do the outputs lead to anticipated outcomes? A well-developed logic model can be useful not only for identifying performance metrics along each step in the chain, but also for uncovering opportunities for improving performance.[7] As we shall see throughout this book, however, developing a useful logic model is often complicated by the uncertainties about cause and effect inherent in many social change efforts.

The third component of a social change model is a *system framing* that positions the organization's interventions within a broader social or institutional context. Take, for instance, an ambulance service that responds to emergencies and delivers patients to a hospital. Even though such a service may operate as an independent enterprise, its effectiveness ultimately hinges on plugging into a larger health-care system so that it can access hospitals and deliver patients to facilities that can meet their needs. Similarly, an organization serving the homeless with meals or overnight shelter is part of a larger ecosystem of actors attempting to address urban poverty. The cases in chapters 4 and 5 of this book illustrate the usefulness of a system framing, especially for organizations that seek to influence public policy or to collaborate with other actors in order to achieve their social goals.

Finally, an effective social change model requires *alignment with its business model* in order to minimize conflict between social and financial performance goals (Ebrahim, Battilana, and Mair 2014). In a highly competitive funding environment, it is not uncommon for organizations to accommodate the wishes of their funders even if that means compromising their social objectives. Even social enterprises that generate revenue directly from their customers can lose sight of their social goals in their efforts to generate revenue, a risk referred to as *mission drift* (Fowler 2000; Jones 2007; Weisbrod 2004). For instance, a health-care business serving low-income communities will constantly be tempted to also serve middle-income populations in order to bolster its bottom line. On one hand, doing so may enable it to expand its services to more low-income communities. On the other hand, it may succumb to mission drift by reducing its services to the poor in order to become more financially successful. This dilemma is further exacerbated by the fact that financial performance is easier to measure and audit than social performance. As such, a key strategic function of performance measurement in the social sector is to ensure that financial performance goals support, rather than overtake, social performance goals.[8]

Accountability

The final pillar of social sector performance is accountability—how the organization plans to hold its own feet to the fire. I focus here on the internal terms of accountability that the organization sets for itself, rather than on the expectations of external actors such as funders. There are two main dimensions of accountability that an organization's leaders must clarify as part of their strategy (Behn 2001; Ebrahim 2016; Kearns 1996; Mulgan 2000; Najam 1996a):

- accountability *for what?*
- accountability *to whom?*

Specifying *for what* the organization is accountable requires identifying the social results (outputs and outcomes) that are most important to its performance. Unlike in the business world where there is general agreement about standard measures of success, accountability in the social sector is complicated by a lack of common standards or benchmarks for measurement, and the general difficulty in comparing social performance across organizations. The task thus falls on leaders and managers to develop metrics that not only capture the organization's value proposition but also can realistically be delivered by the organization's model of social change. For example, it does not make much sense for an emergency medical service to measure long-term health outcomes when all it can reasonably deliver is a short-term response such as delivering a patient to a hospital. On the other hand, without ambitious outcome targets such as ending chronic homelessness, an organization that serves the homeless may fail to achieve its full potential.

Moreover, it is important for organizations to develop internal clarity about *to whom* they owe accountability. Even when an organization has clear measures of its performance, these measures may not satisfy all of its key stakeholders, particularly if their interests are divergent or in conflict.[9] An important task for leadership is to prioritize among various stakeholders and then develop mechanisms through which those central stakeholders can hold them to account.[10] In the absence of such mechanisms, organizations run the risk of defaulting to the interests of their most powerful stakeholders rather than those who are most vulnerable and most important to their missions. Typically, the most powerful stakeholders tend to be donors or investors rather than beneficiaries or clients, because funders can threaten to withhold funding whereas clients often do not have such an exit option or sanctioning mechanism (Hirschman 1970; Najam 1996a). This condition, prevalent in the social sector, is often described as strong "upward" accountability but weak "downward" accountability (Ebrahim 2003a; Edwards and Hulme 1996a), or even as "multiple accountabilities disorder" (Koppell 2005). The case studies in this book show that there are many avenues for strengthening downward accountability, for example, by systematically collecting client feedback on goods or services, allocating decision-making rights to clients in the work of the organization, and building the capacity of clients to engage in policy advocacy. We shall explore these mechanisms through the case studies that follow.

In sum, a key task for leaders is to specify how they will hold their organization's feet to the fire—by clarifying *for what* they are accountable and prioritizing *to whom* they owe accountability. This is the "intelligent forms of accountability" referenced in the opening to this chapter. By setting their own terms of accountability, social sector leaders can establish performance goals for themselves rather than merely being on the receiving end of the accountability demands of funders or other stakeholders. This is an accountability based on strategy rather than compliance.

These three components of social sector performance—value proposition, social change model, and accountability—constitute a virtuous cycle within an organization. A value proposition clarifies the organization's social purpose, its social change model puts that purpose into action, and accountability closes the loop by judging whether that purpose is being achieved.

A Contingency Framework for Measuring Social Performance

With the brief introduction to social sector strategy above, I turn now to the questions of performance measurement at the heart of this book: *What results should social sector organizations measure? What kinds of performance measurement and management systems should they build?*

Conventional wisdom in the social sector suggests that one should measure results as far down the results chain as possible—measuring not only the activities and outputs produced by an organization, but also its long-term social outcomes. This expectation is based on a normative view that organizations working on social problems should be able to demonstrate results in solving societal problems. Yet it is worth pausing to consider whether, and to what degree, such measurement makes sense for all types of social sector organizations. A crude typology of the social sector in the field of poverty alleviation distinguishes among at least three broad types of activities (Najam 1996b; Vakil 1997):

- Emergency relief—activities that address urgent survival needs, such as food and temporary shelter, as well as disaster, crisis and conflict mitigation

- Service delivery—activities that address basic needs, such as education, health care, longer-term shelter, community development, employment and income generation

- Policy and rights advocacy—activities that address structural issues related to rights, public policy, regulation, and societal norms

For instance, many international NGOs—such as the Red Cross and Doctors Without Borders—are engaged in emergency relief work. Measuring the work of such organizations is conceptually fairly straightforward: count the timeliness and delivery of emergency supplies such as tents, food, water, and medical supplies, as well as the numbers of people reached. Emergency relief is thus typically measured in terms of activities and outputs. While it is a complicated activity requiring highly sophisticated coordination and logistics management capabilities, it is focused on meeting immediate survival needs rather than long-term development outcomes. The links between inputs, activities, and outputs follow logically: the organization plans its requirements of supplies and staff (inputs) and the logistics for delivering those supplies (activities) in order to provide relief to the people most affected by the emergency (outputs). When the effort is well planned and executed, the program will be able to orchestrate activities that lead to measurable outputs.

Outcome measurement, on the other hand, requires answers to a more complex causal question: Are the activities and outputs leading to sustained improvements in the lives of affected people? Take the example of an immunization campaign against a contagious disease. A key output measure of an immunization campaign is the number of people vaccinated, against polio for instance. Although each person immunized is important, the most significant impacts are only achieved once a certain "herd immunity threshold" is reached, about 80–86 percent of a population in the case of polio, as this makes it possible for the disease to be eradicated. The metrics are typically expressed as outputs (number or percentage of people vaccinated) and outcomes (declines in illness) in order to get at impacts at scale (prevention, containment, or eradication of a disease). While the causal logic in preventing or eradicating a disease may be relatively well established, executing it turns out to be extremely complicated—it requires having not only a proven vaccine and the technology for distribution but also strategies for community organizing, for addressing cultural norms and fears that may limit immunization uptake, for coordinating public health workers, and for replicating these efforts at scale. Only two diseases, smallpox and rinderpest, have ever been eradicated through immunization campaigns.[11]

Outcome measurement turns out to be uncommon in the social sector for the simple reason that organizations have the most control over their immediate activities and outputs, whereas outcomes are often moderated by events beyond their organizational boundaries. An emergency relief organization that has done excellent work during and after a natural disaster might still fall short on outcomes of rehabilitating and resettling those displaced from their homes and livelihoods, especially if those outcomes depend on extended coordination with local governments, businesses, and nonprofits. Connecting individual-level outcomes to societal-level outcomes, such as a sustained drop in poverty in the region, is even more complex due to the number of additional factors at play—involving the larger political, social, cultural, and economic systems—that are beyond the control of any one entity.

The link between outputs to outcomes turns out to be even more complex in cases of policy advocacy and rights-based work. Well-known organizations like Amnesty International, CARE, Human Rights Watch, Oxfam, and others aim to address the root causes poverty and injustice through their policy-based work. But their abilities to measure long-term results, and to attribute those results to their interventions, are severely limited. Their advocacy campaigns may achieve many successes—for example, in getting the attention of public officials to the rights of children, women, political prisoners, and others; in forming national-level constituencies and coalitions; and in improving public awareness about marginalized groups. However, these measures are largely about activities, processes, and outputs, rather than about ultimate outcomes on rights. This focus on activities and process is due, at least in part, to the complex nature of causality when it comes to shaping public policy and social norms. It is also about the difficulty in attributing any one organizational intervention, among an ecosystem of interventions, to societal outcomes.

These preliminary observations enable us to relate performance measurement to the type of social sector activity:

- Performance in emergency and relief work can be measured in terms of inputs, activities, and outputs.

- Performance in service delivery work can be measured in terms of activities, outputs, and only sometimes outcomes.

- Performance in advocacy and rights-based work can be measured in terms of outputs and possibly "influence" (an interim outcome).

Perhaps what is most surprising about these initial observations is that only one category of intervention can readily be measured at the outcome end of the logic chain—service delivery activities for which the causal link between outputs and outcomes is well established and where the organization can exercise sufficient control over its environment to ensure fidelity to the causal model. In contrast, rights-based and advocacy interventions, despite aiming to address root causes of social problems, cannot easily demonstrate a causal link and are thus typically left with measuring outputs. These constraints on measuring performance also present a dilemma for accountability: many funders increasingly want to see measures of outcomes, whereas it may not be feasible for many organizations to measure performance beyond outputs.

In short, outputs don't necessarily translate to outcomes, and individual outcomes don't necessarily translate to societal outcomes. This much is clear: every organization should at least measure and report on its activities and outputs, as these results are largely within its control. But when should it step forward into the domain of outcomes and impacts?

Two Contingencies: Causal Uncertainty and Control Over Outcomes

Addressing this question requires a deeper understanding of the causal models of social change. In an important conceptual advance, Rogers (2008) differentiates among three categories of causal logics: simple, complicated, and complex (a distinction she credits to Glouberman and Zimmerman [2002] and which is also closely related to Snowden [Snowden and Boone 2007, Snowden and Kurtz 2003]). Most organizations employ a *simple* logic model, which assumes a

linear cause-effect relationship among variables as a basis for setting
performance targets and for evaluating success. She suggests that such
models are best suited to interventions that are tightly controlled, well
understood, and homogenous. Arguably, such interventions presup-
pose rational behavior and are amenable to technocratic control.
Complicated logic models are more useful for interventions that involve
multiple actors in implementation, multiple causal strands that must
operate simultaneously in order to achieve success, or alternative
causal strands where there are different pathways to the same result.

Complex logic models are distinguished by their nonlinearity, where
the causal logics and outcomes are insufficiently understood, interactive, and multidirectional. They may involve disproportional impacts
where small effects can magnify through reinforcing loops or at critical
tipping points. Rogers further suggests that complex causal models are
developed through processes of recursivity, requiring feedback loops
for convergence and negotiation among multiple actors, or through
an emergent process where patterns are gradually identified through
ongoing interaction and analysis. She cautions that the high degree of
uncertainty associated with complex causal logics "can lead managers
and evaluators to seek the reassurance of a simple logic model, even
when this is not appropriate" (Rogers 2008, 45).

Framed another way, simple logic models seem best suited to conditions of rationality within closed systems where knowledge of cause
and effect is well established and where organizations exercise considerable control over each step in the results chain. Complicated logic
models, however, may be more useful for assessing interventions that
play out in rational but open systems where environmental influences
are more difficult to contain, requiring special efforts to integrate
various interventions. And complex logic models may be appropriate
for organizations operating in open systems, but not necessarily fully
rational or technical ones, that require greater recursivity and coordination among external actors for identifying and assessing results and
their causal pathways.[12]

However, this spectrum of logic models—from simple to complicated to complex—merges two distinct factors that are useful to ex-

amine separately: *uncertainty* in cause-effect knowledge for addressing a social problem and *control* over the activities and conditions necessary for producing long-term outcomes. For social interventions, it is necessary to consider these two contingencies in order to identify the types of results an organization can reasonably be expected to produce.[13]

The first of these variables, uncertainty about cause and effect, has been a long-running theme in the management and accounting literature, especially as shaped by contingency theory (Chapman 1997; Chenhall 2003, 2006; Galbraith 1973; Hopwood 1980; Thompson 1967; Thompson and Tuden 1959). One key insight of this research is that high uncertainty in cause-effect relations makes it difficult to specify which behaviors are necessary for achieving desired outcomes prior to task completion, and even to evaluate the appropriateness of behaviors after task completion. This insight substantiates the reservations of evaluation researchers about the usefulness of the ex ante specification of cause-effect models under high causal uncertainty. Under these conditions, there may exist a temptation to use overly simplified linear logic models for program evaluation, which can be valuable for gaining organizational legitimacy but may also create an unintended focus on narrow activities or rationales for an intervention (Blalock 1999, 136–37; Lindgren 2001).

The second contingent factor focuses on the degree to which an organization controls all of the activities and conditions necessary for delivering long-term outcomes. Exercising control over social outcomes is complicated by the fact that it typically requires sequencing and coordination of multiple interventions, or even multiple actors, in an ecosystem. In organization theory, such "interdependence" is seen as a necessary consequence of the division of labor in joint activities (Victor and Blackburn 1987). In their seminal work on power and control in organizations, Pfeffer and Salancik (1978, 40) define interdependence as a phenomenon that "exists whenever one actor does not entirely control all of the conditions necessary for the achievement of an action or for obtaining the outcome desired from the action."[14] The strategic challenge for social sector organizations thus lies in how to integrate or coordinate the constellation of activities and actors that produce collective outcomes. In this book, I explore a number of mechanisms of coordination for increasing control over outcomes.

These two contingent factors form the axes of the contingency framework depicted in Figure 1.3. First consider the vertical dimension of the matrix, which refers to the causal uncertainty underlying an intervention. When there is low uncertainty, the relationships between cause and effect are relatively well understood and stable, and one has fairly complete knowledge of how a set of actions will lead to outcomes. In the social sector, such clarity is most likely to exist for interventions involving a linear or "simple" logic model (Rogers 2008). In contrast, high uncertainty refers to interventions where knowledge about causal pathways is relatively incomplete, and where cause-effect relationships are believed to be "complex" in that they may be nonlinear, interactive, and emergent.

In more commonly used practitioner language, the vertical dimension of Figure 1.3 refers to an organization's theory of change, which

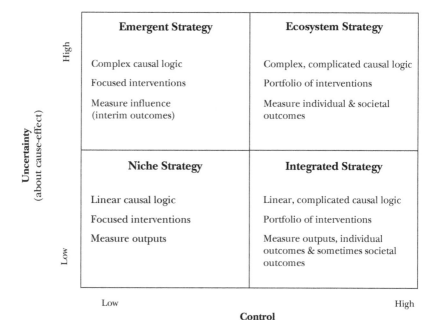

FIGURE 1.3   A Contingency Framework for Social Performance

articulates the causal logic or pathway through which a set of interventions is expected to lead to a long-term goal. How complex is the relationship between cause and effect, and how well is it understood? The bottom half of the matrix refers to settings where the theory of change is well established and is typically linear or simple. The upper half of the matrix applies to settings where the theory of change is complex, such that cause-effect relationships are only weakly understood, and where there may be multiple causal factors at play.

We can apply this reasoning to the examples above of organizations engaged in the delivery of emergency and basic services after a natural disaster such as an earthquake or hurricane. They operate on a clear and well-established causal logic: get shelter, food and water, and medical care to people facing a crisis in order to avert further disaster. Or provide access to clean water and sanitation to prevent outbreaks of waterborne illness and improve human health. In order to deliver aid quickly, they must acquire and stock critical supplies such as blankets, tents, food, water, and medical supplies, while also transporting and distributing those supplies and ensuring that they are delivered equitably and safely on the ground. The supply chain management capabilities needed to deliver such aid can be enormously complicated, but the basic intervention logic is fairly well understood. Similarly, immunization campaigns follow a well-established causal logic based on evidence about the vaccination rates required in order to reduce or eliminate a disease, even though the operational strategy can be very complicated. Such interventions fall in the bottom half of the matrix, as the knowledge about causal mechanisms is fairly well understood. Under such conditions, output measures are useful for assessing performance.

On the other hand, consider efforts by organizations to influence public policy or foster democratization and human rights, such as by Amnesty International, Oxfam, or various civil liberties groups. Their abilities to attribute any long-term changes in public policy or social norms to their interventions are severely limited. These are settings with "complex, foggy chains of causality" where "events evolve rapidly and in a nonlinear fashion, so an effort that doesn't seem to be working might suddenly bear fruit, or one that seemed to be on track can suddenly lose momentum" (Teles and Schmitt 2011). Under these conditions, it would be foolish to attribute outcomes to any one organizational intervention. While an organization may influence or *contribute* to a policy or attitudinal change, it is more difficult to *attribute* that change primarily to its interventions. In such contexts, it is hard to know how much of a difference a particular intervention makes. Causality would be hard to establish, although one could make credible claims about "influence" on a set of outcomes (an interim outcome).

To be sure, attribution and contribution are both about establishing a causal relationship between interventions and an outcome. But they differ in the degree of uncertainty about cause-effect knowledge, and the methods for testing causal claims. A claim of attribution requires specification of: (1) a well-defined intervention or "treatment" applied to a unit or treatment group; (2) an observable outcome; (3) a counterfactual value, that is, the outcome expected in the absence of the intervention; and, (4) a means of assigning units or groups that receive the intervention and those that do not (treatment and control groups).[15] Satisfying these four conditions is important for testing claims of causal attribution; doing so is feasible for many social interventions involving the delivery of goods and services such as medicines, agricultural inputs, or even education and training. The evaluation methods ideally deployed in such contexts are experimental, such as randomized control trials, which enable the assignment of some kind of control group for comparison (Banerjee and Duflo 2009; Imbens and Rubin 2015; White 2006).

But there are many interventions and contexts where these conditions cannot be satisfied. For instance, consider an organization aiming to influence national health-care or labor policy. It may have a well-defined intervention (a lobbying strategy with specific arguments and tactics that target specific legislators) and an outcome it seeks to achieve (passage or changes to proposed legislation). Similarly, an organization seeking to influence negotiations in a civil conflict may have a strategy for influencing key players and a clear outcome in mind. But in neither of these settings is it typically feasible to establish treatment and control groups. These difficulties do not obviate the need for making and testing causal claims. But they require a different toolkit better suited to assessing causality in complex nonlinear contexts, such as methods of "process tracing" used by political scientists and "contribution analysis" developed by evaluators (Bennett and Checkel 2015; George and Bennett 2005; Kane et al. 2017; Lemire, Nielsen, and Dybdal 2012; Mayne 2011, 2012). In Chapter 7, I offer a series of resources for carrying out evaluations using attribution-based and contribution-based methods, and I revisit the conditions to which each is best suited.

Moreover, the distinction between attribution and contribution is not merely methodological or technical. It also has implications for strategy. Any organization that chooses to work collaboratively with other actors must confront the problem of how to "take credit" for its role when communicating with funders. Measurement focused primarily on attribution runs the risk of undermining the collective efforts of actors in an ecosystem when it incentivizes them to seek credit and funding for individual behavior (a zero-sum game) rather than to produce interdependent results (a mutual-gains game). In such contexts, managers and funders alike are better off identifying a constellation of factors that jointly affect a social problem (contribution) rather than obsessing about how to isolate the causal role of each factor or assigning weights to those factors based on statistical correlation (attribution). This distinction is important because it forces managers to be honest about the limitations of their claims of cause-effect, while still taking action under uncertainty. I revisit this distinction in chapters 4 and 5 in order to examine the challenges of measuring results when working with other actors in an ecosystem.

Now consider the horizontal axis of the matrix in Figure 1.3, which refers to an organization's control over outcomes. Under conditions of low control, an organization focuses on delivering a highly specific task or output that, on its own, is insufficient for addressing a social problem. Such an output may provide a necessary service—

such as meals or emergency shelter for the homeless, or job training for the unemployed—but it is unlikely to be sufficient for delivering an outcome such as ending homelessness or providing stable employment to a target population. In contrast, an organization may choose to increase its control over outcomes by combining multiple interventions—such as job training in combination with counseling, job placement, and postplacement coaching—that together are more likely to address the social problem. In practitioner terms, this is the "operational strategy" of the organization: the organization's leaders must choose whether to adopt a highly focused strategy that delivers a limited set of outputs with high quality, or to adopt a portfolio strategy that brings together a wide range of activities that, in combination, are likely to increase its control over outcomes. This is a strategic organizational choice.

Taking into account these contingencies, Figure 1.3 identifies four broad or "ideal types" of strategies that can be undertaken by organizations: niche, integrated, emergent, and ecosystem strategies. These four types should not be read as a normative continuum, but instead as a reflection of the deliberate strategic choices made by social sector actors.

A *niche* strategy is an appropriate choice when there is good knowledge about cause and effect but where control over outcomes is limited. There are two basic kinds of value propositions that fall into this quadrant. The first involves interventions where the desired results are outputs rather than outcomes. For example, emergency and relief services that provide temporary shelter or food aim to deliver a very specific set of outputs. These outputs are valuable in themselves, despite the fact that they do not aim to affect longer-term outcomes for individuals. They may be assessed in terms of the quality and efficiency (outputs/inputs) of the goods or services they provide.

A second kind of value proposition favoring a niche strategy is when evidence about cause and effect is sufficiently well established such that output measures can serve as a reasonable proxy for outcomes, even in the face of low control over those outcomes. For example, a medical intervention that treats children for intestinal worms has been shown to decrease school absenteeism in the developing world and thus increase employment earnings of those participants over time (Baird et al. 2011; Miguel and Kremer 2004). These findings were based on a randomized evaluation of a government deworming program conducted in seventy-five primary schools in a rural district of Kenya, involving over thirty thousand children. A representative sample of about 7,500 respondents was assessed ten years after the intervention. Where such research can establish confidence in the causal links between the outputs and desired long-term outcomes, it is sufficient for the implementing organizations to execute a niche strategy and focus on measuring outputs (numbers of children dewormed) and the quality and efficiency with which those outputs are delivered. Admittedly, such instances remain rare in the social sector, as they typically require meeting the conditions for a randomized control trial.[16]

An *integrated* strategy is characterized by good knowledge about cause and effect, but a need to coordinate among multiple activities or actors in order to increase control over outcomes. Take the example of a job training program that provides technology skills to unemployed youth. The organization may deliver a high-quality training program necessary for helping its clients climb out of poverty. But it does little to influence the actual employment opportunities for those youth or to address the problem that many youth are likely to lose their jobs within several months of being placed in them. To have real impact, additional interventions are needed, such as creating a job placement pipeline with employers, coaching the youth when they have difficulty retaining jobs, and working with employers to provide support when youth underperform (e.g., Chertavian 2012). The niche intervention of a job training program is insufficient and must be delivered in coordination with other upstream and downstream interventions. These additional interventions may be undertaken by the same organization as part of a vertically integrated strategy, or they may be done in collaboration with other organizations. Either way, coordination of the interventions is essential to delivering outcomes.

An *emergent* strategy, in contrast, is appropriate under conditions of relatively poor knowledge about cause and effect and little control over outcomes. A policy advocacy organization, for instance, faces a dual challenge in its efforts to influence public policy: a need to quickly adapt its strategy in order to take advantage of new policy windows or a changing political landscape, and a lack of control over the policy-making process and policy makers. Its strategy is necessarily emergent in that it must learn to respond quickly to changing conditions (Mintzberg 1978), all the while staying focused on its advocacy goals. Performance measurement is especially messy in such settings due to the nonlinear and interactive nature of causality. The organization might claim to have influenced a public policy but could only rarely provide compelling evidence that it was actually responsible for a policy change. Another example lies in the field of higher education. While there is well-established evidence that individuals with college degrees are able to get better-paying jobs than those without such education, the missions of many colleges and universities to advance knowledge, to build an engaged citizenry, and to contribute to society are more difficult to measure due to the cause-effect uncertainties involved, particularly in the liberal arts (Faust 2013; Rosenman 2013). Here, too, modest claims of influence on such outcomes are plausible.

Finally, an *ecosystem* strategy must grapple with complex cause-effect pathways that are poorly understood, while simultaneously seeking to increase its control over outcomes. It does so by orchestrating the interventions of multiple actors in an ecosystem in order to produce outcomes that no single actor could produce alone (Bradach and Grindle 2014; Kania and Kramer 2011; Montgomery, Dacin, and Dacin 2012; Weber 2003; Wei-Skillern and Marciano 2008). Consider a homeless-service provider that feeds its clients a warm breakfast and is focused on immediate outputs (meals), but any longer-term outcomes (getting people out of homelessness) are typically beyond its control. Other organizations in the same city may be providing substance abuse counseling, job training, or shelter. But none can independently reduce or end homelessness. To address this problem, many communities across the United States are increasingly coordinating services by first placing clients in housing and then matching services to their needs. The cause-effect relationship between each intervention and the outcome of reducing homelessness is largely unknown, but their collective impact is measurable. Success hinges on better coordination of previously isolated actors and services within an ecosystem (e.g., Culhane, Metraux, and Hadley 2002; National Alliance to End Homelessness 2006; Tsemberis and Eisenberg 2000).

Taken together, the two axes of the framework embed social performance in relation to an organization's knowledge about cause-effect and its control over outcomes. The vertical dimension of the framework acknowledges the constraints on rationality in organizations, particularly for addressing complex social problems where causal knowledge remains limited. The horizontal dimension differentiates between two kinds of operational choices, where an organization may choose to deliver highly focused interventions or to assemble a portfolio of interdependent interventions for generating outcomes.

Implications of the Contingency Framework

The four types of strategies and their performance measures outlined in Figure 1.3 are not intended as a normative continuum or as mutually exclusive domains, but instead as ideal types reflective of the contingencies faced by social sector actors. This typology leads to a number of implications that I summarize here and explore further in the chapters that follow.

First, and perhaps most important, *it is possible to be high performing in each of the four quadrants of the matrix*, where high performance is defined as "the ability to deliver—over a prolonged period of time—meaningful, measurable, and financially sustainable results for the people or causes the organization is in existence to serve" (Performance Imperative 2015). The yardsticks for what constitutes "meaningful" results must necessarily vary with the contingencies in the matrix. Unless social sector leaders have a grasp of both contingent factors—the state of knowledge about cause and effect for the problem they are trying to address, and their degree of control over outcomes—it will be impossible for them to determine appropriate measures of performance.

Second, the measurement of long-term outcomes is feasible under a limited set of circumstances—in the integrated and ecosystem quadrants of the framework. In such settings, seeking to attribute outcomes to a single intervention does not make much sense. To increase their control over outcomes, organizations face two strategic choices. They can either better integrate a series of interventions in-house (such as a vertically integrated job training program that does job training, job placement, and job retention coaching), or they can better orchestrate a network of service providers. Only in a limited set of circumstances are they likely to have sufficient control over the entire delivery chain to reasonably measure and take credit for outcomes.

Third, outputs can be a valuable measure of social performance, particularly under conditions of low causal uncertainty. For some interventions, such as emergency relief services, the desired results are best captured in terms of outputs. For others, where cause-effect knowledge is well established, outputs can serve as a reasonable proxy for outcomes. This does not, of course, mean that outputs are always a good measure of performance, but only that managers must be clear in their rationale when they use outputs.

Fourth, many organizations will not fit neatly into the quadrants of the matrix, with some traversing many of them. Complex international development organizations like Oxfam or CARE, for instance, are engaged in a portfolio of activities ranging from emergency relief to service delivery to rights-based work. They face the double challenge of measuring performance in each of these areas separately while also integrating across them in order to gauge their possible synergistic effects at an ecosystem level.

And finally, this contingency framing presents a dilemma for accountability: donors and investors increasingly want to see measures of long-term societal outcomes, whereas it may not be appropriate for many operating organizations to measure performance beyond outputs and possibly individual-level outcomes. In other words, there is a gap between what funders and the general public may desire from social sector actors and what they can reasonably be held account-able for. Managers who focus on measuring outputs or influence (as in the niche and emergent quadrants) risk being seen as failing to be accountable to some of their stakeholders, failing to convince funders and citizens that they are making a difference in society, thus risking both their support and their legitimacy. At the same time, managers who seek to take credit for societal outcomes (as in the integrated and ecosystem quadrants) risk overreaching by claiming social changes that may be beyond their actual control and for which they are not solely responsible, potentially undermining their own credibility (Campbell 2002).

In sum, the contingency framework depicted in Figure 1.3 reflects the open systems nature of social change rather than treating it as a closed rational system. Only in a limited set of circumstances are social sector organizations likely to have sufficient clarity about cause and effect, and control over the results chain, to reasonably take credit for long-term outcomes. As a result, we might expect the role and na-ture of performance measurement and management systems to vary with each quadrant of our matrix. Using a diverse range of cases, the next four chapters of this book examine what performance systems might look like in each quadrant of the figure.

Building Systems for Social Performance: An Overview of Four Case Studies

The following four chapters provide in-depth case studies on each type of social change strategy identified in the matrix in Figure 1.3—niche, integrated, emergent, and ecosystem. I summarize each of the four cases below. Readers most interested in a particular type of strategy and its performance measurement system can proceed directly to the relevant chapter. Chapter 6 provides a synthesis of the findings and develops diagnostic frameworks for managers.

Each case study has three objectives: (1) to move from conceptual-izing "what to measure" to examining its operational details, (2) to de-velop general insights on the type of performance measurement and management system best suited to supporting each type of strategy, and (3) to consider the tensions and difficulties common to developing a robust performance system for each type of strategy. The cases have been selected with these three goals in mind. But perhaps what makes the cases most interesting is the continuous struggle within each organization to adapt its performance measurement system to its evolving needs. There is no such thing as perfection in these dynamic contexts, only constant improvement.

Chapter 2 examines the challenges of measurement common among organizations that adopt a *niche* strategy, where the relationship between cause and effect is relatively well understood and the intervention is highly focused. The main argument in this chapter is that, under such conditions, managerial attention is best focused on implementing the intervention with high quality—which requires a focus on short-term metrics of activities and outputs rather than on long-term outcomes. I develop this argument through the case of Ziqitza Health Care Limited, a social enterprise that is one of the fastest growing private ambulance services in India. Ziqitza's experience offers two general insights. First, it illustrates the conditions under which managerial attention is best devoted to tracking short-term outputs. Second, it highlights the role of *standardization* and quality control as a defining feature of an output-focused performance measurement system. The chapter also draws briefly on other examples of niche interventions such as postdisaster emergency response.

Chapter 3 explores the performance systems necessary for supporting an *integrated* strategy, where the relationship between cause and effect is relatively well understood but where multiple interventions must be combined in order to produce outcomes that are greater than the sum of their parts. Here, the core tasks of a performance measurement system is *coordination*, which involves prioritizing and sequencing a portfolio of activities and measuring their synergistic effects. I examine the experience of the Aga Khan Rural Support Programme India, looking at a pipeline of integrated interventions in rural agricultural and natural resource management that aim to increase incomes of smallholder farmers. This portfolio of interventions includes agricultural credit, access to high-quality inputs such as seeds and fertilizers, farmer training, soil and water conservation interventions, and access to markets. I track the organization's challenges in measuring the performance of these interventions over a twenty-year period. This chapter concludes with other examples of integrated strategies, including an even more complex endeavor to assist people living in extreme poverty by BRAC in Bangladesh, and a pipeline of educational interventions developed by the Harlem Children's Zone in New York City.

Chapter 4 shifts the focus to an *emergent* strategy, where the relationship between cause and effect is complex and control over outcomes is very limited. Such organizations are best served by an *adaptation* system that enables quick iteration and adjustment of strategy in response to unexpected opportunities. I draw on a complex case of a global network organization called WIEGO—Women in Informal Employment: Globalizing and Organizing—which advocates for the rights of workers in the informal economy. Such workers include, for instance, street vendors, waste pickers, and domestic workers who typically lack social protections such as working condition standards and minimum wages. I explore the efforts by WIEGO to influence standard setting at the International Labor Organization (ILO). It would be difficult for WIEGO to demonstrate that it has improved the working conditions of informal workers, but it can reasonably claim to have "influenced" the ILO's standards and guidelines on measuring the informal sector, which in turn shape how national governments measure and support their informal sectors. WIEGO's performance system is characterized by constant adaptive learning: quick actions to take advantage of policy windows and recalibration of strategy based on new information, but tempered and guided by clear long-term goals. Such a performance system is not unique to WIEGO but is relevant to a diverse range of organizations engaged in changing social policies and norms. In closing this chapter, I draw parallels to two very different types of interventions—a campaign to prevent teen pregnancy in the United States and a leadership training program in Burundi in the aftermath of a violent ethnic civil conflict.

Chapter 5 turns to an *ecosystem* strategy, where not only are cause-effect relationships complex but also where multiple organizations collaborate in order to increase their control over outcomes. In such settings, causal attribution is nearly impossible because organizations cannot reliably isolate their interventions from those of other actors in the ecosystem. This chapter shows that rather than trying to solve the attribution problem, managers are better served by building an *orchestration* system: developing shared (supraorganizational) performance indicators to chart the progress of the field as a whole, support collective learning, and align individual efforts that aim towards joint goals rather than independent aims. I examine the case of Miriam's Kitchen, an organization that aims to end chronic homelessness in Washington, DC, by fundamentally reconfiguring and aligning efforts of over one hundred nonprofit and public sector actors in the city. In concluding this chapter, I draw on the many developments related to a growing "collective impact" movement in the social sector including, for instance, a major strategic shift undertaken by the United Way of America.

These empirical chapters provide a basis for developing a general framework for designing performance measurement and management systems for social change, which I summarize in Chapter 6. They also offer many insights on the roles of funders, which I consider in Chapter 7, in supporting the building of performance measurement and management systems.

Chapter 2

NICHE STRATEGY

niche: a role taken by a type of
organism within its community.[1]

In 2004, if you dialed 102 (the government
ambulance service), you were connected to
the cremation ground. Ninety percent [of]
ambulances then were used as hearse vans.
SWETA MANGAL, COFOUNDER AND CHIEF EXECUTIVE,
ZIQITZA HEALTH CARE LIMITED, INDIA[2]

ON NOVEMBER 26, 2008, the city of Mumbai was the target of twelve coordinated shooting and bombing attacks that lasted four days. At two
of these sites, the first emergency responders on the scene, even prior
to the police and media, were ambulances from Ziqitza Health Care
Limited (ZHL). Over the next three days, ZHL transported 126 victims to health-care facilities with thirty ambulances and 24/7 operations (Bellman 2008). Ziqitza had begun its service barely four years
prior to that day with two ambulances. Within a decade, it would
grow to nearly three thousand ambulances with operations in several
states across the country.

This chapter examines Ziqitza's strategy in which the two dimensions discussed in the opening chapter—causal uncertainty and control over outcomes—are both low. From the perspective of managers
running such an organization, how should they assess performance?
How can performance be measured, monitored, and improved? Contrary to conventional wisdom, I argue that high performance for a

niche strategy is achieved through a relentless focus on delivering short-term outputs rather than long-term outcomes. The case of Ziqitza illustrates the critical role of standardization and quality control systems in generating meaningful outputs.

The field of ecology offers a useful metaphor, the niche, for understanding the highly focused interventions of social sector actors like ZHL. The ambulance service offered by this organization fills a well-defined niche in an ecosystem, a tightly bounded role within a larger community of interventions and organizations engaged in health care. In the preceding chapter, I identified two categories of value propositions suitable for a niche strategy. The first involves interventions where the organization serves an immediate or critical need, where its intended results are outputs rather than outcomes. For example, emergency services—such as ambulances, homeless shelters, soup kitchens, food banks, crisis hotlines, and disaster response services—generally aim to deliver immediate short-term benefits, rather than long-term outcomes, to an affected population. They can, of course, influence long-term outcomes but that is not their primary purpose.

In the second type of niche strategy, there is a tight causal link between the outputs of an intervention and its intended outcomes, such that measures of output can serve as a proxy for longer term results. I provided the example of a government deworming program in Kenya (see Chapter 1), where a randomized evaluation provided strong evidence of a link between children who received treatment for intestinal worms (outputs) and their long-term educational attainment and income (outcomes). In both of these types of niche strategies—where the purpose of the intervention is to satisfy an immediate need, or where there is strong evidence of a direct link between the intervention and intended outcomes—outputs provide the primary measure of performance.

To be sure, a focus on outputs does not let managers off the hook for developing robust metrics and measurement systems. On the contrary, an emphasis on outputs requires managers to pay enormous attention to building systems to reliably deliver outputs of high quality.

The main objective of this chapter is to illustrate the critical relationship between the delivery of outputs and the design of performance systems focused on standardization and quality control. To do so, I focus primarily on the case of Ziqitza's emergency ambulance services in India, with special attention to its systems for monitoring quality. In closing, I draw generalizable lessons from this case, introducing other examples of niche strategies and the common challenges they pose for managers in delivering standardized high-quality outputs.

Building a Niche Value Proposition and Business Model

Ziqitza Health Care Limited was established in 2002 by a group of young entrepreneurs—Naresh Jain, Ravi Krishna, Sweta Mangal, Shaffi Mather,[3] and Manish Sancheti. Their value proposition was to create a world-class ambulance service in India that would be on par with 911 in the United States and 999 in the United Kingdom, and that would serve the public irrespective of one's ability to pay. ZHL began operations in Mumbai, and gradually expanded to over 2,900 ambulances servicing 16 states across the country by early 2018. At this time, the company employed 8,610 individuals, had served over 12.5 million people through its services, and was playing an increasingly important role in shaping the country's health care system.

The company was born from two contrasting personal experiences. In 2004, Shaffi Mather awoke in the night to the sound of his mother choking in her sleep in the family's home in Kerala, India. Not knowing whom to call, and feeling alarmed and helpless, Mather drove his mother to the hospital where she was stabilized in the intensive care unit. A few days later, the mother of his childhood friend, Ravi Krishna, collapsed in New York City. However, she was attended to by an ambulance within minutes of calling 911.

These life-changing personal events, coupled with a deep rooted belief in the Gandhian philosophy that saving a life is one of the most rewarding experiences in a person's life, motivated the founding team.

A number of the founders gave up lucrative careers in the private sector for the challenge of creating a standardized emergency medical service accessible to people across income groups in India.

The company's name Ziqitza was derived from the Sanskrit words *chikitsa*, meaning medical treatment, and *jigyasa*, which meant quest for knowledge or curiosity. "We were a bunch of people who wanted to provide medical aid; and we didn't know anything about it but we were curious to know how to do it," said Sweta Mangal, explaining the moniker (Acumen 2013). ZHL's vision was to be the leading ambulance service provider in the developing world. It was committed to meeting international standards of quality in emergency medical services, staying accessible to people regardless of income and becoming financially self-sustainable. Their vision was a far cry from the status quo. One of the founders recalled:

> If you needed an ambulance in 2002, you had to know someone who knew somebody with an ambulance. This person would have to vouch for you. Then you would have to deposit anywhere from INR 5,000 to INR 10,000[4] before the ambulance arrived to pick up the patient. . . .
>
> As far as hospitals were concerned it was a money-losing proposition to run an ambulance. Drivers were difficult to deal with, their vehicles were not maintained properly, [and] when you need one you will never find one. (Ravi Krishna, cofounder and director, July 10, 2015)

ZHL's founders had identified a very specific niche in the healthcare ecosystem that they wanted to transform. The larger ecosystem of public and private hospitals, medical professionals, insurance companies, and government regulators was too complex to tackle by a single intervention. But they felt they could target a piece of that system by focusing on emergency response services, and particularly ambulances. Their ambition was not only to create an effective ambulance service but also to change prevailing cultural norms about it, taking what was a prepaid and inaccessible service to one that was postpaid and widely accessible. The founders pooled their savings to establish ZHL, initially as a nonprofit organization:

> Our original intent was *not* to be a for-profit entity because we felt it is impossible to put a price on human life. (Naresh Jain, cofounder and director, July 10, 2015)

They expected that nonprofit status would help them to access grants and private donations. Since ambulance service was a capital intensive business, grants could help offset capital outlays and manage cash flows. But philanthropic support turned out to be slow to materialize and insufficient for fueling growth. The founders thus began to consider market-based options:

> For us it was never about earning money. Our aim was to offer compassionate service and raise the value of human life. When we started out . . . we were looking to be an enterprise that was self-sustaining on revenue generated by the services provided to people who could afford the fee, and subsidizing the people who could not afford the fee. (Ravi Krishna, July 10, 2015)

The founders recognized that without private investment, they would be unable to grow ZHL's operations to achieve greater social impact. The company began to seek private loans and equity investments, while cognizant of the potential risk to social mission posed by the profit motive. Its former CEO was clear:

> [We follow] a values-based approach that sees revenue generation as a means, not an end. . . . Private ambulance services that are out-and-out commercial will only provide a service to you if you are willing to pay for it. But my objective as a social enterprise is first to save a life and second to be sustainable. (Sweta Mangal, as quoted in Balch [2014])

In 2007, Ziqitza accepted its first external investment from Acumen, a nonprofit impact investing firm based in New York. This investment of $1.5 million in equity capital spurred ZHL to grow, while tracking both its financial and social performance. Over the next few years, ZHL raised additional funding by taking on more equity investors including the Housing Development Finance Corporation, Infrastructure Development Finance Company, and India Value Fund

Advisors.[5] Growing the fleet of ambulances required ongoing infusions of capital, which was initially provided by equity investors and later by state governments.

ZHL established a head office in Mumbai, and gradually opened regional offices in the states of Bihar, Jharkhand, Kerala, Madhya Pradesh, Maharashtra, Odisha, and Punjab. It designed two main business models: one based on private payment directly from customers, and the other on partnerships with state governments.[6]

Private-Pay Model

The company initially launched a private service that offered emergency medical services for a fee. Branded "1298," users could call this number 24/7 from their landline and cellular phones to access an ambulance. Once the ambulance reached the location, trained paramedics would transport the patient to a hospital of their choice, or to the nearest facility in case of accidents and disasters.

ZHL charged users a fee, determined by ambulance type and distance traveled by the patient in the ambulance.[7] Patients or their families would pay for the service only after they reached the hospital. And payments would be reduced or waived if patients were unable to pay. Accident and trauma victims were transported free of charge to the nearest government-run hospital. This way the service remained accessible and flexible to meet user needs.

Ziqitza met its capital and operational costs through a combination of user fees, advertising (on vehicle exteriors), private donations, and its own funds. In the private-pay model, ZHL estimated that each ambulance would have to serve 2.5 patients per day to break even on operational expenses. Despite initial expectations that this cross-subsidy for-profit model would generate enough surplus to grow the company, in reality it barely broke even. But it demonstrated that a private-pay model could operate effectively in Indian cities and cover most of its operational costs. For instance, in 2015, ZHL operated 112 vehicles and employed 556 people under this model, generating annual revenues of $2 million with a net loss of $163 thousand (see Table 2.1, under size of Operations and financial performance).

TABLE 2.1   Summary Table on ZHL's Business Models (FY 2014–15)

	Private Pay Model	Public-Private Partnerships
Size of Operations		
Employees	556	5903
Fleet size	112	1056
Fleet utilization (number of trips per ambulance)	152.90	956.04
Operational Performance		
Number of dispatches	17,125	1,009,582
Calls availed	16,011 (93.49%)	909,693 (90.11%)
Calls not availed	1,114 (6.51%)	99,889 (9.89%)
Average Response Time (hh:mm:ss)	00:21:00	00:23:54
Average Cycle Time (hh:mm:ss)	05:54:11	02:22:21
Social Performance		
Patients served (excluding pregnant women)	18,772	561,758
Pregnant women served	0	364,679
Babies delivered on board	0	1,800
Free or subsidized trips	68	NA
% served from low-income groups	NA	77% (Punjab) 78% (Odisha)*
Financial Performance		
Cost of operations (USD)	2.20 million	17.92 million
Billed kilometers	456,794	NA
Unbilled kilometers	570,904	NA
Revenue from operations (USD)	2.03 million	18.80 million
Operating profit (USD)	(162,918)	878,634

Source: Data compiled from company documents and Choudhury (2014).*

Public-Private Partnership Model

Ziqitza's primary growth model lay in partnerships with state governments. The organization had been urging state governments to hold a transparent and competitive bidding process for ambulance services, and in 2007, it won seven of eleven contracts with state governments through a transparent bidding process (Meera 2013). Widely known as the "108" service, citizens in these states could dial 108 to get free prehospital care and emergency transportation to a nearby government hospital, focusing on patients requiring critical care and accident victims. Starting with a fleet of 10 ambulances in 2009, this business expanded rapidly to more than 1,000 ambulances and nearly 5,000 employees within 6 years, operating medical care and transportation services in the states of Kerala, Punjab, Bihar, Odisha, and the National Capital Region (the region surrounding New Delhi) by 2015.

Unlike the private-pay model where revenues from user fees fluctuated month to month based on usage, ZHL received a fixed remuneration from state governments to deliver this service. As part of this fixed remuneration, all capital expenditure was financed by state governments and operational expenditure was partially defrayed. The extent of support for operational costs varied from state to state. Some states also permitted ZHL to levy a nominal user fee for certain income groups. Any remaining costs were recovered through advertising.

Building a Social Change Model and Accountability for Outputs

Ziqitza's aim was to provide a quality ambulance service in India regardless of ability to pay. What did this mean in terms of a theory of change? What were the internal metrics to which the enterprise would hold itself accountable?

The organization's theory of change was based on a linear causal logic drawn from the experiences of ambulance services in the United States and United Kingdom:

> It is a well-accepted fact that a patient who receives basic care from trained professionals and is transported to the nearest healthcare facility within 15–20 minutes of an emergency has the greatest chance of survival. (ZHL 2017)

> Ambulance services in India follow the "scoop and run" approach, where ambulances gather the patient and rush them to the nearest facility. Thus the speed of transportation has a potential impact on a patient's clinical outcome. (Ravi Krishna, July 10, 2015)

In the language of logic models, these claims posited a causal link between an output measure (time to respond to an emergency) and an outcome (patient survival), and were largely substantiated by the medical research on emergency response. For instance, considerable research had shown that a survival benefit was associated with a shorter response time for patients with intermediate or high risk of mortality as in the case of cardiac arrests (O'Keeffe et al. 2011; Pell et al. 2001; Pons et al. 2005), and that increased EMS prehospital time was associated with higher mortality rates (Gonzales et al. 2009).[8] Taking this causal reasoning—that speed of emergency response can increase patient survival rates—ZHL set two key social performance objectives for itself:

- to meet international standards in emergency medical service
- to provide accessibility to all people regardless of income

The first objective clarified "for what" the organization was accountable, while the second objective identified "to whom" it was primarily accountable. Together, they constituted the organization's value proposition.

The performance measurement challenge lay in establishing clear metrics and targets for each objective. For the first objective, Ziqitza developed a pair of output metrics: "response time," which was defined as the time taken from when a call was received to when an ambulance reached the scene; and "cycle time," which was the entire time an ambulance was deployed for a medical event (i.e., response time, plus time to deliver the patient to a medical facility, plus time to return to a base location for cleaning and maintenance before being redeployed). ZHL began to routinely gather and report on both metrics (see Table 2.1, under operational performance).

The company benchmarked its performance against national and international standards of response times, while recognizing that the conditions of Indian roads and traffic differed considerably from the United States or United Kingdom. For instance, one study recommended a target response time of 18 minutes for "serious but not life threatening" emergencies, and 8 minutes for "immediately life threatening" emergencies (Knight and Harper 2012). These targets would be nearly impossible to achieve in many parts of urban India under prevailing conditions, but provided an external benchmark that would push the organization to constantly improve performance. The company established average target response times for ambulances in the different settings it operated—urban, semiurban, rural, and remote—based on requirements of state governments, constantly seeking to improve upon this key performance indicator. For example, the target was 20 minutes in most urban settings (with 10 minutes in the state of Kerala), and 30–35 minutes in rural areas where distances were large and infrastructure was poor. Table 2.2 provides a list of permissible response times in four Indian states, and a comparison to London and New York. And as Table 2.1 shows, the actual average response time was about 21 to 24 minutes in 2015. The company was transparent about this shortfall, recognizing its value for motivating improvement.

It is notable that ZHL chose to focus on outputs (response and cycle times) as its key performance metrics rather than the outcome

TABLE 2.2 Permissible Response Time (in Minutes) for Emergency Medical Response Services in Select Indian States

	Rajasthan	Kerala	Odisha	Punjab
urban	20	10	20	20
semiurban	—	20	25	—
rural	30	30	35	30
remote areas	—	30	—	—

International Response Times

London Ambulance Service (999)
For immediately life-threatening situations: 75% of calls within 8 minutes and 95% of calls within 19 minutes
New York City Emergency Medical Response (911) (2013 data)
For life-threatening medical emergencies: 9 minutes and 22 seconds (based on actual average response time)

Source: State Governments of Kerala, Rajasthan, Punjab, Odisha; London Ambulance Service; New York City Department of Investigation.

of patient survival. Two of the founders were candid about their constraints:

> Just because you brought a patient in an ambulance to the hospital doesn't mean the life was saved, because the patient can die in the hospital. . . . It is very difficult because we don't track the entire progress to wellness . . . and it is a very long tracking window. So that is one handicap we have. (Ravi Krishna, July 10, 2015)

> We do not track patients postdelivery because the cost is heavy. (Shaffi Mather, cofounder and director, January 30, 2015)

Given ZHL's low control over outcomes, coupled with a reasonable scientific basis for linking outputs to outcomes and the constraints of time and cost in tracking outcomes, they chose to do what any pragmatic manager would do: focus on delivering outputs reliably. Moreover, ZHL's leadership understood that their organization occupied a niche within a much larger ecosystem; their niche was responsible for producing quality outputs, but it was the larger system that generated outcomes.

For tracking progress towards its second objective—accessibility to all people regardless of income—Ziqitza tracked a second type of output: numbers of patients served, particularly among low-income or underserved groups and pregnant women. Table 2.1 provides aggregate numbers for one fiscal year (see the subsection on social performance). For example, through a survey administered through its call centers, the organization estimated that 77 percent of users in the state of Punjab and 78 percent in Odisha were living under the government poverty line of $2.50 per day, thereby confirming that the vast majority of its users were from low-income households (Choudhury 2014). However, the survey also indicated that ZHL's rural operations in Odisha were not reaching as many poor clients as in the urban parts of Odisha or Punjab. Despite the fact that over three-quarters of ZHL's customers in these two states were below the poverty line, the company's leadership found this proportion to be inadequate given the high poverty levels in the region:

It should be closer to 90 percent. We are actually missing out [on a] huge chunk of people because they are so poor [that] they can't afford [a] mobile phone. We are completely missing out [on] that segment. We haven't quite figured out how to connect [to] them. (Ravi Krishna, July 10, 2015)

Another founder explained the importance of this finding for improving the organization's service to indigenous "tribal" communities who were barely using it:

[We tried] to understand why it was so. The tribal population in that region assumes that these ambulances [are] "not for them." They don't call the ambulance when they need it, assuming they don't have access to it. Now we are undertaking campaigns with the tribal population to explain and make them aware [of the service]. (Shaffi Mather, as quoted in Inclusive Business Action Network [2014])

Along with increasing its outreach, ZHL also used the results of the survey to reexamine its ambulance deployment strategy in rural Odisha, in order to better locate vehicles near low-income populations. Once again, these metrics of social performance were exclusively focused on outputs—how many people were being served and in what demographic segments. ZHL also kept a running tally of such aggregate outputs on its homepage. For example, at the time of this writing, the company reported having served 12.5 million patients since its founding, of which 4.3 million were pregnant women, and delivering over fourteen thousand babies on board its ambulances (ZHL 2018).

In building its model of social change, ZHL also faced two challenges common among social enterprises: how to generate sustainable revenue streams, and how to ensure alignment between financial and social performance objectives. On the first of these challenges, the company found that its initial private-pay model, in which wealthier customers subsidized the fees of lower-income customers, was proving difficult to replicate outside of major cities, generating only about 10 percent of total company revenues. Even in Mumbai, this private-pay service had reached only a modest scale. As a result, ZHL's scaling plans increasingly shifted away from this cross-subsidy model and towards public sector contracting. Government contracts in the form of public-private partnerships thus became the company's largest income source by far—90 percent of total revenue in 2015, with an increase in 33 percent over the previous year alone (see Table 2.1, under financial performance, for a comparison of the two models).

The second challenge experienced by ZHL, common among social enterprises, was the potential for conflict between financial and social performance objectives. For managers at the private-pay call centers who were responsible for deploying ambulances, the balance between generating revenue and serving low-income patients was a daily struggle. In cities such as Mumbai, managers often had weekly and monthly financial targets. ZHL estimated that each ambulance needed to serve 2.5 fully paying people per day to break even on operational costs; managers thus sometimes accepted calls that were not emergencies but where a patient needed a means of conveyance to a hospital and was willing to pay for it. So long as such opportunities were undertaken during slack periods and did not come at the cost of responding to an emergency, they were considered acceptable. But such decisions required regular monitoring in order to ensure that financial targets did not overtake social ones.

This tension was less of a concern in the public-private partnership model because the company was paid a fixed fee by state governments rather than a fee per service. There was thus no financial incentive to prioritize patients who could pay over those who could not. But while these public partnerships allowed ZHL to reach more people across income segments, they also exposed the organization to the vagaries of the political process. Because the company insisted on a transparent bidding process for government contracts, the time frames for securing state contracts were often long, requiring multiple years of effort and resistance to corruption. The payoffs were potentially large, however, not only in terms of the numbers of people Ziqitza could directly reach, but also in terms of derivative services. For instance, as a result of ZHL's finding that there was a great need for services for pregnant women, especially in semiurban and rural areas, many state governments launched a "102" service to offer basic transportation to pregnant women, newborn babies, and sick infants to medical centers. This service aimed to promote in-hospital deliveries and reduce infant and maternal mortality rates. Many women in rural and remote communities preferred to deliver children at home due to lack of transportation and to avoid hospital expenditure. But under the 102 service, they could avail of free transport to and from a government facility for delivery and pre-, post-, and neonatal checkups.

In addition, in an environment where there was a paucity of high-quality epidemiological information or data on incidence rates of diseases, ZHL was able to inform public and private health systems on why patients were seeking emergency care, with the data broken down by demography and gender. For instance, its patient surveys showed that there was a high incidence of abdominal pains in Odisha, likely due to poor access to clean drinking water. Its mobile medical units routinely provided information on common infections and disease outbreaks in its areas of operation, allowing the government to better design its vaccination programs and outreach efforts. For all of these reasons—a more sustainable revenue stream, better alignment between social and financial objectives, and opportunities to influence other public services—ZHL chose to prioritize its public-private partnership model over its private-pay model.

Designing a Performance System: Standardization and Quality Control

> If your system is flawed, then you have to correct the system. But you have to first have evidence that your system is flawed. Otherwise, stick to the system.
>
> RAVI KRISHNA, JULY 10, 2015

In executing its social change model, Ziqitza faced a performance challenge common among organizations with a niche strategy: building a system to produce outputs consistently. To deliver its outputs, ZHL developed a system focused on standardization of tasks and quality control. It standardized four key activities in its value chain: call handling and dispatch, patient transport and delivery, vehicle maintenance, and patient follow-up.

Ziqitza's experience offers a number of general lessons for other types of organizations with niche strategies in identifying and designing:

- key activities or tasks that can be standardized

- quality control: standard procedures for each activity, supported by accountability and learning mechanisms

- key performance indicators for each activity (outputs)

These components of ZHL's standardization system are elaborated below and summarized in Table 2.3.

Call Handling and Dispatch

Every call that ZHL received was automatically routed through its nearest call center, also known as contact desk center (CDC). Typically ZHL established a CDC for every fifty ambulances in an area. CDCs were operational 24/7. They were staffed with agents who were supervised by an operational manager and assistant manager for that area. Calls were picked up by trained CDC agents in the shortest time possible, typically within two rings. Agents then followed a series of standard questions to ascertain and accurately capture the caller's request, the patient's chief medical complaint, location of the patient, and the medical facility to which the patient was to be transferred. CDC agents determined the type of ambulance (basic life support (BLS) or advanced life support (ALS); see note 7) to be deployed based on the patient's medical complaint.

Once they determined ambulance type, CDC agents checked the availability and location of the nearest ambulance. With all ZHL ambulances fitted with a global positioning satellite system (GPS) that transmitted their position in real time, agents were able to track the location of the fleet on a mapping system in the CDC. The GPS system also allowed them to determine if an ambulance's ignition system was

TABLE 2.3 Ziqitza's Standardization System

Key Activity	Quality Control: Standard Procedures	Quality Control: Accountability & Learning	Key Performance Indicators (Outputs)
Call Handling and Dispatch	• call script • on-site supervision at call centers	• review of recorded calls by quality management team, assessment of "good and bad calls," followed by feedback and coaching of call agents	• time to answer call • time to dispatch vehicle
Patient Transport and Delivery	• GPS mapping of traffic and location • EMT certification • physician backup • patient care record (PCR) • handover protocol at hospital	• surprise audits by quality analysts of patient care records and hospital handover documents • review of patient care records by physicians, followed by feedback and training for underperforming paramedics • monthly operational reviews at the cluster (field) level • third-party audits of records and finances • quality scorecards	• time to reach patient • time of admission to hospital • Key metrics: • *response & cycle time* by setting (urban, semi-urban, rural, remote)
Vehicle Maintenance and Inventory	• maintenance check • hygiene check • inventory/log check	• surprise audits by quality analysts • remote monitoring of fuel consumption	• meets standards consistently • no corruption
Patient Follow Up	• user feedback calls on service quality, timeliness, targeted services • poverty probability index (PPI) survey	• review of feedback by call center heads and quality management team at headquarters • training and quality checks by Grameen Foundation PPI experts	• patient satisfaction • patient demographics • Key metric: *poverty level of patients* (BoP)

on or off, if an ambulance was stationary or moving, and the speed at which it was moving.

Upon identifying the nearest ambulance, CDC agents estimated the time to reach the patient, after factoring in traffic data that was available through online services such as Google Maps. For the private-pay service, they also estimated the approximate service fee to transport the patient to a medical facility of their choice. The service was then logged into the dispatch system and an ambulance was deployed. The time taken for call handling and dispatch was automatically recorded. Ziqitza's senior quality manager, Vasim Qureshi, who was responsible for overseeing the entire process, explained:

> [T]he moment the call starts, the moment it rang and picked up, the timer starts . . . the call is assigned to an ambulance and within a minute the driver starts moving. (July 10, 2015)

Once the ambulance was en route, CDC agents continued to remotely track its location and monitor response time. In the unlikely event that an ambulance was delayed, agents called back the caller/patient to provide an updated response time. If a ZHL ambulance was not available or ZHL response was not likely to be timely, agents referred the patient to other ambulance providers in the area, and offered to transfer the call. All calls were audio recorded and logged into the dispatch system. Assistant operational managers provided real-time supervision of call handling and dispatch to avoid fatal errors in the process. They also ensured that patient location and condition were accurately defined.

In addition to creating scripts and procedures for CDC agents, ZHL tracked time to answer calls (number of phone rings), time to dispatch the vehicle and to reach the patient (response time), overall cycle time, distance traveled by the ambulance to reach the patient (unbillable kilometers), distance traveled when transporting a patient (billable kilometers), and overall accuracy of dispatch (correct type of ambulance and correctly capturing patient condition and location). Dispatch and response times were often stipulated by governments in their contracts with ZHL. Qureshi explained using the example of the state of Odisha:

[For] dispatch time I have 90 seconds, . . . I am given a response time [for urban areas of] 20 or 25 minutes, semiurban I need to be [there] in 25 minutes, rural I need to be there in 35 minutes. (July 10, 2015)

As discussed above, these performance targets were quite different from international benchmarks used by 911 in the United States and 999 in the United Kingdom that, according to Qureshi, set the platinum standard for response time at approximately nine minutes, and the gold standard at nineteen minutes (see Table 2.2). He knew that these targets would be impossible to achieve given the infrastructure in India, but this made it even more critical to measure response times and to station ambulances in locations where that time could be minimized. Qureshi went on:

It is not very complicated. . . . In most places it's a government facility like a hospital or police station where the ambulance would be stationed. . . . [And it] is based on experience, distance, as well as the infrastructure. With GPS technology, it is easier for the dispatcher to locate the nearest ambulance in order to reduce response time and to deliver the patient to the nearest government hospital. (July 10, 2015)

Under Qureshi's supervision, cases with slower than expected response times were analyzed by an internal quality management team, and areas for improvement pinpointed. Audio recordings were also examined, and accuracy and adherence to protocols were reinforced through agent feedback and coaching. In this manner, performance of CDC agents was continuously reviewed and evaluated. Their performance was also tracked and scored using an internal performance evaluation tool, and agents who failed to achieve a score of 80–85 percent were shifted to a performance improvement plan. New recruits were trained for six months and were similarly assessed after their training period.

Patient Transport and Delivery

On arrival at the scene, ZHL paramedics took over to meet patient needs and transport them to the nearest medical facility (or facility of patient's choice). They were supported by qualified physicians, who typically held degrees from five-year medical schools and twenty to twenty-five years of work experience and who provided expertise in case a patient's condition demanded clinical support beyond the capability of paramedics. These physicians, directly employed by ZHL, were often present in the CDC and were available 24/7 to guide paramedics on specific protocols.

Paramedics followed a series of protocols to ensure patient safety and care. When transporting patients, paramedics obtained and recorded vital signs every fifteen minutes. They also gathered patient history, performed physical assessments, and provided emergency care for an array of situations. For instance, in case of fractures, paramedics immobilized affected joints and bones during transportation. In many cases, they controlled bleeding and provided treatments for shock. Data were recorded in a patient care record (PCR). This was a paper-based form that was used to document patient contact and care services. ZHL trained its paramedics to complete a PCR for each patient transported in a ZHL ambulance. PCRs captured patient demographic data, medical diagnosis (reasons for seeking prehospital emergency care), clinical data (patient's heart rate, blood pressure, etc.), and also ZHL staff's interventions to stabilize the patient until transported to a hospital or an advanced care facility.

When they arrived at the hospital, ZHL paramedics communicated the patient's history along with relevant details to the attending staff at the hospital, and recorded the time of admission and attending staff details in the PCR. Sections of the PCR were completed with self-reported information from the patient or his or her caregiver. Other sections relied on accurate observations and descriptions provided by ZHL paramedics.

Completed PCRs were reviewed on a daily basis by a team of ZHL physicians for completeness as part of a regular quality control process. Physicians typically reviewed ten to twenty forms per paramedic and deliberately sampled PCRs of different types of patients (trauma, accident victims, pregnant women, etc.). They checked to see if important patient conditions were accurately recorded, patient vitals were recorded at the stipulated frequency, and medicine usage was correctly logged. By triangulating information from various fields in the PCR, physicians also ensured that paramedics were not forging information. Reviewed PCRs were then classified into three categories (A, B, and C). Paramedics with PCRs in the C category were offered additional feedback and training by ZHL physicians. Physicians also developed ideas for refresher training courses for all paramedics based on their review of these PCRs. They also used audio recordings from actual calls to improve efficiency in patient transport and handover.

In addition, as an anticorruption measure for the private-pay service, the ambulance driver recorded and reported the vehicle's odometer reading to the patient or caregiver at two points in time. The first reading was provided once the patient was transferred into the ambulance, and the second upon delivery of the patient to the medical facility. These readings ensured that patients or their families would be billed only for the distance the patient was transported.

Vehicle Maintenance and Inventory Check

Routine hygiene servicing of vehicles was critical for ensuring patient safety and preventing the spread of infections. ZHL developed a cleaning checklist for its vehicles, and there was a mandatory fumigation of vehicles between patients at a dedicated facility. This process required taking ambulances off the road between patients, spraying fumigants, and extensively cleaning the vehicle. This process on average took between forty-five minutes and three hours, including travel time to the fumigation facility. Acknowledging that this process could affect ZHL's vehicle deployment plans, a manager emphasized its significance: "Failure to do this will increase the risk of transmission of infection to both patients and staff. And we don't want to forsake care and hygiene for increased business" (Tony D'souza, head of operations, ZHL western region, July 11, 2015). There were similar protocols for paramedics during patient contact.

Each vehicle also underwent a routine inventory check at this time for equipment functionality, supplies such as syringes and sterile pads, and medicines. The two different types of ambulances (BLS and ALS) had different checklists. Paramedics and their helpers were required to keep a log of medicines used on board, while ensuring that they were kept under proper cooling and had not expired.

Patient Follow-up

Most importantly for performance improvement, ZHL made extensive use of its call centers to gather structured customer feedback on all of its services. Every ZHL call center had a dedicated agent for these feedback calls. Patients or their families typically received this phone call within the first week of availing the service. "It was important that we reached out while they could still recall details, yet we couldn't call them the very next day since in many instances they were probably still in the hospital," explained Qureshi, the senior quality manager.

There were a number of different types of feedback calls that ZHL carried out. First, patients who had used ZHL's service received a standard feedback phone call. Once patients confirmed their willingness to participate in the survey, the ZHL agent asked them a series of questions. Each call averaged between four and five minutes. User feedback was solicited on multiple parameters such as responsiveness of call centers, time taken for the ambulance to arrive, cleanliness of the ambulance, conduct of ZHL paramedics and staff, amount paid for the service, and drop off location. Users were also asked how they had heard of ZHL. Finally, they were asked to rate ZHL's service on a scale of one to five. Responses were manually entered into a paper form and later transferred to an Excel-based format. As a first check, responses were reviewed by the head of the call center. All responses that received an unsatisfactory rating were reviewed in detail.

A second type of feedback call targeted callers who had contacted ZHL through its emergency number but did not avail the ambulance service. The feedback process sought to uncover the reasons the service was not utilized. For example, delays in responding to a call or locating an address or other operational factors sometimes resulted in patients making alternative arrangements. At times the patient was stabilized before or on arrival on scene, thereby not requiring transportation to a hospital. In these instances, the ZHL paramedic completed a separate form to state that the service was not availed. These feedback calls followed a standard script of questions. User responses were manually transferred from paper to the Excel format, and the collected information was reviewed, cross-checked, and analyzed for patterns.

Third, ZHL collected feedback from specific target groups, such as pregnant women who used its 108 or 102 service. In the case of expectant mothers, the calls tracked the number of times women visited health facilities for prenatal care, their expected date of delivery, and preferred health facility at the time of delivery. ZHL used this information to assess and manage its level of preparedness for emergency and nonemergency obstetric care.

Finally, in its most ambitious feedback survey, ZHL sought to better assess the socioeconomic profile of its customers, in order to determine how effectively it was serving low-income households. In 2014, through a partnership with one of its investors, Acumen, and the Grameen Foundation India, ZHL conducted a phone survey based on a Poverty Probability Index (PPI).[9] It interviewed approximately one thousand users in the states of Punjab and Odisha to measure the proportion who were living below national and international poverty lines. ZHL administered the PPI questions at the end of its regular feedback calls to improve uptake and ease administration. It also administered in-house surveys for 5 percent of respondents to validate data gathered through the phone surveys. Sample size and sampling strategies in both states were informed by state-level characteristics along with ZHL's call history. The Grameen Foundation India trained ZHL agents on the process for administering the survey and analyzing results. Responses were collected and tracked in an Excel format.

Taken together, these various customer feedback calls provided critical insight into the company's operations, the demographic profiles of its users, and opportunities for improvement. Most importantly, the calls made use of ZHL's existing technology (call centers) and customer contact points (its regular feedback calls) and were thus easily integrated into the company's daily operations without needing additional resources.

Quality Control: Accountability and Learning Mechanisms

In order to maintain quality across all four components of the value chain described above, ZHL created a series of accountability and learning mechanisms carried out by an internal quality management team in concert with external auditors (see Table 2.3, third column). Accountability mechanisms such as audits and reviews were designed to assess performance and to identify shortfalls; learning mechanisms such as feedback and coaching processes were designed to improve performance. Accountability and learning thus went hand-in-hand, serving not only to verify compliance against company standards and protocols but also to enable continuous improvement.

Most internal audits were carried out by ZHL's quality management team (QMT). This team was headed by Vasim Qureshi, the senior quality manager based at headquarters in Mumbai. Qureshi joined ZHL in 2012 after seven years as a medical insurance advisor with a multinational company. The motivation to provide high-quality services at affordable prices to Indians across income groups appealed to him: "When I was initially approached by ZHL, I dismissed them as a typical private fee-for-service ambulance provider. But I later saw their profile and recalled how they were the first ambulance service to arrive at the Taj and Trident hotels during the Mumbai terrorist attacks in 2008" (July 10, 2015).

Qureshi's team included quality auditors and analysts of different types. For example, one set of analysts audited call handling by CDC agents, while another team conducted surprise audits of ambulances, and a third team of trained physicians audited the patient care records completed by EMS staff. The work of the QMT was guided by a quality plan that defined its key quality functions, objectives, processes, and policies.

Quality analysts conducted audits at each of the stages described above: call handling, patient transport, and vehicle maintenance. At the first of these stages, the QMT audited phone calls received at the emergency call centers. Each member of the team was assigned a target of auditing three calls per CDC agent per week. The process was designed to provide rapid feedback to the call agent by a team coach and quality analyst:

> [W]e try to do it in real time, as soon as possible, so that the person has a very short learning curve. If I [provide] feedback two days or three days or four days later, the person is going to continue that same . . . mistake again and again. . . . [A coach and quality analyst] will make them listen to the call, they will highlight the mistake and coach them. (Vasim Qureshi, July 10, 2015)

This process was supplemented by team-wide discussions at each call center, using a method dubbed "good and bad calls." The head manager of the call center, supported by a member of the QMT, would play a series of recorded calls over a loudspeaker, and would then ask the call agents to identify the "dos and don'ts" on the call, that is, what was done well and what could be improved. In order to successfully conduct these sessions, Qureshi and his QMT needed first to agree on what constituted a good call or a bad call. Team leaders and quality analysts across the country needed be on the same page. This required a process of regular discussion among them. To do so, Qureshi and his team organized call listening sessions once every two weeks. Audio recordings of calls were assigned for review prior to the session. During the session, led by a master calibrator (a role assigned on a rotational basis), the team analyzed and discussed the quality and efficiency of call handling in the audio recording. Qureshi elaborated:

> Two days prior to the call [a quality analyst] will send out some recordings, . . . you listen to the call and mark down [your assessment] on the quality sheet. Then what we do is we come together and discuss—on this call Vasim has an opinion [of] 90 percent, then my colleague has 80 percent. So there is a debate . . . [and] by the end, everybody leaving

> the room . . . is on the same page and is calibrated. So this is something
> we [do] for team leaders and the team coaches but now I think . . . we
> should do it for the [call] agents as well. (July 10, 2015)

The purpose of this process was to foster collective learning, improve coaching and feedback techniques, and revise call-handling protocols.

Furthermore, the QMT's quality auditors conducted audits of ambulances in the field. Their job was to check on ambulances across the state, often conducting surprise audits, in order to ensure that quality standards were being maintained. Using an audit sheet, they reviewed patient care records for completeness and accuracy, and they inspected and inventoried equipment and medicines on board all ambulances (BLS and ALS ambulances had different checklists). They checked if ZHL paramedics and helpers maintained a comprehensive log of medicines that were used on board, including checks on the expiration dates of medicines. And they inspected the cleanliness of vehicles, along with its maintenance schedule to avoid unexpected breakdown or repair. Quality auditors had monthly targets for surprise audits, traveling independently from state to state to complete these checks and meet targets. Their responses were entered into a quality audit spreadsheet, generating a vast amount of data that was further collated by regional managers in each state and assistant managers in the ZHL head office into a short scorecard. This monthly scorecard (see Table 2.4) allowed Qureshi to swiftly ascertain if a particular ambulance or site was not meeting routine quality parameters:

> I can just have a glance at the scorecard, it's a two-page sheet and I can
> come to know is everything fine with this particular ambulance or there
> is something wrong. If there is something wrong, the scorecard will
> pinpoint [what] I need to focus on. . . . Then I can go into detail and
> dig [into] all those audit sheets. (July 10, 2015)

Moreover, ZHL ambulances were equipped with fuel sensors to support remote monitoring of fuel consumption across its fleet. These tamperproof sensors, fitted inside fuel tanks, periodically transmitted data on fuel levels within the tank via satellite network to ZHL's information

TABLE 2.4 Sample Monthly Scorecard for a Private-Pay Site (June 2015)

	West	East	South	North	Total
Fleet					
Number of Ambulances	6	1	13	1	21
Number of Backup Ambulances	3	0	2	0	5
Number of Ambulances on Road	6	0	12	0	17
Ambulance Utilization (hours utilized as % of total hours/week)	46.15%	0.00%	15.35%	0.74%	15.56%
Number of People Served	233	9	459	1	702
Calls					
Number of Calls Received	5,146	9	9,647	10	14,812
Availed Calls	233	9	460	1	703
ALS Calls/BLS Calls	99/134	9/0	341/119	1/0	450/253
Unavailed Calls	0	0	16	0	16
Total Calls Dispatched	233	9	476	1	719
Service Calls	34	0	326	4	364
Quality Parameters					
Average Dispatch Time (hh:mm:ss)	0:06:17	0:01:28	0:00:42	0:01:00	0:02:22
Average Response Time	0:25:19	1:05:34	0:28:31	0:50:00	0:42:21
Average Cycle Time for Availed Calls	1:01:18	11:01:16	5:00:31	4:45:00	5:27:01
Average Cycle Time for Unavailed Calls	—	—	1:20:16	NA	1:20:16
Operational Performance					
Total Distance Traveled (km)	16,460	1,611	60,691	119	78,881
Local Distance Traveled (km)	4,463	94	46,958	119	51,634
Long Distance Traveled (km)	11,997	1,517	13,494	0	27,008
Distance Traveled, Unavailed calls (km)	0	0	239	0	239
Average Distance Traveled per Trip (km)	70.64	179.00	127.50	119.00	109.71

TABLE 2.4 (*continued*)

	West	East	South	North	Total
Fuel, Mileage, and Service Calls					
Total Fuel Consumption (liters)	2,433	233	7,812	0	10,478
Total Fuel Expenditure (INR)	142,283	13,356	449,949	0	605,588
Average Distance Traveled per Ambulance	2,970.64	0.00	5,788.79	0.00	4,969.33
Mileage	6.93	7.91	8.60	0.00	8.19
Distance Traveled on Service Call (km)	902	0	4978	200	6080
Revenue					
Local Trips (INR)	334,012	12,000	2,223,650	2,500	2,572,162
Long-Distance Trips (INR)	255,116	42,707	316,900	0	614,723
Special Events (e.g., sport events) (INR)	506,614	0	9,000	0	515,614
Unavailed Calls (INR)	0	0	3,500	0	3,500
Total Discount Provided (INR)	14,676	0	1,000	0	15,676
Total Revenue (INR)	1,081,066	54,707	2,552,050	2,500	3,690,323
Average Revenue Per Day (INR) (Revenue/No. of Ambulances on Road)	6,346	0	7,333	0	7,119

Source: Excerpted from scorecard sample provided by ZHL.

technology department. The data were cross-checked by Qureshi's team with data generated from routine operations. This measure contributed significantly to reducing fuel pilferage and loss across operations.

In addition, ZHL held monthly cluster-level reviews. Clusters were geographic units, each with about twenty ambulances. Each cluster was headed by a cluster leader (CL) who reported to an operations manager, who was in turn overseen by a project head. The CL served as a single point of contact for field staff management. In addition to field operations, the CL was also responsible for carrying out ambulance audits at the cluster level. This was in addition to the surprise audit undertaken by QMT auditors. Every ambulance in a cluster was audited at least once every month by the CL. The monthly cluster reviews were designed to allow key individuals responsible for service quality to reflect on quality parameters. Patient care records, patient feedback, and scorecards were all reviewed and analyzed.

Finally, ZHL's board of directors put in place its own mechanisms for auditing company operations and finances. The board's audit committee, composed of three members including two independent directors, appointed an independent audit agency to regularly examine operations and finances, identify risks, and quantify potential losses to the company in the absence of appropriate risk mitigation systems. "This team is not connected to anyone in operations. In fact, if anyone from that team walked into our head office today, no one would even recognize them," explained Krishna, one of the founders. This team maintained its anonymity, sent its information requests via e-mail and reported directly to the company's chief financial officer and audit committee. Reports from this independent audit were submitted to the committee twice a year. Management was often called to respond to queries or offer clarification on issues that were flagged in this report. For instance, in 2013, the audit report raised concerns when fuel consumption exceeded fuel tank capacity for some ambulances in the state of Odisha. Further investigation showed that the mismatch was a result of a precautionary measure taken by the team ahead of a tropical storm (Cyclone Phailin). To avoid a fuel shortage, the team refilled fuel tanks, and stored additional fuel in jerry cans.

Ultimately, the aim of all of the above accountability and learning mechanisms—call quality audits and feedback, ambulance quality audits and scorecards, cluster-level reviews, and third-party audits of operations and finances—was to create reliability and consistency in operations. One of ZHL's founders summarized the organization's approach, emphasizing adherence to standard procedures and quality systems rather than improvisation:

> [T]he moment you deviate, you create problems. . . . [Y]ou can't have *jugaad* [improvisation] in ambulance [service]. You have to [follow] the system, because you are responsible for people's lives. And if your *jugaad* goes wrong, you are putting people's lives [at] risk. (Ravi Krishna, July 10, 2015)

Conclusions: Performance Management for a Niche Strategy

What can we learn from Ziqitza's experience that might be more broadly generalizable to other social change organizations? The focus of this chapter has been on a niche strategy—where an organization has the advantage of good knowledge about cause and effect but has little control over long-term outcomes. Within this context, the chapter offers a series of insights about the importance of outputs as the primary measure of performance, and the key role of standardization systems in ensuring the consistent delivery of outputs.

As the case of Ziqitza illustrates, a focus on outputs does not obviate the need for careful measurement. On the contrary, the standardization of performance processes, supported by quality control and accountability systems, is critical to delivering results. This case offers several generalizable lessons that are supported by a vast literature on the management processes required for standardization of quality, including total quality management (TQM), lean manufacturing, and their variations.[10] In particular, three core components of a standardization system remain underdeveloped in many social sector organizations: standardization of activities or tasks; quality control processes, which include accountability and learning mechanisms; and key performance indicators focused on well-defined outputs.

In terms of *standardized activities or tasks*, ZHL illustrates how a service delivery organization can establish clear roles for every stage of its operational work: call handling and dispatch, patient transport and delivery, vehicle maintenance, and patient follow-up. Each step in the process has well-defined responsibilities and qualifications, performance indicators, and audit mechanisms for ensuring that protocols are followed (as summarized in Table 2.3). Employees know their roles and understand the standards of quality expected of them.

The heart of the performance system is a *process of quality control* that emphasizes standard procedures supported by accountability and learning mechanisms. Call center agents receive a script that guides them in handling calls, supported by on site-supervision and one-on-one feedback on their calls. Ambulance teams receive regular training and are supported by staff at the call centers, including doctors who are on call to advise paramedics. A series of surprise audits monitors whether protocols are being followed, for example, in the accurate completion of patient care records, stocking of medicines, use of medical equipment, and the maintenance of vehicles. The mechanisms of accountability and learning touch every level of the organization: assessments of "good and bad calls" made by call agents, biweekly listening sessions for team leaders, surprise audits of ambulances and finances by quality analysts and third-party auditors, and monthly aggregate scorecards at the cluster level. Employees such as call agents or paramedics who perform poorly, rather than being sanctioned, receive additional support and training. Sanctions are imposed only when poor performance persists despite training and coaching. And support is provided both by an internal quality management team and by external experts like the Grameen Foundation India.

Finally, a standardized system requires well-defined *outputs as the key performance indicators*. ZHL's key metrics are centered on the beneficiary or client: how quickly the ambulance reaches the patient and delivers her to the hospital (response time and total cycle time), and the customer segment the organization is serving (poverty level of patients). The organization commits resources to gathering feedback from clients on a daily basis. Feedback calls, conducted four days after an emergency event, systematically gather data on the patient's experience with special attention to timeliness and quality of service.

More generally, it is important to note that the three features of a standardization system are not limited to emergency services like ambulances or disaster response. They apply across diverse types of interventions. Consider an example from the field of education and community development. Communities In Schools (CIS) is an organization that works with school children in low-income communities in the United States to prevent dropouts and promote graduation. It has developed a distinct model in which it works with school leadership to identify critical support needs, and then connects them to key resources in their communities such as tutors, coaches, counselors, and parent support groups, to name just a few. An evaluation conducted in collaboration with an external firm found that the CIS model was effective but that it was not executed consistently across its network of 217 affiliate organizations (ICF International 2010). As a result, CIS launched a "total quality system" (TQS) to ensure the consistent quality in the delivery of its model across affiliates. The process was painful: about 40 percent of affiliates dropped out of the network in the ensuing years. The organization's then-president wrote about the tradeoff at the time:

> That kind of mass defection might seem like a fatal blow, but we found just the opposite to be true. When we embarked upon TQS, our 217 affiliates were serving 1.24 million students. Seven years later, we have 165 affiliates serving nearly 1.5 million students. . . . The entire TQS process began with a focus on the individual child, so for us, the happiest result of all has been our ability to serve more students despite—or perhaps because of—our smaller footprint. (Cardinali 2015)

The purpose of CIS's quality system was to execute its model with fidelity. Once CIS developed its standardized quality system, it also saw gains in efficiency, reaching more students through fewer affiliates.

Organizations in the social sector are often torn between delivering interventions that work (effectiveness) and doing so at lower cost (efficiency). Only when consistent quality is possible does it make sense to measure efficiency. For a niche strategy, efficiency provides a valuable measure of the costs of delivering outputs, helping to identify opportunities for reaching more clients with the same resources. But in settings where knowledge about cause and effect is weak (as we shall see in chapters 4 and 5), efficiency is not a very meaningful measure, as one does not even know if the output produced actually matters for achieving the goals of the organization (Thompson 1967, 86).

To summarize: for a niche strategy, performance management is best focused on the measurement of outputs, supported by systems of standardization and quality control. There are two general types of interventions where such a focus makes sense. The first involves interventions where the targeted results are outputs rather than outcomes.

Ziqitza's ambulance service is a case in point. More generally, such interventions include emergency and relief services in disaster or crisis contexts, such as earthquakes or military conflict. Key outputs may include the provision of temporary shelter, food, water, clothing, or medicines to an affected population. These outputs are valuable in themselves, despite the fact that they do not aim to affect longer-term outcomes for individuals. Many international NGOs—such as Oxfam, Doctors Without Borders, CARE, Save the Children, World Vision, and the Red Cross—are engaged in emergency relief work. Increasingly, private sector corporations also provide services in emergencies, such as Walmart's use of its distribution capabilities to supply bottled water, food, and clothing in the wake of hurricanes (Barbaro and Gillis 2005).

Of course, the work of emergency service providers can provide a basis for longer-term results. When an ambulance delivers a patient to a hospital, it is handing off that patient to another niche in the ecosystem that is better equipped to consider health outcomes. Similarly, homeless shelters and soup kitchens occupy critical niches that are part of a longer chain of interventions for assisting homeless individuals. And organizations that respond to disasters and crises are also often engaged in postemergency community development work. However, that work is better assessed separately from their emergency response work. In chapters 3 and 5, we will turn to the question of how a series of niche interventions can add up to longer-term outcomes.

The second type of niche intervention arises where the link between outputs and outcomes is well established, such that delivery of the key outputs is likely to lead to the outcome. Examples of such interventions are especially abundant in the field of medicine, where there is a long history of scientific research, often through randomized control trials, linking medical interventions to their health outcomes. Two scholars of international development have emphasized this point:

> Is there a knowledge gap on the efficacy of the measles vaccine? Perhaps we're ignorant of the medical literature, but we believe the answer

is *no*. Thus an NGO vaccinating children need not run a randomized trial to measure the impact of the measles vaccine. . . . [R]esearchers should run experiments only when there is real uncertainty over impacts. In fact, it would be an unethical expenditure, as the money could go to pay for more vaccines! (Gugerty and Karlan 2014)

A similar view is offered by a former chief investment officer at Acumen, one of the first equity investors in Ziqitza's ambulance service:

Moving from outputs . . . to understanding outcomes and proving impact is extremely complicated. . . . So our strategy has been to review the literature and consult the experts, to establish the clarity and certainty of a specific output's link to impacts, and to focus on counting those outputs. (Trelstad 2008, 109)

The key message here is that where research has established a causal link between outputs and desired long-term outcomes, it is sufficient for the implementing organization to measure outputs as a proxy for outcomes. Organizations delivering proven vaccines do not need to measure the effectiveness of the vaccines. Ambulance services such as Ziqitza do not need to measure health outcomes at the hospital. But both need to pay a great deal of attention to the quality of their services, such as whether the vaccines are being delivered under suitable conditions, or whether the emergency response time is quick enough to increase the chances of patient survival. Part of the challenge for managers and investors alike lies in identifying the relevant research, in order to judge whether there is enough existing evidence to rely on the measurement of outputs.[11]

In short, this chapter illustrates the conditions under which it is sensible to focus on outputs as the primary measure of social performance. To be clear: concentrating on outputs does not let managers off the hook for measuring performance. On the contrary, it increases their responsibility to develop standardized processes capable of delivering those outputs efficiently and with consistently high quality.

Chapter 3

INTEGRATED STRATEGY

integrate: to put or bring together (parts or elements)
so as to form one whole; to combine into a whole.[1]

Transforming a life is interdependent on so many
things. It's not only irrigation, it's not only alternate
energy . . . there are so many interdependencies.
**NAVEEN PATIDAR, CHIEF OPERATING OFFICER, AGA KHAN
RURAL SUPPORT PROGRAMME INDIA**

OVER THE PAST TWENTY-FIVE YEARS, I've had the good fortune of observing a prominent rural development organization in western India at key moments in its evolution. This organization, the Aga Khan Rural Support Programme India (AKRSP),[2] works with smallholder farmers and landless households on some of the most difficult problems they face: severe and recurring drought, saltwater contamination of water resources, and lack of access to institutions such as banks and markets. During the monsoons from mid-June to early September, it is not uncommon for rivers in the region to swell and flood, eroding farms and hillsides, only to flow out to sea and leave the land parched for the remaining nine months of the year. To make matters worse, the region is often hit by years of extended drought. Attempts by farmers to tap deep underground aquifers have further depleted natural resource by overextracting groundwater to such an extent that saltwater has been sucked in from the sea, contaminating the precious remaining freshwater.

AKRSP began operations in three districts of Gujarat state, western India, in 1985. I first visited the NGO as a young intern from 1991 to 1992 when it was still an early-stage enterprise developing its model of social change. I then returned as a doctoral researcher gathering data for my dissertation in 1996 to 1997 during a phase of rapid organizational growth fueled by international aid, which was later documented in a book (Ebrahim 2003b).[3] A subsequent project on participatory approaches to natural resource management took me to the region again in 2007. And finally, for research on this book, I visited AKRSP during the summer of 2015. By this time the NGO had grown into an enterprise with nearly 340 staff, operations in three states across the country, and serving over 192,000 households and 1.4 million people.

In this chapter, I tell a story of how AKRSP's social change model and its performance systems have evolved over time. At first glance, its work looks like series of niche interventions focused on irrigation, soil and water conservation, and agricultural support. But the heart of the model lies in its distinctively grassroots approach to integrating these efforts, in which community-level institutions prioritize, manage, and oversee the natural resources in their villages. It exemplifies an "integrated strategy" of social change where a series of discrete interventions, delivered in a coordinated fashion, produce outcomes that are greater than the sum of their parts. These are contexts where knowledge about cause and effect is relatively well developed, but there are many moving parts that must be coordinated in order to increase control over outcomes.

My primary aim in narrating AKRSP's story is to unpack the key components of an integrated strategy and its performance systems. At the end of this chapter, I draw parallels between AKRSP's experience and other types of integrated interventions in order to draw general lessons. In addition, I seek to place the development of a performance system within an historical trajectory, framing it as a dynamic organizational process. What systems of performance measurement did the organization build as it grew? How did it routinize its model of social change so that it could be delivered at scale? What were the roles of funders in enabling, or impeding, the development of performance systems? What general insights can we extract about the design of an integrated strategy and its performance system?

Evolution of an Integrated Strategy: The Aga Khan Rural Support Programme India

The early 1980s marked the launch of a period of unprecedented growth in NGOs throughout the developing world. The preceding two decades had seen large increases in agricultural productivity in India and elsewhere as a result of green revolution technologies. But these modern farming techniques had favored regions with irrigation and infrastructure, contributing to the emergence of a class of rich modernized farmers, a growth in income disparities between regions, and an increased marginalization of the rural poor (Bernstein 1992; Breman 1985; Ghosh and Bharadwaj 1992). On the heels of these growing disparities, a range of participatory and grassroots approaches to development began to gain traction among activists as well as global funders (e.g., Chambers 1983; Chambers, Saxena, and Shah 1989; Freire 1973; Fals-Borda and Rahman 1991; Rahnema 1997).

It was in this context that AKRSP emerged. With a startup endowment from the Aga Khan Foundation (AKF)[4] based in Geneva, it was set up as a nonprofit company with a board of directors composed of prominent figures from Indian industry, government, and civil society, thereby giving it immediate national visibility. The board recruited, as its first chief executive officer, an influential public official who had recently retired from the post of secretary for rural development in the Government of Gujarat. With this prominent leadership and a growing cadre of professional staff recruited from the country's leading rural development management schools, the organization quickly established itself as a reputable rural development actor in India. Grants from international aid agencies soon followed, including from the Canadian International Development Agency, the UK Department for International Development, the European Commission

(EC), and the Ford Foundation, as well as from many state and federal agencies in India.

Building a Social Change Model, 1984–1994

From its inception, AKRSP sought to develop a value proposition based on two key pillars: sustainable natural resource use and organizing rural communities for collective action. The underlying premise was that organized communities would be better able to address problems of natural resource degradation and thus to generate opportunities for social and economic improvement. AKRSP's first decade of operations focused on developing and testing a model of social change that would operationalize this value proposition.

The organization's model began to coalesce within its first few years of operations. There were two main elements: technical interventions in water and land management that aimed to achieve "optimal long-term use . . . at high levels of productivity," coupled with the creation of community-level institutions that would "decide, execute and manage the development programmes" (AKRSP 1990, 2). This model of social change, which eventually came to be called *Community Based Natural Resource Management* (CBNRM), is illustrated in Figure 3.1.

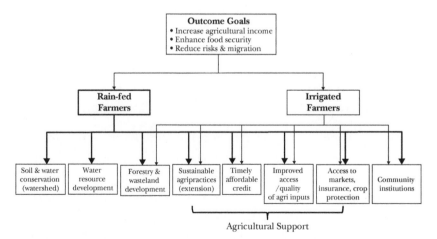

FIGURE 3.1   Community-Based Natural Resources Management (CBNRM)
Adapted from AKRSP internal documents, 2015.

Water and Land Management

More specifically, the organization developed four main types of technical interventions focused on natural resource use.[5]

Soil and Water Conservation. A variety of structures and techniques were used to reduce soil erosion and water loss from farmland, particularly on unirrigated land. For instance, stone or earthen bunds were built along land contours and field boundaries to reduce soil loss during the monsoons and to slow water drainage from sloping fields. Small stone dams were built across gullies or ravines during the rains in order to reduce erosion damage. In some cases, land was leveled or terraced, and farmers were trained to plow following the natural contours of the land to reduce moisture loss. This work was part of a larger "watershed approach," which involved treatment of tracts of private land as well as public land on the basis of hydrogeological boundaries.

Water Resource Development. AKRSP constructed small-scale infrastructure for improving water storage and irrigation. For example, check dams or small concrete and masonry structures moderated the flow of rivers during monsoons, resulting in small reservoirs that often retained water for several months after the rains. Along rivers with adequate water storage, the organization built irrigation facilities that would "lift" water via pump-houses to a high point in the topography, from where it would be distributed by gravity to farmers' fields. A suite of other technical structures (percolation tanks, spreading canals, farm ponds, and recharge wells) were also constructed to capture rainfall during the monsoons and to recharge groundwater supplies.

Forestry, Wasteland Development, and Alternative Energy. Tree-planting programs sought to reduce soil erosion, while providing income-earning opportunities through horticulture and other tree products. Members of a village, usually women, were hired to run nurseries to raise seedlings until they were fit to be sold to local farmers. These efforts were supplemented by afforestation of "wasteland" or unused government land, either with hardy species or those that had commercial or household value. Alternative energy projects used cow manure to generate methane for cooking (biogas) in order to reduce fuelwood extraction from forests while providing cleaner energy. AKRSP was among the first organizations in Gujarat to establish a joint forest management program in which rural communities partnered with the state Forest Department to manage and protect publicly controlled land.

Agricultural Support: Extension, Input Supply and Marketing. The organization worked with farmers to improve agricultural practices, access timely and affordable credit and other inputs, and provide access to markets and crop protection insurance. A cadre of local extension volunteers provided training on sustainable practices such as integrated pest management, drip irrigation, root intensification, and production of indigenous bio-pesticides and organic fertilizers. The extension workers encouraged farmers to try new practices, to share local knowledge and to aid in distributing inputs. Farmers' associations were linked up with local banks to secure credit for purchasing inputs, especially to support newly irrigated villages.

Community Institutions

The execution of these technical interventions in natural resources and agriculture all hinged on the establishment of integration mechanisms at the community level.

All of the above activities were carried out through community-level associations nurtured by AKRSP and responsible for prioritizing among the many interventions, raising local resources (in cash or kind) for the interventions, coordinating among interventions and groups, maintaining and managing the resource, and resolving conflicts. For instance, the operation of lift irrigation systems involved the establishment of local user groups to distribute water, collect user fees, and maintain and manage the infrastructure. Similarly, in regions near government irrigation canals, AKRSP pioneered the transfer of those canals to farmer groups to manage and maintain the systems. Other associations enabled their members to develop group-specific goals such as increasing household savings, securing and negotiating credit from local banks for agricultural inputs and supplies, and even lobbying elected officials for better services.

The ultimate goal of these two main components of the CBNRM model—interventions in natural resources, integrated through community institutions—was to improve the lives of farmers by increasing agricultural incomes, reducing food insecurity, and potentially even reducing the need for farmer to migrate in search of work. (These outcomes are listed in the top box of Figure 3.1.)

During its first decade, AKRSP concentrated on building this model of social change. Notably, the organization did not develop this social change model in isolation, but had substantial support from international funders and consultants who introduced new ideas and advances from other parts of the world. For example, soil and water conservation activities were introduced in 1989 by a watershed expert hired by the Aga Khan Foundation. Similarly, consultants from the United States and Honduras motivated AKRSP to develop an agricultural training and experimentation approach in collaboration with farmers on their own fields rather than at separate research sites, a practice known as farmer-to-farmer extension. And AKRSP's work in irrigation management was heavily influenced by the experience of the Ford Foundation in the Philippines that had demonstrated the power of participatory and community-based management of canals.[6]

Global funders also played an important role in transmitting ideas about community institutions. For example, the Aga Khan Foundation arranged for several visits by specialists in participatory methodologies. AKRSP was deeply influenced by the work of Robert Chambers of the Institute for Development Studies[7] on bottom-up approaches to development, eventually leading to the establishment of an approach, Participatory Rural Appraisal (PRA), as a cornerstone methodology for interacting with rural communities. PRA consists of a series of interactive tools and mapping methods for gathering information about a community or its resources (e.g., about local forest or water resources, community wealth and social rankings, local priorities and concerns, and so on), and ranking local priorities, while simultaneously facilitating the establishment of rapport between researchers and community members (Chambers 1994). AKRSP's experimentation with PRA techniques led to a transformation in its engagement with rural communities, enabling greater voice and downward accountability to its clients. As a methodology, PRA demanded that villagers be seen as experts and agents in their own right. The organization even developed training manuals on the method and offered training workshops to other organizations (AKRSP n.d.).

By the mid-1990s, this model of social change was well established in the organization's DNA. The next challenge lay in developing performance systems to help deliver the model systematically at scale.

Designing a Coordination System, 1994–2012

The second phase of AKRSP's evolution was a period of rapid growth, fueled by two large grants from the EC that lasted nearly two decades. During this time, the organization became more systematic in planning and delivering its key interventions, eventually expanding to other states in India. The key building blocks of its performance system—what might be called a coordination system—began to emerge at this time. It consisted of three main parts:

- standardizing the delivery of outputs
- combining those outputs in a systematic way
- assessing interdependent outcomes

Standardizing Output Delivery

AKRSP secured an eight-year grant from the EC from 1994 to 2001. It was the largest ever grant from the EC to the NGO sector at the time, and provided nearly three-quarters of AKRSP's budget.[8] The project, dubbed Community Management of Natural Resources in Gujarat (CMNR), aimed to provide rural communities with "income earning opportunities through improved and sustainable management of natural resources by VIs [village institutions]" (Weir and Shah 1994, Appendix 3.1). Over the course of the project, AKRSP sought to triple the number of community institutions it worked with in Gujarat state, while also reaching more beneficiaries per village.

The influx of resources, and the external scrutiny that accompanied the EC grant, placed great pressure on AKRSP to improve its planning procedures in order to reliably set and meet quantifiable targets. The 1990s were characterized by a struggle in the organization to develop planning procedures to enable the rapid delivery of outputs and also to forecast budgets more accurately. Tensions between AKRSP and its intermediary funder, AKF, sometimes flared up as a result of the NGO's poor planning and its submission of reports that contained inconsistent quantifications of its target achievements.

One of the organization's main challenges lay in planning and monitoring the delivery of outputs, particularly in its water resource and soil conservation work. During its first several years of operation, the organization's planning systems were ad hoc, with target planning dependent on personal interaction and adjustment by individuals at the spearhead team level.[9] The foundations for a centralized system were laid by a series of consultants hired by AKF who recommended redesigning the organization's reporting to allow for a comparison of quantifiable achievements with planned objectives, and further developing its impact studies to include regular collection of agricultural data, project baselines, and use of participatory rural appraisals (Hampshire 1991; Poate 1989).

For routinizing monitoring and impact assessment, the consultants introduced a project management tool known as "logical framework analysis" (LFA or log frame), which is a variation of the now-ubiquitous logic model (see Chapter 1 for a brief introduction). The logical framework is a matrix in which a project's objectives and expected results are clearly identified, along with a list of indicators that are to be used in measuring and verifying progress towards achieving those objectives and results.

AKRSP's logical framework for the CMNR project ended up including eighty-nine indicators for monitoring progress![10] Table 3.1

provides an excerpt of this logical framework. The "project purpose" specifies the longer-term outcomes expected by the project, whereas the "results" specify the activities and short-term outputs (such as village institutions strengthened and built, watershed area developed, check dams constructed, and so on). For brevity, I include in the table only the first two of a total of twelve such "results" or outputs—showing only thirteen of eighty-nine output indicators that the organization tracked on a semiannual basis. The third and fourth columns specify how progress towards these results was to be measured and the information sources needed for this verification. The last column articulates key assumptions in the model's theory of change.[11]

This logical framework served not only as a tool for codifying AKRSP's development model but, perhaps more importantly, for focusing the attention of program staff and managers on producing outputs in a systematic, quantifiable, and predictable fashion. A few years into the grant, a senior executive explained how this shift in attention had affected his work:

> [In] the last three years, I've had only one mission—it was like a bloody cricket match—and that was to reach 100 percent target achievement. . . . What you review determines very much what you do. If you review targets, you end up doing targets. (February 28, 1997)

This attention to meeting quantitative targets permeated the entire organization. AKRSP's chief executive at the time elaborated:

> I put pressure on staff [and] say we must be more accurate in forming targets and predictions. Once targets are set, yes, [there is] pressure on field [staff] to achieve them. . . . We've landed a big grant and are expected to scale up. Everybody in the organization knows we must achieve more every year until we reach a plateau. (March 18, 1996)

Reflecting back many years later, another executive recalled the systematic improvements in program delivery achieved at the time:

> The organization developed a streamlined procedure for implementing programs, which included community organizing and procurement. . . .

TABLE 3.1 Excerpt of Logical Framework for the CMNR Project (1994–2001)

	Intervention Logic	Objectively Verifiable Indicators	Sources of Verification	Assumptions
Project Purpose	Improved income earning opportunities through improved and sustainable management of natural resources by VIs in four districts of Gujarat	• increase in income earning opportunities and employment for participating villagers • increased income from individual and group savings • sustained increase in the productivity of natural resources, including crop yields • reduction in distress out-migration • increase in the number of mature VIs	• baseline and impact surveys, credit records, surveys • baseline and impact surveys, NGO and VI records, agricultural census data • baseline and impact surveys, case studies • case studies • VI maturity/performance index	• Improved management of natural resources is sufficient to increase income earning • natural resource base can support population • population growth rate will not increase significantly • there are no severe droughts or other natural disasters during the project period
Results (1)	Existing Village Institutions (VIs) strengthened and new ones established	• Number of new VIs established as proportion of targets • Number of existing VIs operating effectively as proportion of total • Number of VIs ceasing to operate	• VI and NGO Records • Annual analysis of VI records; 10% sample surveys of VI members • case studies	• Vested interests opposed to VIs can be neutralized • government policies on formation and operation of VIs remain favorable

Results (2)	Micro-watersheds developed	• Area of watershed developed as proportion of targets	• VI and NGO Records	• Government policies on use of common property resources remain favorable
		• number of water harvesting structures constructed as proportion of targets	• NGO Records	• farmers in treated watersheds agree to communal management
		• number of micro-watersheds completely treated as proportion of targets	• NGO Records	
		• number of micro-watersheds partially treated as proportion of targets	• NGO Records	
		• increase in cultivated area and changes in cropping patterns	• Baseline and impact surveys	
		• increase in area under supplementary irrigation	• Baseline and impact surveys	
		• rates of soil deposition	• VI records / technical studies	
		• proportion of structures well maintained by farmers in the watersheds	• Participatory Rural Appraisals (PRAs)	
		• increase in groundwater recharge	• VI Records/technical studies	
		• proportion of cost contributed by farmers	• VI Records/PRAs	

Adapted and excerpted from Weir and Shah (1994, Appendix 3.1, LFA Version 2.0, 1–2).

> Even in the check dam program, we know what to do, how to approach
> people, how to float the tender, how to find the vendor to supply the
> material, how to [allocate] the work. . . . [This] reduces uncertainties
> and you can achieve the numbers. . . . (Umesh Desai, director, Water
> Resources, July 14, 2015)

By the end of the CMNR project in 2001, AKRSP reported
achieving most of its output targets in the construction of water resource infrastructure, although it fell short in its soil and water conservation efforts, possibly due to overly ambitious target setting prior
to the project. Overall, however, an external evaluation by the EC
expressed satisfaction with the progress of both AKRSP and another
partner NGO:

> The final and general recommendation, taking into account the lessons
> learnt and the positive results of the CMNR project is to fine-tune and
> replicate the activities elsewhere in semi arid regions of India having
> similar conditions. . . . In view of the very successful achievements of
> the two implementing NGOs, both . . . deserve to be supported in their
> activities by funding organisations in the future. (European Commis-
> sion 2001, 49)

In brief, during the eight years of the CMNR grant, AKRSP had
developed a standard set of outputs and had put in place a system
for better planning and delivering those key interventions. What remained underdeveloped, however, was how best to combine or integrate those outputs in order to generate synergistic outcomes.

Combining Outputs in a Systematic Way

The success of the CMNR grant led to an even larger subsequent
grant from the EC that provided another ten years of support, from
2002 to 2012, for further replicating and scaling AKRSP's social
change model.[12] This project, titled Sustainable Community Based
Approaches to Livelihood Enhancement (SCALE), retained the core
emphasis on natural resource management through village organiza-

tions. But its emphasis on the latter—on building community institutions—was stronger and more explicit:

> These grass roots organisations identify and prioritise local problems, participate in all phases of building the project, negotiate with and lobby appropriate government agencies for better policies and funding[,] and assure its sustainability with participatory management and full responsibility at the village level for the maintenance of physical infrastructure. (Funding proposal, Aga Khan Foundation 2001, iii)

In its early years, AKRSP often tried to create a single organization in each village—the Gram Vikas Mandal (Village Development Committee)—that was responsible for planning and implementing all interventions in that village while also ensuring fair distribution of benefits, conflict resolution, oversight, and management of accounts. But as AKRSP gained experience working in rural communities, this model evolved in three respects. First, it learned that village-level organizations were prone to capture by community elites, sometimes failing to represent the interests of its most marginalized members such as the landless, women, and lower castes. This made it necessary to create institutions at the subvillage level that catered to specific groups. Second, AKRSP learned that the management of different natural resources such as surface water, ground water, and forests required specific skills and tasks, making it necessary to create resource-specific institutions. And third, the organization learned that the effectiveness and power of community institutions could be scaled by connecting them to one another, for example, by forming federations across a region with greater political power. Over time, AKRSP thus began to differentiate among four broad categories of community institutions—subvillage, village, multivillage, and apex—which are described in Table 3.2.

The organization's work in the Meghal River Basin in western Gujarat illustrates the central role of community institutions in prioritizing and coordinating interventions (AKRSP 2011). During the 1990s, AKRSP constructed over sixty small check dams along the Meghal

TABLE 3.2 Types of Community Institutions Created by AKRSP

Level	General Purpose	Institution Type	Specific Purpose
Subvillage	Address the needs of a particular marginalized group within a village	Mahila Vikas Mandals (Women's development committees) & Self-Help Groups	Provide savings and credit support, and address various needs determined by group, such as savings and credit, health and reproductive care, income-generating activities, etc.
		Tola Vikas Mandal (Hamlet development committee)	Promote interests of subgroups in a village, typically by caste or occupation such as farming, goat rearing, Maldharis (cowherds), who require fodder supply and savings.
		Jal Bachao Juth (Water-saving group) Community Interest Groups	Promote water storage and conservation efforts at a hamlet level.
Village	Address village-level development needs	Gram Vikas Mandal (Village development committee)	Set village-wide priorities and coordination, such as water resource development, soil conservation, agricultural extension, and input supply.
		Lift Irrigation Cooperative Societies	Manage and maintain irrigation equipment and ensure fair and timely distribution of water; collect user fees; manage conflicts.
		Pani Samiti (Water user group; Drinking water committee)	Promote and maintain drinking water and sanitation, for example, through roof rainwater harvesting systems.
		Kissan Vikas Samiti (Farmer development group)	Support farmers through agricultural extension and access to inputs and credit.
Multivillage	Address multivillage natural resources	Canal Irrigation Society Watershed or River Basin associations (e.g, Meghal River Core Group)	Manage, maintain, and coordinate water resource infrastructure that serves a cluster of villages; ensure fair and timely distribution of water; collect user fees; manage conflicts; liaise with public agencies.
Apex	Build capacity of member organizations, and represent their collective interests	Federation of Canal Irrigation Societies	Collective of canal irrigation societies to coordinate canal water flow and liaise with irrigation department.
		Mahila Manch (women's federation)	Collective of women's groups to represent their interests in dealings with service providers such as banks or health clinics, while also backing efforts to increase the visibility and power of women in other institutions.
		Producer Company	Collective of farmers' groups for purchase of inputs and joint marketing of products.

Sources: Compiled from information in AKRSP (2000, 2008).

River and its tributaries, but these were built largely in isolation from one another and provided benefits only to the farms in the immediate vicinity of the dams. They were essentially niche interventions. But from 2002 to 2012, following a period of severe drought, the organization began to coordinate its work both within and across villages in the river basin.

This coordination was accomplished in two ways. First, AKRSP's water resource staff began to map out the river and its watersheds in order to view the river basin as an integrated hydrological system. They identified sixty-four villages in the basin, eventually working with fifty-four of them on water resource management through local Jal Bachao Juths (water saving groups). These local groups, which operated at a neighborhood level such as a hamlet, were explicitly tasked with "program planning, integration and implementation" of water resource activities in their localities, combined with "awareness building" and "acting as a pressure group" to galvanize action in the community (AKRSP 2008, 13). Over the course of a decade, AKRSP worked with these local groups to build over three hundred water resource structures such as check dams and other smaller structures, supplementing efforts by governmental agencies on the river. Figure 3.2 is a map of the river basin, with its major villages, large government dams, and hundreds of check dams.

In addition, AKRSP convened a pan-basin coordination committee known as the Meghal River Core Group. Because the building of infrastructure upstream would reduce the flow of water downstream, a coordination mechanism was essential for minimizing potential inequity and managing conflict. With AKRSP's support and initial facilitation, the Meghal River Core Group became responsible for scheduling and coordinating interventions across the entire river basin. AKRSP provided technical expertise, management support to the community institutions, and financial support to each village. The costs of construction were equally shared between AKRSP and local communities. Furthermore, AKRSP introduced soil conservation and drip irrigation technologies as a complement to the water resource

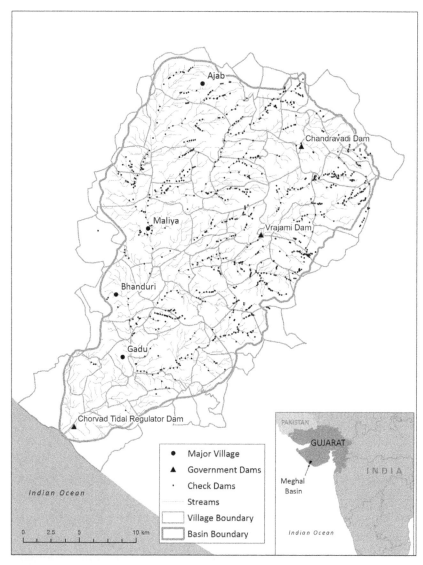

FIGURE 3.2 Meghal River Basin and Its Villages, Gujarat, India

Sources: Verma, Krishnan, and Joshi (2011) for village and basin boundaries, check and government dams; Esri Data and Maps for state boundaries; SRTM for rivers. Map by Thais Rodrigues de Oliveira and Jeff Blossom, Center for Geographic Analysis, Harvard University.

structures on the river. This was achieved by taking the Core Group on an exposure visit to soil and water conservation projects in other parts of the state, using a peer-to-peer model where they learned directly from other farmers of the benefits and costs of such interventions.

An external evaluation team hired by the EC at the end of the SCALE project commented on the impact of this effort:

> Where activities are concentrated in river basin areas, dramatic results are possible, as with the Meghal River Basin, where AKRSP supported construction of about a quarter of the structures built (306 of 1,146). Clear evidence of improved drought proofing has been found, with improved water security for drinking water and agriculture. There are also visible changes, as the river now flows for 10-12 months of the year, when previously it was present for only 6–7 months. . . . Gross value of agricultural production in the basin is estimated to have increased from INR 1,466 million in 2000-1 to INR 3,926 million in 2010–11 . . . [and an] increased capacity of the area to support a winter and in some cases summer crop. (COWI and Atkins 2013, 53–54)[13]

The Meghal River experience, while remarkable, was not unique. AKRSP was engaged in multiple efforts that required coordination, for instance, in the management of irrigation canals and forested lands that traversed multiple villages, and in soil and water conservation efforts that were often undertaken at a watershed level rather than on a village basis. Even AKRSP's organizational structure at the field level reflected this integrative orientation. Field staff were divided into "cluster teams" that were typically responsible for twenty to thirty villages, with the clusters often defined by watershed boundaries rather than political ones, and comprising five to ten staff with a mix of technical and social mobilization skills.

Yet, despite the importance of community institutions to AKRSP's development model, the organization had not yet learned how to assess or support them. A key performance measurement challenge lay in assessing the quality of these various groups in order to most effectively provide support. An internal strategic review conducted in 1999 was blunt about this shortfall:

Though AKRSP(I) has been a pioneer in promoting different kinds of community organisations, . . . the lack of targets for VI [village institution] development, the lack of time frames, the lack of quantification, have all been worrying issues which have prevented AKRSP(I) from adequately allocating resources. (AKRSP 1999, 14–15)

The SCALE project, with its emphasis on community institutions, provided an opportunity to begin gathering data more systematically on the functioning of these various types of groups. AKRSP began to develop a framework for monitoring and evaluating the health and maturity of community institutions, to serve as a complementary tool to the standard logical framework (AKRSP 2000). A new Social Process Team was created at the central office to develop assessment and rating tools for use by the field teams, where they would be implemented by front-line staff. The core task was to develop instruments that would yield reliable data and yet be feasible to implement by field staff, the development organizers (DOs). This involved a process of trial and error over a period of several years. The head of the Social Process Team explained:

[We developed] an institutional maturity index . . . but it was much too idealistic and much too complicated. . . . The DO was not able to understand that. It was [also] very time consuming . . . [so] we devised a simpler kind of assessment format. . . .

[Now] we have different kinds of assessment formats for different institutions—for SHGs [self-help groups], federations, Pani Samitis, and Gram Vikas Mandals. . . . [Staff] do assessments based on the criteria for that institution. (Falguni Lokhil, July 15, 2015)

To illustrate how such an assessment might be designed, Table 3.3 provides scoring criteria developed by AKRSP for assessing Pani Samitis (water user groups). The criteria covered several categories that staff found useful for assessing quality and determining how to provide further support—ranging from governance criteria such as meeting regularity and participation of members, to financial management, quality and reliability of service, conflict resolution, and external alliances. Each group was assessed by the development organizer tasked with supporting it on an annual basis. For instance, under the first category of "group formation," the group was rated (on a scale of 1 to 5) on whether it had followed a set of standards provided by AKRSP in ensuring the representation of marginalized groups. The group was assessed on numerous metrics during its formation and planning stages, plus additional metrics once it commenced operations.

AKRSP's regional teams also periodically conducted aggregate assessments of community institutions. For instance, one team assessed a sample of 425 community institutions, ranking them into five categories—self-reliant, active, redundant, dormant, and defunct—that represented a spectrum of institutional quality (AKRSP 2008). At one end of the spectrum, self-reliant organizations ran independently without any need for further support from AKRSP; at the other end, defunct organizations had either collapsed or been supplanted by another type of community institution. Notably, only 19 of the 425 community institutions were rated as self-reliant, in that they were independently managing their own affairs, allowing AKRSP to exit from the intervention. Most of them (71 percent) were ranked as active, needing varying degrees of support from the NGO. About one-quarter were weak or no longer operating (dormant/defunct), requiring the development organizer to either provide enhanced support or to cut losses. The value for AKRSP in collecting these data lay in targeting its support more effectively and in deepening its own understanding of what support to provide for each type of institution.

In addition, the SCALE project also set a series of explicit goals with respect to the building of community institutions. The project identified three main "results": (1) Community institutions are managing natural resources in an improved and more equitable manner (in irrigation, groundwater management, soil and water conservation, etc.); (2) Community institutions are managing the provision of basic amenities (such as drinking water, alternative energy, sanitation); and, (3) Community institutions are managing interventions for improving

TABLE 3.3 Quality Assessment Tool for *Pani Samitis* (Water User Groups)

Quality Metrics		Scores	
	5	3	1
Prior to Project Commencement			
Group Formation	As per standards, with representatives from marginalized groups including women	As per standards	Group formed but did not follow standards
Group Leadership	Leadership based on courtyard/community/party basis; Women leaders	Leadership based on courtyard/community/ party basis	Lack of leadership
Roles and Responsibilities	Responsibilities of members are fixed; there is regular supervision of members	Responsibilities assigned only for 1–2 members; there is no regular supervision	No clear roles and responsibilities and no supervision
Meetings	Regular with agenda Member attendance over 80%	Regular with agenda Member attendance under 80%	Intermittent/irregular
Women's Participation	Attendance more than 80%	Attendance less than 80%	Irregular
Planning	Project planned in the *Gram Sabha* (village meeting) with inputs from different sections of the community	The planning is made by *pani samiti*	The planning is made by some of the committee members

	During Operations	Financial Contribution	95% of community members contributed and receipts were issued	50% of community members contributed	10% of community members contributed

	Category	Column 1	Column 2	Column 3
During Operations	Financial Contribution	95% of community members contributed and receipts were issued	50% of community members contributed	10% of community members contributed
	Audit of Accounts	Internal audit was undertaken and accounts were submitted in the *Gram Sabha* (village meeting)	Internal audit was undertaken and accounts were submitted in the *pani samiti*	Internal audit was undertaken and accounts only shared with few members
	Conflict Resolution	Conflicts are addressed in a timely manner	Conflicts are not adequately addressed	Conflicts prevail
	Awareness Programs	Awareness programs organized regularly on health, water, and sanitation issues	Awareness programs organized intermittently	Awareness programs organized rarely
	Operator	Operator is appointed, regularly paid, and monitored	Operator is appointed, but not paid regularly	Operators are frequently changed
	Regular Water Service	All segments/community get sufficient and timely water; committee members undertake this responsibility	All segments/community get timely water; responsibility remains with operator, not committee	Operator provides the water but with partiality
	Sanitation	Water committee makes efforts minimize wastage of and dirt in water; Takes responsibility for regular sanitation/chlorination of water tank	Operator makes efforts minimize wastage of and dirt in water; Regular sanitation/chlorination of water tank	Operator makes efforts to minimize wastage of and dirt in water; Irregular sanitation/chlorination of water tank
	External Alliances	Alliances with Water Supply Division, other government departments, and village organizations	Alliance with Water Supply Division (of government)	No alliances

Source: Adapted and excerpted from Social Process Team documents; translated from Gujarati.

nonfarm livelihoods (such as through financial services, self-help groups, and the agricultural value chain) (COWI and Atkins 2013, 92–93).[14] AKRSP set measurable targets for each of these goals. For illustrative purposes, Table 3.4 shows the targets and indicators for the first of these three results, along with its key performance indicators. Each indicator was further divided into specific activity targets (not shown). For example, the first indicator on groundwater management was supported by physical targets for the numbers of check dams, percolation tanks, wells, and so on, to be managed by community institutions. Progress was tracked every six months and reported by the field teams to AKRSP's headquarters, and then aggregated and sent on to AKF and the EC.

While most of the targets were met, an evaluation carried out by a third party hired by the EC expressed concern about community

TABLE 3.4   Performance Targets and Achievements, SCALE Project (2002–2012)

		Target	*Achieved*
Result 1	**Community institutions (CIs) are managing natural resources in an improved and more equitable manner**		
Indicators	1. CIs are actively participating in groundwater management initiatives	160 villages	153 villages
	2. Water-efficient irrigation technologies are adopted	7,000 households	9,333 households
	3. Improved and diversified cropping patterns adopted	15,000 households	31,991 households
	4. CIs are undertaking agricultural input supply and marketing interventions	400 villages	697 villages
	5. CIs are managing soil and water conservation	300 villages/18,000 hectares	294 villages/ 13,640 hectares
	6. CIs are managing wasteland regeneration	100 villages/4,000 hectares	76 villages/4,432 hectares
	7. CIs are undertaking participatory irrigation management	10,000 hectares	12,035

Source: Adapted and excerpted from logical framework for SCALE project, AKRSP internal documents; COWI and Atkins 2013, 27–28, 103–7.

institutions, noting "some reduction in the number of functioning groups" and the "potential to enhance the vibrancy of some of these groups." For example, the evaluation team noted that only 59 percent of self-help groups that provided loans to their members had linkages with external financing institutions such as banks (COWI and Atkins 2013, 44). It was at about this time that AKRSP renewed its efforts to develop quality assessment metrics for community institutions in order to better support them.

In sum, AKRSP's performance systems now served two main functions in support of its integrated strategy. The first was standardizing the delivery of outputs. By the end of the first EC grant in 2001, the organization had put in place a well-oiled process for producing technical outputs such as check dams, irrigation systems, or land treatment with soil and water conservation techniques. The key tool for measuring, monitoring, and reporting progress was the logical framework (Table 3.1). Second, the organization began to develop a complementary set of measures and tools for assessing and improving the quality of its community institutions (Tables 3.3 and 3.4). These institutions were the vehicles through which key interventions were systematically prioritized, sequenced, executed, and coordinated, not only at a village level but also across multiple villages. As such, they served to integrate a set of outputs that would otherwise be delivered in isolation from one another.

Assessing Interdependent Outcomes

AKRSP's development model was premised on an integrative theory of change: *if farmers were to be provided with a series of natural resource and agricultural interventions, prioritized and managed by community institutions, then there would be improvements in outcomes for farmers.* But what were these interdependent outcomes, and were they actually produced?

It was not until the CMNR project (implemented from 1994 to 2001 in 460 villages) that AKRSP explicitly articulated a set of measurable outcomes: to increase incomes of beneficiary households to above the poverty threshold, to improve land productivity, and to reduce seasonal out-migration (Aga Khan Foundation 1994, 4–5;

AKRSP 2002, 5). A more general formulation of these outcomes, developed some years later, is listed at the top of Figure 3.1—increase agricultural income, enhance food security, and reduce risks and migration (AKRSP 2013).

Two teams of consultants hired by the EC helped the organization design baseline surveys and create a database for tracking progress on output and outcome indicators (Weir et al. 1995; Weir and Shah 1994). The first of these teams recommended establishing a control group as part of the baseline data in order to have a basis for comparing outcomes in communities that received AKRSP interventions and those that did not (i.e., a counterfactual). AKRSP also hired academics from local institutions to conduct further surveys on specific programs.[15] Notably, most of the output measurement was done in-house and documented in spreadsheets based on the logical framework for the project (with eighty-nine indicators, some of which are shown in Table 3.2), whereas the outcome measurement was largely contracted out, with the exception of a few cases studies conducted at a village level.

A final evaluation of the CMNR project, conducted by the EC in 2001, noted substantial achievements in terms of the outcome goals, observing "an enormous drop in out-migration, in certain project areas from 90 to 10%" and increases in income and land productivity in agriculture such that "irrigators managed on average to double their income, while those who had their land and water conditions improved were able to increase their rain fed yield and income by 20–25%." The evaluation did not, however, explicitly address the question of whether income increases were above a defined "poverty threshold." The evaluation also noted improvements in natural resources, where "check dams and watershed treatment activities have to a large extent contributed to the recharge of the ground water levels (1 to 3 meters), soil erosion has been reduced and the soils contain more moisture, resulting in higher yields as well as a better drinking water supply" (European Commission 2001, 7).

The subsequent SCALE project (implemented from 2002 to 2012 in 1,242 villages), also reported considerable positive outcomes as a result of the integrated efforts—although, surprisingly, these claims appear to have been made without reliable baseline data.[16] A final evaluation noted that the "combined effects" of various water re-source treatments such as check dams, farm bunds, gully plugs, and participatory irrigation management activities, "has helped both re-duce cultivation risks and increase production levels" (COWI and Atkins 2013, 4–5). As evidence, the evaluation cited various reports and case studies produced or contracted by AKRSP that claimed, for example, an "increase in production on private land of 15-20% for some 5,561 households, out of which 68% of beneficiary households are small and marginal farmers." Another report cited in the evalua-tion claimed that "the majority of beneficiaries covered under SCALE have crossed the poverty line as their earnings have risen above [INR] 8,000 per year in a sustainable manner. The increased income from the project supported activities have effectively reduced the distress migration, [and] increased security to their families. . . . " (COWI and Atkins 2013, 4–5).

Lessons Learned in Assessing Outcomes

A number of general lessons, positive and cautionary, stand out from AKRSP's experience with assessing outcomes. First, the organization implemented a number of best practices for outcome measurement during the CMNR, the first EC grant. For instance, it identified a set of clear and measurable outcomes that were explicitly linked to its theory of change. It was also systematic in tracking progress on both outputs and outcomes. And, it sought support from consultants for tasks that were beyond its expertise, such as in developing a base-line and identifying control groups (i.e., villages that did not receive AKRSP's interventions), so that there would be a basis for comparing any changes in outcomes (i.e., a counterfactual).

Second, as a practical matter, AKRSP separated the task of out-put measurement from outcome assessment. As noted, most of the output measurement was done in-house as part of a regular moni-toring process codified in the logical framework for the project. The organization's own monitoring and evaluation team was responsible for gathering this data and reporting it to senior management and the funder. Outcome assessment, on the other hand, was largely contracted out, either to local academic institutions or to consultants. This separation of tasks enabled the organization to focus on executing its work and use output measurement to monitor progress according to targets, while leaving the complex outcome assessment work to hired social scientists and external evaluators.

Third, on a more cautionary note, the organization's attention to assessing outcomes appears to have declined over time. AKRSP's first large grant from the EC required it to specify outcomes and to collect baseline data. As these external demands diminished over time, so too did the organization's attention to outcomes. The second EC grant, for instance, had neither a reliable baseline nor a systematic plan for assessing outcomes. This decline in attention to outcomes is troubling for an organization with an integrated strategy, where its model of social change aims to produce interdependent outcomes. Moreover, for an enterprise that operates at substantial scale—in thousands of villages—it would not have been infeasible for it to gather baseline data and establish control groups.

What might explain this decline in attention to outcome measurement, despite the importance of outcomes to AKRSP's social change model? As I discuss below, AKRSP is representative of a deeper malaise common among organizations dependent on their funders: a myopic view of accountability focused on compliance with funder expectations rather than an accountability driven by their own strategies for social change (Campbell 2002; Ebrahim 2005; Edwards and Hulme 1996a; Najam 1996a). AKRSP was eventually forced to confront this problem with the end of EC funding.

Towards a Strategy-Driven Accountability, 2012–2015

Both the CMNR and SCALE grants provided AKRSP with nearly two decades of stable long-term funding, a luxury that made it possible to plan for growth and to execute its integrated development model in thousands of communities and to reach over a million people. But by 2010, bilateral aid was on the decline and NGOs were no longer its key recipients. As the era of EC funding came to an end, AKRSP entered a phase of uncertainty and turbulence.

The organization began to diversify its funding sources, seeking increasing support from a wide range of government sources, philanthropic foundations, corporations, and community institutions. AKRSP had depended on the EC for nearly 75 percent of its budget under the CMNR grant and almost 50 percent under SCALE. Over a period of several years, it succeeded in diversifying and growing its funding base to over forty different donors by 2015 from a range of public, philanthropic, and corporate sources (see Figure 3.3 for a comparison of funding sources in 2010 and 2014). Corporate foundations were an important new player in Indian philanthropy, spurred by the Indian Companies Act of 2013 that required all corporations exceeding a certain size to spend at least 2 percent of their average net profit made in the preceding three years on corporate social responsibility.[17] A growing number of corporate foundations thus began to emerge, each seeking recipient organizations with the capacity to absorb their donations. AKRSP was well positioned to tap this emerging pool of capital.

Although AKRSP succeeded in diversifying its funding during this period, the effects of this balkanized funding environment on its performance systems were less positive. Each new funder had different demands for accountability. The organization's internal monitoring and evaluation (M&E) unit gradually became marginalized, as grant proposal writing and reporting increasingly fell to individual department heads rather than the M&E team. Output and outcome measurement now proceeded largely on an as-needed basis depending on the idiosyncratic requirements of an increasingly varied pool of funders. A comprehensive management information system established during the two decades of EC support was abandoned in favor of separate reporting for each grant. The head of AKRSP's water resource department described this shift in stark terms:

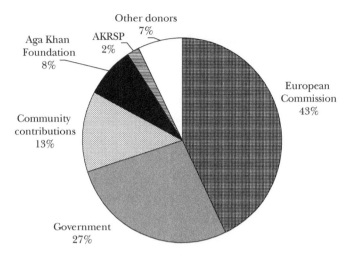

FIGURE 3.3A AKRSP's Funding Sources by Utilization, 2010

Source: AKRSP(I) Annual Report, 2010 (2011).

Note: Other donors include philanthropic and corporate foundations, and bilateral aid agencies other than the EC. AKRSP's own contributions include interest income and income from operations. Government refers to the central and state governments in India.

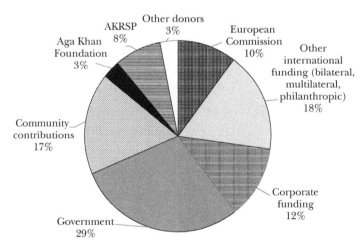

FIGURE 3.3B AKRSP's Funding Sources by Utilization, 2014

Source: AKRSP(I) Annual Report, 2014 (2015).

In the early years of the organization, there was greater freedom to work—to just "do it"—because of flexibility internally as well as externally. Now, in the current situation, there are lots of standard procedures that need to be followed, often as part of donor requirements. (Umesh Desai, director, Water Resources, July 14, 2015)

For instance, a grant from a corporate donor for building check dams and groundwater recharge structures was very particular about the type of data to be gathered. The head of AKRSP's M&E team elaborated:

> They are very keen [to count] every drop [of water] that is collected or harvested—what happens to it, how much [groundwater] recharge is there, and how many times does the check dam fill up. . . . [We] have to even measure the amount of soil that is deposited in certain structures. (Niraj Joshi, July 14, 2015)

The effects of these piecemeal grants on AKRSP's community-based approach to development were palpable. A middle manager in the soil and water conservation program explained:

> Our programs are now-a-days becoming more donor-oriented rather than community-oriented. So we need to satisfy the donors [with] timely reporting under their audit compliance [procedures]. [And] . . . they are coming to the field [to] cross verify the measurements. (John P. Inchakalody, manager, Water Resources and Soil and Water Conservation, July 14, 2015)

The deeper risk to AKRSP was the potential loss of a coherent purpose, that its integrated development model would become eroded into a series of isolated niche interventions. The head of M&E and a middle manager were both concerned:

> [Y]ou will not see a sequenced intervention. You would more likely see some bit of soil conservation work, some bit of agriculture work, some bit of dairy, and some bit of integration. All the pieces of the jigsaw will not . . . fit in. (Niraj Joshi, head of M&E team, July 15, 2015)

[M]ost of the staff are now focused towards implementation only: I need to complete fifty hectares of soil-water management activities within this one or two months. They are not thinking beyond that as to what is the impact of that fifty hectares. So internally we need to capacitate our staff to see the activities [from] this [wider] angle. That is [a] major internal rectification we need to do. (John P. Inchakalody, manager, Water Resources and Soil and Water Conservation, July 14, 2015)

These concerns and their consequences were not lost on the organization's leadership. Possibly for the first time in two decades, AKRSP began to look inward for strategic direction and focus. The organization's chief executive officer was candid:

AKRSP has to now reemphasize its mission and values much, much more than earlier. . . . [T]here are so many donors . . . and they all have different approaches and theories of change, so you need to make sure that your guys are all anchored. (Apoorva Oza, July 17, 2015)

Similarly, the organization's chief operating officer saw the primary challenge as internal rather than external. For him, the way ahead lay in creating a "framework in the minds of our grassroots people and middle managers and senior managers" that would enable them to realize the "transformational" potential of an integrated strategy rather than merely the "transactional" nature of piecemeal projects driven by funding (Naveen Patidar, COO, July 13, 2015).

AKRSP's leadership introduced a series of new efforts to refocus the organization's work, to provide its staff with purpose and coherence. For instance, one such mechanism was an annual reflection workshop. The basic idea was straightforward: gather the field teams in each region to articulate a five-year vision for their region; discuss how this vision links to AKRSP's mission and values; and then use the insights to assess the work of the past year and plan for the coming year. The workshops typically lasted two to three days, and were led by the CEO and COO, with all the top management participating alongside field staff. Five such workshops were held for the first time in early 2015. The very idea of asking field staff and managers to take the time to reflect was countercultural in an organization that prided itself on action:

> [W]e are driven by *doing*. The organizational DNA is *doing*, the person who *does* is respected . . . that's where the energy and invention and growth is. . . . So you have to dedicate within a year some time where you are saying *don't do but reflect*. We don't expect you to *do*. The organization values you *not doing* that at that time. (Apoorva Oza, CEO, July 17, 2015)

A second mechanism focused on aligning donor funding with mission. Any senior manager who wanted to accept donor support for a project would have to articulate how that project was necessary for AKRSP's mission. This basic requirement was intended to serve not only as a screen for filtering potential donors but also as a means of forcing managers to position their own work within a coherent organizational strategy. Doing so would also enable greater clarity around metrics, as the managers were required to specify their own performance measures, not just those of the donor:

> [W]e have come up with our own thing, that from now onwards, any new project which is sanctioned by a donor, has to be converted into AKRSP's own project. So okay, [here] are the two to three indicators which [the] donor will look at. But what [will] AKRSP look at? . . . So from day one, [managers] have to say very clearly how this project will contribute to AKRSP's mission. (Naveen Patidar, COO, July 13, 2015).

Perhaps the silver lining in the loss of EC funding was the fact that it forced AKRSP to reflect inwards, refocus on its mission, and design performance metrics aligned with that purpose. The two new mechanisms described above—annual reflection workshops and mission alignment formats—were among a wave of new experiments in the organization, all intended to create strategic focus. Whether they will gain traction and become incorporated in the organization's culture remains to be seen. But the common thread is that they were internally driven, with performance measurement focused on serving strategy rather than funding.

AKRSP's experience further suggests that an integrated strategy—which combines many interventions to achieve outcomes that are greater than the sum of their parts—requires substantial long-term commitment and flexibility in the relationship between funders and grantees. This is different from a transactional relationship that can be executed through performance-based contracts that specify activities and outputs for auditing on a quarterly or annual basis. In contrast, an integrated strategy, or what AKRSP's chief operating officer calls "transformational" work, requires flexibility in funding coupled with a long-term commitment to outcomes. In other words, the quality of the relationship between the grantee and funder matters at least as much as the quantity of funding.

Conclusions: Performance Management for an Integrated Strategy

In summary, the experience of AKRSP offers a number of general insights on performance measurement and management for an integrated strategy. This is a strategy in which the organization delivers a series of outputs that, in combination, produce outcomes that are greater than the sum of their parts. In order to generate these interdependent outcomes, an organization needs a coordination system that accomplishes three main tasks:

- *Standardize the delivery of outputs.* Each department or program in the organization is responsible for creating outputs of consistent quality, setting multiyear targets, and building tracking systems for delivering those outputs. Logical frameworks, for instance, are widely used instruments for setting and tracking such targets on a regular basis.

- *Combine outputs in a systematic way.* The central challenge of an integrated strategy lies in how best to combine interventions rather than delivering them in isolation from one another. This is the task of coordination, and it involves prioritizing, sequencing, and managing multiple outputs over time.

- *Assess interdependent outcomes.* Any integrated strategy must specify the outcomes that it expects to achieve. Assessing these outcomes typically follows standard social science methods of gathering baseline data, identifying control groups, and measuring specific outcomes over time. Where implementing organizations do not have the expertise or capabilities for systematically tracking outcomes, this task may be contracted out to external consultants or local academic institutions.

This performance system may be captured metaphorically as a "coordinated pipeline." The content flowing through the pipeline consists of various programmatic outputs, delivered in a particular sequence or combination. In the case of AKRSP, this coordination was achieved through two mechanisms: a vertically integrated social change model and its execution through community institutions. The social change model determined the content flowing through the pipeline, such as soil and water conservation interventions, irrigation systems, agricultural credit and marketing services, and so on. The community institutions played a critical role in prioritizing and sequencing those interventions, as well as maintaining them and distributing benefits among stakeholders over time.

To illustrate how the above lessons on an integrated strategy translate to other contexts, I close this chapter with two very different examples. First, consider the case of the Harlem Children's Zone (HCZ) in New York City, a nonprofit organization that provides disadvantaged children with individualized support through various stages of educational development. The organization describes its work in integrated terms—as a "pipeline" of interventions "from cradle to college to community" that includes prenatal programs for parents, early childhood and after-school programs for children, charter academies at the middle- and high-school levels, tutoring in public schools, vocational training and college preparation, and a range of support services to college students who are the first in their families to attend higher education.[18] The HCZ's model of social change is premised on continuous educational support to children from preschool through high school, in order to produce interdependent outcomes such as college entry and societal integration.

In order to provide this pipeline of interventions, the HCZ has concentrated its activities in a narrow geographical region of nearly one hundred city blocks of Harlem, under the assumption that it will be better able to control the child's overall environment. In 1998 before the HCZ scaled its programs across Harlem, 60 percent of the children lived in poverty and only 20 percent of children in elementary schools were able to read at grade level. In 2011, based on the organization's internal reporting, the sixth graders in its two main charter schools had shown significant improvements: approximately 80 percent were at or above grade level in statewide math exams, and 48–67 percent (depending on the school) were at or above grade level in English. Moreover, 95 percent of seniors in public schools who attended HCZ after-school programs were accepted into college (Harlem Children's Zone 2011). The grade level metrics are short-term measures, while college acceptance may be considered long-term outcome measure. The time horizon for these interventions is five to nineteen years; the organization is undertaking longitudinal studies, with external support, to better assess its outcomes.

The HCZ is similar to AKRSP in terms of how it exercises control over outcomes: by vertically integrating a sequenced set of interventions (its pipeline from cradle to college) in a tightly bounded geographic space (one hundred city blocks). This control within a physical boundary is similar to AKRSP's control over a watershed or river basin, within which it can concentrate its efforts in order to saturate the region. Unlike AKRSP, however, the HCZ itself is the community institution that serves as the coordination mechanism, responsible for prioritizing, sequencing, and executing services and distributing benefits. The experience of both of these organizations suggests that pursuing outcomes is feasible when the range of integrated interventions needed to achieve those outcomes is within the control of the organization.

What is not clear, however, is whether some interventions may be more important than others in producing outcomes. External evaluators, for instance, have found that the HCZ's charter schools have succeeded in narrowing the educational achievement gap (as measured by student performance on statewide standardized test) but that other aspects of its community pipeline make no difference (Dobbie and Fryer 2009; Whitehurst and Croft 2010). Such studies have largely been silent on other outcomes related to social integration.

Another illustration of an integrated model is an effort by BRAC in Bangladesh, one of the world's largest NGOs, to assist people living in extreme poverty. These are people who typically have no land or assets and must spend the majority of their total expenditures on food. The organization pioneered a "graduation" model to support this segment of the poor in getting out of extreme poverty, consisting of five sequenced interventions: (1) consumption support such as a small cash stipend or foodstuffs; (2) assistance in learning to save money, for example through a self-help group, bank account, or financial literacy training; (3) an asset transfer, such as livestock or inventory for a small business, based on a local market analysis; (4) technical skills training on caring for the asset or business; and, (5) life skills coaching to build self-confidence and social capital, while supporting other individual needs such as business planning, money management, and access to health services. This model was replicated at ten sites in eight countries with support from the Ford Foundation and the Consultative Group to Assist the Poor (CGAP) between 2006 and 2014 (Montesquiou et al. 2014).

A "how-to" manual developed to disseminate the graduation model could just as easily have been describing AKRSP's integrated model or HCZ's pipeline:

> We were intrigued by the idea that with the right mix of interventions, offered in the right sequence, the extreme poor could "graduate" from extreme poverty into a sustainable livelihood within a defined time period. . . .
>
> Graduation programs adapt the building blocks to the local context— prioritizing, sequencing, and shaping the elements to the priority needs

of the poorest and to the reality of the markets in the various program sites. The key is for the implementing partners, especially the participant-facing staff, to understand the core logic of the Approach and to know how and when to bring in flexibility. The overarching goal across all the pilot programs was to help people onto a pathway out of extreme poverty ((Montesquiou et al. 2014, 2, 26)

Randomized control trials were conducted in six of the countries where the program was implemented (Ethiopia, Ghana, Honduras, India, Pakistan, and Peru). The trials engaged 10,495 participants, with about half assigned to treatment and the other half to control. Outcomes were assessed using a baseline survey of participants and two endline surveys, one about twenty-four months after the start of the intervention and a second a year later. The findings showed significant gains in outcomes for treatment participants, particularly on the key variables of consumption, household assets, and food security. The researchers concluded that "a multifaceted approach to increasing income and well-being for the ultra-poor is sustainable and cost-effective" (Banerjee et al. 2015).

These examples of integrated strategies—community-based natural resource management by AKRSP, a pipeline for urban child education by the HCZ, and a graduation path to self-employment for the extremely poor by BRAC—illustrate the diverse contexts in which a series of coordinated outputs can produce outcomes for the poor. All three integrated models are premised on a logic (a theory of change) that their outputs are both necessary and sufficient to reliably produce outcomes. In order to test this logic, it is essential to build a performance system that accomplishes the three tasks detailed in this chapter: standardize the delivery of outputs, combine those outputs in an integrated way, and assess interdependent outcomes.

Finally, this chapter provides a series of managerial insights on the role of external and internal drivers of performance measurement and accountability. External actors, such as funders, can play an enormously important role in supporting performance measurement in social sector organizations. In the case of AKRSP, the European Commission and the Aga Khan Foundation provided over two decades of support in helping the organization to develop its social change model and to build its performance measurement systems. Yet that extensive external support proved of limited value and durability in the absence of an internal culture of performance measurement. Ironically it was the loss of that support, coupled with a proliferation of accountability demands from a range of new corporate funders, that motivated AKRSP to develop internally driven measurement systems. The organization's CEO looked back on that experience:

> I find that much of what we are doing now, including a new internal management information system . . . uses indicators which we had drawn up and internalized during those two decades. So those efforts and systems of performance monitoring are now slowly making a comeback. (Apoorva Oza, e-mail communication, March 10, 2018)

Thirty years after its founding, AKRSP had begun to transition from an accountability based on compliance to one driven by its own strategy. This is the "intelligent accountability" advocated by Onora O'Neill in the opening chapter to this book, and it offers a painful but enduring lesson for any mission-driven organization.

Chapter 4

EMERGENT STRATEGY

emergent: arising unexpectedly; arising as an
effect of complex causes and not analyzable
simply as the sum of their effects.[1]

The end game overall is that the informal [economy]
should be seen as normal, and it shouldn't be
stigmatized, penalized and criminalized. . . . That's
our job, to turn the paradigm on its head.
**MARTY CHEN, COFOUNDER AND INTERNATIONAL
COORDINATOR, WIEGO**

EVERY YEAR IN JUNE, the International Labour Organization (ILO) of
the United Nations convenes an "international parliament of labour"
in Geneva to set global standards on labor and its role in the economy.[2] This convening, known as the International Labour Conference (ILC), brings together three types of representatives from each
member state: governmental representatives such as cabinet ministers,
delegates of workers, and representatives of employers nominated by
their own national associations.

The voice of one group—informal workers—had historically been
excluded from such standard-setting discussions. Informal workers are
ubiquitous and yet invisible in many parts of the world. In cities of the
global South, they typically include street vendors, waste pickers or
garbage recyclers, goods carriers, rickshaw pullers, domestic workers,
individuals who work from home for the garment and food industries
(known as home-based workers), and day laborers in the construction

industry. In wealthier countries of the global North, they often include domestic workers, migrant laborers in agriculture and construction, truck drivers, and a growing body of workers in the so-called gig economy such as drivers for ride-hailing services.[3] What all of these workers lack is employment-based social protection, such as employer contributions to health insurance or retirement pensions. Many also lack the protections afforded by national labor laws such as working condition standards or minimum wages and hours. They are often self-employed, working individually or in small enterprises.

Beginning in 2002, however, delegations of informal workers began participating in the annual ILCs with the support of an unusual organization called Women in Informal Employment: Globalizing and Organizing (WIEGO). Over a period of two decades, WIEGO facilitated delegations of informal workers to twenty global forums, including eight ILC meetings as well as several climate change negotiations and UN Habitat summits. Moreover, WIEGO's pathbreaking statistical work, conducted with the ILO, had shown that informal workers constitute an enormous proportion of the working poor worldwide, making up over 50 percent of nonagricultural workers in most of the developing world, and over 80 percent in much of South Asia and parts of sub-Saharan Africa (Vanek et al. 2014). And yet, national governments routinely failed to account for the role of informal work in their economies, much less to develop public policies to improve the conditions of informal workers. Part of this failure lay in the fact that there were no guidelines or standards for statisticians, economists, and policy makers on how to measure the informal economy, to estimate its contribution to GDP, or to formulate policies relevant to it.

At the ILCs of 2014 and 2015, a global delegation of twenty representatives of informal workers went to Geneva to engage in a standard-setting discussion on the gradual transition from the informal to the formal economy. Representatives of informal workers, many of whom had never previously traveled outside of their home countries, spoke in Geneva about their own labor conditions and their contributions to their economies. They also presented their perspectives on how to formalize their sector, not only by registration and taxation, but also through legal and social protections and support for informal businesses. WIEGO provided coaching and training to these worker representatives in preparing their statements, backed up by data that the organization had been compiling for over a decade. In preparing for these discussions, WIEGO convened three regional workshops with fifty-five organizations of informal workers from twenty-four countries, ultimately generating a common platform—from the perspectives of informal workers—on the formalization of informal work. By the end of the convening, over 50 percent of their proposed amendments to the negotiating document of the ILC were adopted, setting the stage for policy guidance to national governments on how to better support their informal sectors (ILO 2013b, 2015).

In this chapter I explore how WIEGO achieved such influence, drawing lessons for other organizations engaged in influencing public policies and standards. WIEGO's experience is broadly relevant to a range of interventions, especially in policy advocacy, where the "complex, foggy chains of causality" require "long periods of trial and error, during which the policy landscape, and what strategies work within it, may change significantly" (Teles and Schmitt 2011, 39-40). These are settings where little can be achieved by any organization acting alone because outcomes are largely in the hands of other actors. They are also highly dynamic contexts, where organizations must adapt and evolve with the other players in their environment because an action that worked at one point in time or place may not work in another.

In the language of this book, organizations like WIEGO operate under conditions of high uncertainty about cause and effect, coupled with low control over outcomes. Making progress under these conditions requires an "emergent" strategy characterized by constant adaptation and guided by clear long-term goals. This idea builds on the work of management scholar Henry Mintzberg (1978) who differentiated between deliberate and emergent strategies; the former are planned strategies that get executed as intended, while the latter are less predictable in their planning and execution. The central challenge for organizations working in complex environments, where strategies are highly unlikely to unfold as planned, is how to design for emergence. I use the term *emergent strategy* to refer to a *deliberate* approach to managing performance under high uncertainty about causal mechanisms and outcomes. What are the key features of an emergent strategy? What kinds of performance measurement and management systems do managers need in such contexts?

I begin with a narrative of WIEGO's efforts, over a period of nearly two decades, to influence the development of standards at the ILO on informal employment. I then analyze these efforts for insights on the design of emergent strategies and their performance systems.

Making the Invisible Visible: Building WIEGO's Statistics Program

At the time of WIEGO's founding in 1997, there was little data available on the informal economy. The organization was created by a group of ten specialists on the informal economy who were concerned about this dearth of data and the resulting lack of attention by policy makers to the informal sector.[4] At their first meeting, held at the Rockefeller Foundation's conference and study center in Bellagio, Italy, this founding group converged on a framing for the problem they sought to address:

> In many countries, a majority of workers (particularly women) earn their living in the informal sector. Yet, official statistics and economic plans still fail to adequately count these workers or measure their contribution to national economies. As a result, little attention is paid to how policies affect women in the informal sector or how their situation can be improved. . . .
>
> [T]he ultimate goal [of WIEGO] is not only to target specific policies or programmes to the informal sector, or to women within the sector, but to integrate the sector into official policy in order to include informal sector workers and entrepreneurs in plans for economic development. (WIEGO 1997, 1, 3-4).

It was an ambitious value proposition—to integrate the informal sector into official statistics and policy. Only by making the "invisible visible," reasoned the founders, would the concerns of informal workers be taken seriously by policy makers. Delivering on this value proposition would require a strategy that was both highly technical and political. On the technical side, it would require collaborating with global experts in statistics to develop precise definitions and terminology on the informal economy, as well as methods of data collection and analysis that could consistently be applied by national statisticians around the world. On the political side, it would require sustained effort to get access to global standard-setting bodies to increase the voice of informal workers in shaping their agendas and decision making, and ultimately to getting new standards and methods adopted by key global and national actors.

One of the founders of WIEGO, Martha Alter Chen, coordinated the effort. Chen had strong relationships across multiple networks: with grassroots organizations of informal workers such as the Self-Employed Women's Association in India (with over 1.5 million members), with global philanthropic and development actors such as the Ford and Rockefeller Foundations, and with researchers in the academic community through her position as a lecturer at Harvard University. She sought to build a global organization with a large network of influence by hiring program directors that were well connected and respected in their own professional networks.

Chen and her cofounders believed that WIEGO needed to lead the way in developing statistical expertise on the informal economy. To create a statistics program, she reached out to Joann Vanek, a sociologist who had worked for twenty years in the United Nations Statistics Division in New York City.[5] Vanek knew the key players in the UN system and was highly regarded for her expertise and collaborative style. She had joined the UN in 1980, at the start of the UN Decade for Women, at a time when the organization was under substantial pressure to produce credible data on national labor statistics disaggregated by sex. She co-led the charge to bring together the work of different UN organizations in order to produce a report, *The World's Women: Trends and Statistics*, which quickly became one the best-selling publications the UN research division had ever produced (United Nations 1991, 1995).

As a sociologist, Vanek viewed official statistics as reflecting a country's norms and priorities, not merely as hard technical facts:

> There are some things about statistics that many people have a hard time understanding. . . . [C]hanging statistics is often a matter of changing mindsets, and most people just see this [statistics] as a kind of technical product. . . . (August 2, 2016)

Her understanding of the power of statistics echoed that of the French social theorist and historian Michel Foucault, who had charted the historical emergence of statistics—a term that meant "science of the state"—as a form of governmental knowledge in early seventeenth-century Europe. Foucault's work had illuminated how statistics functioned as a *savoir*, or know-how, of the emerging state, a kind of rationality or science that enabled rulers to better define and quantify a "population" within their territory, capturing, for example, its aggregate contribution to labor and wealth, and its rates of death and disease. Foucault showed that the collection of such data had enabled a powerful shift in the purpose or "end" of government during the eighteenth century, ultimately giving rise to the welfare state:

> [P]opulation comes to appear above all else as the ultimate end of government. In contrast to sovereignty, government has as its purpose not the act of government itself, but the welfare of the population, the improvement of its condition, the increase of its wealth, longevity, health, etc. . . . The population now represents more the end of government than the power of the sovereign. (Foucault 1991, 100)

The task for WIEGO's statistics program, as Vanek and Chen saw it, was to develop and then deploy statistics, or the science of the state, to make visible a population that nearly every state had heretofore ignored or dismissed. Vanek's work on gender statistics had made it impossible for national statisticians to ignore the differential effects of economic policies on women and men. WIEGO felt a similar approach was needed for increasing the visibility of workers in the informal economy.

Mapping the Ecosystem

The statistics program began with an understanding of the ecosystem of actors that it sought to influence. Figure 4.1 is a mapping, from WIEGO's perspective, of the main global actors engaged in the production of labor statistics. WIEGO grouped these actors into three types of activities necessary for developing statistics on the informal economy: developing the *methods and training* for generating informal employment statistics, *collecting* these data at a national level, and, *compiling and disseminating* statistics to make them accessible to a wide set of users ranging from policy makers to advocates. The International Labour Organization sat at the core of the required changes:

> We knew from the beginning, even before we started WIEGO . . . [that] we had to work with the ILO because under the international statistical system, they are responsible for labor force statistics. We also knew we had to work with the UN Statistics Division. . . . [W]e knew exactly who the key players were. Now, whether these organizations wanted to work with us was another question. But we knew who we wanted and needed to work with—there was no question. (Marty Chen, June 3, 2015)

Within this international ecosystem, the key standard-setting body for labor statistics was the International Conference of Labour Statisticians (ICLS). Established in 1923, the ICLS made recommendations (in the format of resolutions and guidelines) that represented the best practices related to the measurement of labor. Specifically this body set the standards on how to define informal employment and its components, how to mainstream gender in labor statistics, and how to classify different kinds of occupations among other aspects of labor statistics.

At its conferences, held approximately every five years, the ICLS discussed selected topics of labor statistics, sending its recommenda-

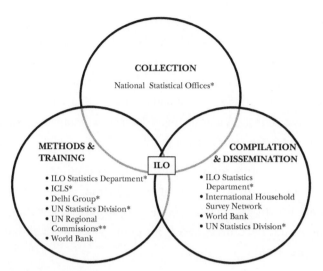

COLLECTION

National Statistical Offices*

METHODS & TRAINING

ILO

- ILO Statistics Department*
- ICLS*
- Delhi Group*
- UN Statistics Division*
- UN Regional Commissions**
- World Bank

COMPILATION & DISSEMINATION

- ILO Statistics Department*
- International Household Survey Network
- World Bank
- UN Statistics Division*

*Actors with whom WIEGO is a collaborator
**UN Regional Commissions include: Economic Commission for Europe,* Economic and Social Commission for Asia and the Pacific and the Statistical Institute for Asia and the Pacific, Economic and and Social Commission for Western Asia

FIGURE 4.1   Labor Statistics Ecosystem
Source: WIEGO (2016).

tions to the governing body of the ILO for approval.[6] Although not binding on members and intended primarily as "best practice," resolutions and guidelines adopted by the ILO carried normative and pragmatic weight, as they shaped globally not only the way the labor force was measured in national statistical systems but also informed the development of national economic policies related to labor and employment. To an outsider, the work carried out by the ICLS could seem arcane, highly technical, and far removed from the lives of informal workers. But by targeting the global actors responsible for setting standards on labor statistics, WIEGO sought to shape the very basis of how the informal economy and its workers were measured and thus perceived. It was a normative goal, with potentially large practical ramifications.

Through her earlier work on gender statistics at the UN, Vanek had developed an understanding of how international and national statistical systems develop and change:

[T]he UN has a decentralized statistical system with the specialized agencies such as the ILO, WHO, UNICEF responsible for data in their area of concern.[7] If you wanted to know the status of women, you had to go to each of the specialized agencies for the data on their specialized area of statistics; no one had put the data together in a common database, so that became an important part in improving the availability of gender statistics. (September 12, 2015)

The opportunity for WIEGO lay in positioning itself as an expert resource on the measurement of the informal economy, as well as an advocate for the importance of developing these statistics. This positioning would become the basis for gaining access to global standard-setting processes.

Key Advances, 1997–2015

In order to influence the employment statistics ecosystem, WIEGO developed a strategy that eventually became part of its DNA: scan the environment for opportunities to engage with key influencers, gain entry to key decision forums by establishing WIEGO's expertise in producing high-quality research, secure a long-term seat at the table, and continue to push for research and evidence to change policies and mindsets.

In practice, the first step of scanning the environment meant building strong relationships with senior statisticians in the system, at both a global and country level, in order to be alerted to opportunities. In recruiting Vanek, WIEGO had someone who not only was respected within the international statistical system but who also understood its inner workings:

When I transitioned [from the UN] to WIEGO, I continued to be able to link to the advocates and the statisticians who I worked with in my former job. I was often called on to take part in ongoing projects relevant to WIEGO's work and could use regular meetings of the [UN] Statistical Commission to meet with statisticians from countries around the world. (August 2, 2016)

Figure 4.2 provides a timeline of key advances towards WIEGO's goal of integrating informal employment into national employment statistics. One of WIEGO's early concerns centered on promoting a worker-based perspective on how informal employment was defined. In 1993, the ICLS had adopted an enterprise-based definition of the "informal sector" as comprising unincorporated small or unregistered enterprises (Chen 2012; Vanek et al. 2014). Under this enterprise-based definition, a person working in an unregistered enterprise was considered an informal worker. But this definition ignored the many workers in formal enterprises and households who had no benefits or legal rights in their employment. It did not include, for example, contributing family workers in household enterprises, domestic workers with no benefits, and employees in formal enterprises who had no social protections or rights.

In 1997, the year of WIEGO's founding, the United Nations Statistical Commission created an international expert group on informal

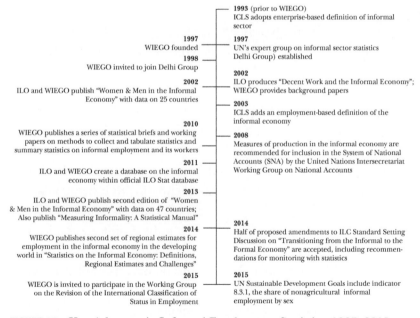

FIGURE 4.2   Key Advances in Informal Employment Statistics, 1997–2015

sector statistics known as the Delhi Group (named after the city where it first met). Vanek and Chen knew this body could be influential in developing and promoting a worker-based approach to informal employment, and they acted quickly and opportunistically to participate in this group:

> We really wanted to get this broader definition [of informal employment]. The Delhi Group was part of the way to do it. . . . Early on, WIEGO invited the chief statistician of India [who headed the Delhi Group] to the first WIEGO meeting on statistics. There we planned with him and later sponsored statistical research to be presented at the Delhi Group, and [we] supported the participation of these analysts. WIEGO developed a partnership with the Delhi Group which is even stronger today.[8] (Joann Vanek, August 2, 2016)

> [We] presented these technical papers to the Delhi Group. . . . It established us as a very credible player. (Marty Chen, August 3, 2016)

Shortly afterwards, WIEGO was invited to join the Delhi Group as its only NGO member. It was a highly unusual invitation, given that all the other members were national statisticians. WIEGO wasted no time in commissioning further research to shape the deliberations of the group.

In an important advance, a statistician at the ILO developed a conceptual framework on the informal economy (Hussmanns 2001), and Vanek worked with him to promote it. The preparatory materials for an important ILC meeting in 2002 drew on this conceptual framing, and also included two other papers prepared by WIEGO.[9] WIEGO's active contributions subsequently led to it being asked by the ILO to prepare a major publication, *Women and Men in the Informal Economy: A Statistical Picture* (ILO 2002b), to be produced as a lead-up to the critical ICLS meeting in 2003. Like Vanek's earlier pioneering report at the UN on gender statistics, this report was similar in format but with the informal economy as its subject. National data at the time were very limited. The report included statistics on twenty-five countries, but with direct measurements of informal employment in only three countries. Despite the limited data availability, the report demonstrated that the informal economy could be measured with credible statistics across countries with the resulting statistics yielding valuable information for policy making. Moreover, the report, which was written largely by WIEGO, began to establish the organization's reputation as a valuable source of expertise to the ILO and to national statistical offices. As Vanek put it:

> We wanted statistical standards to be informed by the on-the-ground experience of informal workers. WIEGO is part of the discussion to do this. Even the statisticians from developing countries do not have the expertise on these workers that WIEGO does (September 12, 2015).

In a landmark resolution in 2003, the ICLS endorsed guidelines on a statistical definition of informal employment as "all employment arrangements that do not provide individuals with legal or social protection through their work, thereby leaving them more exposed to economic risk than the others, whether or not the economic units they work for or operate in are formal enterprises, informal enterprises or households" (ILO 2013c, 3). It was a big win. An external evaluation of the WIEGO statistics program, conducted by a former head of the ILO's Department of Statistics, highlighted WIEGO's role in the adoption of these new guidelines:

> Perhaps, the best indicator of the effectiveness of the statistical advocacy of WIEGO is the adoption of the *Guidelines concerning a statistical definition of informal employment*, adopted by the International Conference of Labour Statisticians in 2003. . . .
>
> The analytical work of WIEGO . . . has provided its constituents with strong evidence-based arguments, bringing visibility and understanding of the informal economy. It has also clarified a number of misconceptions about the relationship between poverty, gender and informal employment. (Mehran 2009, 16)

The broader definition adopted by the ICLS had substantial consequences for measuring the informal economy. Most significantly, it provided for a more complete measurement of informal employment, including not only in the informal sector but also informal employment in the formal sector. Moreover, under the new definition, data on informal employment could be more easily integrated into household-based labor force surveys conducted by national statistical offices (ILO 2013c, 3–4). WIEGO subsequently collaborated with the ILO to support data collection and compilation for dozens of countries, all located in an ILO/WIEGO database on informal employment. The second edition of *Women and Men in the Informal Economy* (ILO 2013c), issued a decade later and based on this database, provided a far more detailed picture of informal employment based on direct measures for forty-seven developing countries and territories and indirect measures for eighty-one countries. Based on these data WIEGO also produced regional estimates of informal employment and employment in the informal sector (Vanek et al. 2014) which have been widely used as benchmarks of informal employment in developing countries. Such data on informal employment (and employment in the informal sector) are now integrated into the main ILO statistical database, ILOSTAT.[10]

The resulting data have had substantial policy significance. For instance, Figure 4.3 illustrates the percentage of workers in informal employment outside of agriculture for a selection of countries where there were sufficient data (gathered between 2004 and 2010). In the majority of countries, informal employment constituted more than half of all nonagricultural employment. In some countries, this figure was even higher. For example it was 75 percent or more in India, Mali, Pakistan, Tanzania, and Bolivia. Informal employment also constituted a substantial portion of work in many of the world's major emerging economies, including 34 percent in China (based on six cities; not shown in the figure), 33 percent in South Africa, and 42 percent in Brazil.

In the decade between the two editions of *Women and Men in the Informal Economy*, international labor statisticians and economists began to take the informal economy seriously. The opening lines of the second edition captured the start of this normative shift (ILO 2013c, v):

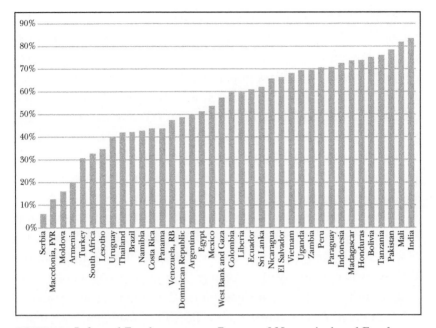

FIGURE 4.3   Informal Employment as a Percent of Nonagricultural Employment. Selected Countries, 2004/10
Source: Vanek et al. (2014). Reproduced with permission.

The informal economy is a major source of employment and livelihood in many countries and interacts closely with the formal economy.
Given its importance, countries are paying increasing attention to the
informal economy in collecting labour force and other economic data.
In 2013, the tripartite constituents of the International Labour Organization defined eight areas of critical importance for the Organization,
one of which is the formalization of the informal economy.

These reports further demonstrated that data on the informal economy could be gathered in a consistent, rigorous, and useful manner:

The comprehensive statistics on the informal economy were collected,
compiled and analysed based on the conceptual framework . . . adopted
by the International Conference on Labour Statisticians (ICLS) in 1993
and 2003, respectively. The resulting analysis confirms the feasibility
and usefulness of these frameworks as a basis for the development of
statistics and for data analysis for policy-making. (ILO 2013c, v)

At about the same time, WIEGO and other members of the Delhi Group worked with the ILO to produce a manual, years in the making, on how to measure informality (ILO 2013a). The manual was designed to assist countries in planning data collection on the informal economy, including guidance in survey design, execution, data analysis, dissemination, and incorporation of data into national accounts. WIEGO further supplemented this manual by producing its own guidance documents that were shorter and more accessible to its wider constituency of policy makers and membership-based organizations (Vanek et al. 2014; Vanek, Chen, and Raveendran 2015).

A further implication of better data on informal employment was that it was now possible to measure the contributions of informal employment to a country's gross domestic product (GDP). In 2008, the UN Statistical Commission produced an update to its guidance on how countries should report their national accounts (Commission of the European Communities et al. 2008). This document included a chapter on the informal economy and made a case for including data on the informal sector as important to providing "a more exhaustive measure" of a country's GDP (ILO 2013c, 4). WIEGO, through the Delhi Group, had encouraged the inclusion of this content, followed by more detailed guidance on its measurement and use (ILO 2013a). A handful of countries, with Mexico in the lead, had begun to report on the contribution of the informal economy to the overall economy.

And in an especially important advance, statisticians engaged in the development of indicators for the UN's Sustainable Development Goals (SDGs) in late 2015 included an indicator—proportion of informal employment in nonagricultural employment, by sex—as part of the SDG goal of promoting decent work and economic growth:[11]

> A major factor [in] the adoption of the [SDG] indicator . . . was that several members of the selection committee recognized that the concept [of informal employment] applied to developed as well as developing countries. WIEGO had initiated work on this and thus was recognized as having an important role in the inclusion of this indica-

tor. . . . Who would have guessed that our work would have led to that! (Joann Vanek, August 2, 2016)

WIEGO's influence continued to grow. For a major review of international classifications of employment undertaken by the ILO,[12] WIEGO was selected to participate in the review group, which would lead to a proposal to be presented at the 2018 International Conference of Labour Statisticians. This was a significant advance in its influence, positioning the organization in a consultative role with the ILO. Moreover, WIEGO was the only NGO on the revision team that otherwise consisted of government statisticians.

In sum, it would not be an overstatement to conclude that WIEGO's statistics program was influential in integrating the informal economy into official statistics at the national, regional, and international levels. This influence was the result of nearly two decades of steady relationship building with the ILO, the Delhi Group, regional commissions, expert groups, and a vast network of associations of informal workers around the world. An external evaluation of WIEGO's statistics program summed up the organization's strategy of influence:

> WIEGO has been particularly intelligent in choosing its partners to achieve its statistical goals. The ILO Bureau of Statistics (now Department of Statistics), the UN Statistical Division, [and] the Delhi Group on Informal Sector Statistics are all institutions with mandates in promoting international statistics. Associating with them, first to influence their agenda, then to set international statistical standards on informal employment, and finally to assist national statistical systems to collect and analyze data on the topic has been a clever strategy and probably the main reason for the statistical success of WIEGO. (Mehran 2009, 16)

The time horizon for change was long. It had taken nearly six years for the International Labour Conference to broaden its definition of the informal economy. And it took a sustained effort over a period of fifteen years for WIEGO and the ILO to collaboratively produce landmark reports on the informal economy, to create a database housed within official ILO labor statistics, to generate manuals and guidance documents on how to measure the informal sector and informal employment, and to begin building the capacities of national statistical bureaus to carry out this work.

These were not merely technical accomplishments, but also normative ones. Informal employment was no longer perceived by many labor statisticians through the reductionist lens of illegality or criminality, but was increasingly seen as a critical and substantial part of national economies. This visibility was a basic step towards improving conditions for informal workers. Much remained to be done, as national-level data collection was still limited in both volume and quality. Asked what success might look like in ten years, Vanek did not hesitate:

> [W]e want the main ILO database to include informal employment statistics, to have data for more countries, and [to] include developed countries. . . . Further[more], the main standards and classifications on employment should apply to informal workers. We should have as much data on workers in informal employment as on workers in [formal] jobs. (September 2, 2015)

The key aim of WIEGO's statistics program articulated nearly twenty years beforehand—to integrate informal employment statistics into standard national statistics around the world—was on its way to being achieved and remained the driving force of the program.

Designing a Performance System: Adaptation

WIEGO's statistics program illustrates the use of an emergent strategy—a strategy where leaders may know their destination, but they do not know what pathways will take them there. Such a strategy requires a capacity to iterate and adjust actions in response to new opportunities, all the while staying focused on long-term objectives. WIEGO's statistics program was constantly on the lookout for policy windows to engage key influencers, to gain entry to standard-setting forums where they could shape deliberations, and to identify opportunities for helping national actors adopt new standards and guidelines.

An emergent strategy requires performance systems that are very different from those examined in the preceding chapters. Organizations with an emergent strategy typically do not deliver a standardized product or service (like emergency medical response or agricultural services discussed in chapters 2 and 3), but instead seek to customize or adapt their actions to a constantly changing social and political context. Moreover, they often cannot achieve their goals alone, as their success depends on influencing the behaviors of other actors in a system.

The performance system required for making progress under such conditions is an adaptive one made up of three main parts:

- *System framing* that clearly identifies key actors, interactions, and structures to be targeted for action
- *Accountability* for interim outcomes using contribution analysis
- *Aligning* emergent actions with long-term goals

I elaborate each of these components below, both in general terms applicable to a range of organizations and more specifically with examples from WIEGO.

System Framing: Identifying Key Actors, Interactions, and Structures

A critical task facing actors in complex contexts is to articulate the "system" they seek to influence. I offer below two definitions of systems, the first from a pioneering scientist of systems thinking and the second from an organization that maps systems in order to improve democratic processes:

> A set of elements or parts that is coherently organized and interconnected in a pattern or structure that produces a characteristic set of

behaviors, often classified as its "function" or "purpose." (Meadows 2008, 188)

A diverse set of parts that interact with each other and their environment in ways that are dynamic and often hard to predict—and that can be studied, mapped, and influenced. (Democracy Fund 2016)

The first definition emphasizes the coherence of systems, while the second notes their dynamic nature. But both definitions suggest that understanding a system requires identifying its key parts, how they interact, and the effects they produce. The core features of any social system can be identified by answering four basic questions:

- What are its key *parts or actors* (individuals, organizations, communities)?
- What are the *interactions* among those parts (roles, relationships, and processes)?
- What are the *structures* or institutions that shape those interactions (social norms, relations of power, policies, and standards)?
- What are its persistent *effects* over time, both positive and negative (behaviors and outcomes)?

Because a system that involves many actors and processes can become overwhelmingly complex, these questions help to specify the boundaries of a system—that is, its most critical actors, interactions, and structures to target for action.[13] These boundaries necessarily shape how one perceives the social problem to be addressed and the range of possible action.

For example, WIEGO's statistics program focused on the "system of labor statistics." The boundaries of this system were determined by identifying the key persons, organizations, and processes that shape the standards for measuring employment and thus for influencing the visibility of informal workers. These were divided into three main functions as shown in the Venn diagram in Figure 4.1: the ILO was identified as the nexus of the entire system, the ICLS as the key standard-setting body (with the Delhi Group playing an influential advisory role), and national statistical offices of governments as the collectors of labor statistics. A key challenge for WIEGO lay in gaining access to the ILO–ICLS–Delhi Group (the key actors) in order to ultimately influence their standard-setting deliberations (interactions), and then to build the capacities of the national statistical offices to adopt the new standards and guidelines (structures). WIEGO's experience suggests that a system framing need not be overly complicated or exhaustive, so long as it articulates boundaries of the system (actors, interactions, structures) in a way that provides a shared understanding among the agents of change of the system and its effects. This systems framing is important for then identifying how to intervene.[14] Chen put it succinctly:

> [T]he other actors in the system have a shared understanding already—WIEGO's success in interacting with this system is that we too understood what they understood. (November 30, 2017)

Identifying the most critical actors in a system and their interactions, however, is not always a straightforward process. Research on complex systems in international development has shown that different actors are likely to perceive aspects of a system and its boundaries differently, such that the process of articulating a system often requires reconciling diverse viewpoints (Burns 2012; Burns and Worsley 2015). Through workshops with social sector actors in diverse settings around the world, Danny Burns and Stuart Worsley have developed a generalizable process for "seeing the system," or what they call *participatory systemic inquiry*. The process involves two main parts:

- *Multistakeholder inquiry*. Diverse constituents are brought together in order to identify key issues, facts, conflicts, and perceptions related to a social problem.

- *System dynamics maps*. Participants are engaged in creating "messy" maps that depict core issues and their relationships, then distilling those maps into a more concise depiction of key system interactions and their perceived effects. These maps can be further validated by testing them with new participants, and can be developed with the assistance of data visualization platforms.[15]

In the case of WIEGO, multistakeholder engagement was a standard part of its governance. The organization's board was made up of representatives from three distinct constituencies: membership-based organizations (MBOs) of informal workers, such as trade unions, cooperatives, and worker associations;[16] researchers and statisticians who study or measure the informal economy, including at the ILO and national statistical bureaus; and development practitioners from nongovernmental organizations and development agencies such as the World Bank. WIEGO engaged systematically with these three constituencies through their representation on the WIEGO governing board and at the "general assemblies" of its members that WIEGO convened every four years in order to take stock of progress and to set future goals. An important underlying goal of WIEGO was to ensure that its core constituency, the organizations of informal workers, understood and were empowered to engage with and intervene in the systems—of key actors, interactions, and structures—of key domains of its policy work, not only statistics but also law, social protection, and urban policies.

WIEGO did not develop system dynamics maps of the labor statistics ecosystem in advance of its efforts to influence that system, given Vanek's in-depth knowledge of it. However, in evaluating its statistics program, WIEGO developed a series of retrospective mappings to document the actions it had taken over time, and the possible effects of those actions in improving the quality and availability of statistics on informal employment. Figure 4.4 provides a simplified illustration of such a map. The boxes summarize key events or actions undertaken by WIEGO in collaboration with workers' organizations (left-hand side), in order to influence decision making at a series of International Labour Conferences between 2011 and 2014 (right-hand side). This retrospective analysis was developed by WIEGO through a series of workshops led by an external consultant as part of an evaluation for the Swedish International Development Cooperation Agency (Sida) (Klugman 2014a, 15–17). Using a participatory process that engaged staff across the organization, the consultant created nine maps or chains like the one illustrated in Figure 4.4 for a range of WIEGO's

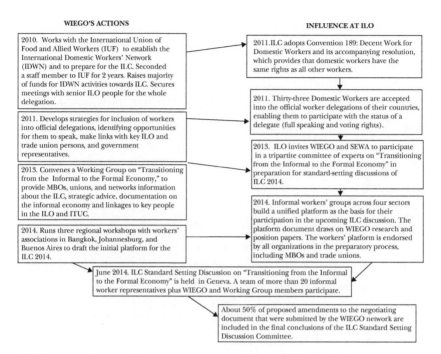

WIEGO'S ACTIONS

INFLUENCE AT ILO

2010. Works with the International Union of Food and Allied Workers (IUF) to establish the International Domestic Workers' Network (IDWN) and to prepare for the ILC. Seconded a staff member to IUF for 2 years. Raises majority of funds for IDWN activities towards ILC. Secures meetings with senior ILO people for the whole delegation.

2011. ILC adopts Convention 189: Decent Work for Domestic Workers and its accompanying resolution, which provides that domestic workers have the same rights as all other workers.

2011. Thirty-three Domestic Workers are accepted into the official worker delegations of their countries, enabling them to participate with the status of a delegate (full speaking and voting rights).

2011. Develops strategies for inclusion of workers into official delegations, identifying opportunities for them to speak, make links with key ILO and trade union persons, and government representatives.

2013. ILO invites WIEGO and SEWA to participate in a tripartite committee of experts on "Transitioning from the Informal to the Formal Economy" in preparation for standard-setting discussions of ILC 2014.

2013. Convenes a Working Group on "Transitioning from the Informal to the Formal Economy," to provide MBOs, unions, and networks information about the ILC, strategic advice, documentation on the informal economy and linkages to key people in the ILO and ITUC.

2014. Informal workers' groups across four sectors build a unified platform as the basis for their participation in the upcoming ILC discussion. The platform document draws on WIEGO research and position papers. The workers' platform is endorsed by all organizations in the preparatory process, including MBOs and trade unions.

2014. Runs three regional workshops with workers' associations in Bangkok, Johannesburg, and Buenos Aires to draft the initial platform for the ILC 2014.

June 2014. ILC Standard Setting Discussion on "Transitioning from the Informal to the Formal Economy" is held in Geneva. A team of more than 20 informal worker representatives plus WIEGO and Working Group members participate.

About 50% of proposed amendments to the negotiating document that were submitted by the WIEGO network are included in the final conclusions of the ILC Standard Setting Discussion Committee.

FIGURE 4.4 Influence Map: Advocacy with Informal Worker Delegations to International Labour Conferences, 2011–2014
Excerpted and adapted from Klugman (2014) for WIEGO.

programs. The process pushed staff to articulate and challenge their implicit assumptions about causality in their programs, while also being frank about what changes did and did not materialize, and the time frames required for change.

The methodology used by WIEGO for developing this mapping of actions and results, known as *outcome harvesting*, was created by a group of evaluation practitioners specifically for complex contexts where cause-effect relationships are poorly understood, such as in policy advocacy and campaigning work.[17] Its developers emphasized that the process "does not measure progress towards predetermined outcomes or objectives" but instead "works backward to determine whether and how the project or intervention contributed to the change" (Wilson-Grau and Britt 2012, 1). Outcome harvesting is part of a suite of methodologies useful for mapping complex social systems and pathways to results; I further explore some of these methodologies in Chapter 7 and provide several useful resources in the Appendix to this book.

Accountability: Interim Outcomes Using Contribution Analysis

Even with a clear framing of the labor statistics system that WIEGO sought to influence, there remains the challenge of how to assess WIEGO's performance. For what results should its managers and constituents hold it to account? Organizations operating under conditions of high causal uncertainty cannot reliably predict the sequence of actions that will lead to their desired outcomes. Nor can they claim to achieve long-term outcomes on their own, given the many other actors in its system. Under such circumstances, performance measurement is best focused on two assessments:

- measures of *interim* outcomes rather than long-term outcomes
- assessment of *contribution* (rather than attribution) to a set of system outcomes

In the case of WIEGO, the organization identified three interim outcomes for all of its work—to increase the "visibility, voice, and validity" of informal workers, which it saw as necessary for ultimately improving the lives of informal workers. This chapter has focused primarily on *visibility*, the first of these "three Vs," which is produced by improving official labor force and other economic statistics on informal employment. It is the key objective of WIEGO's statistics program; Table 4.1 lists a set of key performance indicators used by the organization for measuring progress on this interim outcome.

The second interim outcome, increasing the *voice* of informal workers, is to be produced by strengthening the capacities of organizations of the working poor in the informal economy (i.e., the MBOs) to gain representation in policy-making and rule-setting bodies that affect their work and lives. And the third objective of increasing the *validity* or legitimacy of informal workers is to be achieved by promoting mainstream recognition of them as economic agents who contrib-

TABLE 4.1   Interim Outcome Measures for WIEGO's Statistics Program

Key Interim Outcome	Interim Outcome Indicators	Output Indicators
To increase the **visibility** of informal workers	• more accurate statistics at the national, regional, and global levels on the informal economy • improved country-to-country, regional, and global comparisons • increased visibility of the informal economy among statisticians, mainstream economists, researchers, and development practitioners • improved data analysis capacity among those responsible for analyzing the informal economy	• National statistics departments around the world have access to a manual on survey methods on the informal sector/informal employment, and are trained on how to use these methods • Developing and developed countries are using a common statistical framework to gather statistics on the informal economy • Key partners and grassroots activists have access to an updated version of *Women and Men in the Informal Economy: A Statistical Picture* as a tool in their organizing and policy-change efforts • Researchers and data analysts in various countries network internationally to share information and methods

Source: Excerpted and adapted from Klugman 2014b, Appendix A: Outcomes, Methods & Sources; WIEGO, Monitoring, Learning and Evaluation (MLE) Plan; Record of Progress Against Stated Outcomes for Final Evaluation.

ute to the overall economy and integration of their organizations into policy-making and rule-setting processes.

Together, these three Vs constitute the foundation of WIEGO's theory of change, which can be summarized as follows: *If one increases the visibility, voice, and validity of informal workers (interim outcomes), they will be able to shape the policy and regulatory environment that affects their work (interim outcomes), and then there will ultimately be long-term improvements in well-being, incomes, and risks facing workers (individual and societal outcomes).*[18] Note that there are two stages of interim outcomes in this theory of change; WIEGO refers to the former as "enabling conditions" that lead to the latter, both of which are necessary for ultimately producing outcomes.

In some of its city-level work, WIEGO has been able to document a link between the enabling conditions, interim outcomes, and outcomes on the lives of workers. For example, WIEGO's support of efforts by local organizations to increase the visibility and voice of waste-picker groups in Bogotá, Colombia, helped those groups to get formally integrated into the public waste management and payment system, ultimately leading to better pay, better working conditions, and more stable employment (Abizaid 2015; Táutiva and Olaya 2013; WIEGO 2015b). And its work with street vendors, market traders, and market porters in Accra, Ghana, was influential in achieving better occupational health and safety conditions (Dogbe and Annan 2015; WIEGO 2015a).[19] Such outcomes have been far more difficult to document in WIEGO's global-level work on statistics for the simple reason that the link between global statistical standards and the lives of workers is causally more complex and uncertain. But WIEGO and its member organizations know, from experience, that statistics on the size, composition, and contribution of informal workers are needed for effective negotiations.

In addition to its focus on interim outcomes, WIEGO's experience raises the question of whether organizations intervening in complex systems can reasonably claim to "attribute" any successes to their work. WIEGO has generally resisted making such claims for two reasons. First, the organization is cognizant of the uncertainties of cause and effect inherent in its theory of change. And second, given that it works closely with workers' organizations and many other actors in its ecosystem, any claims of attribution could undermine the collective spirit of its work. Instead, the organization has chosen to make claims of "contribution" that establish a plausible association between its work, in relation to interventions by many other actors, and a set of outcomes.[20] To be sure, claims of contribution rely on a logic of cause and effect just as much as claims of attribution; the difference lies in a high degree of uncertainty about the causal mechanisms and a greater interdependence with other actors in delivering results.

Recent advances in the field of evaluation research provide insights on both of the above challenges: how to identify what interim outcomes to measure, and how to assess contribution (rather than attribution) to a set of system-level outcomes with some degree of rigor. First, the work of Julia Coffman and her colleagues provides useful guidance on identifying different types of results that commonly arise from advocacy (Beer and Coffman 2015; Coffman 2009; Coffman and Beer 2015; Stachowiak 2013). In particular, Coffman and Beer (2015, 11) identify three broad categories of interim outcomes in policy work: changes in awareness, will, and action. They also identify three types of audiences or targets for advocacy: members of the public, key influencers within a system, and decision makers. The resulting matrix of interim outcomes is shown in Figure 4.5.

Applied to WIEGO's statistics program, this matrix helps clarify that the organization's target audience (the horizontal axis) is influencers and decision makers within the labor force and economic statistics ecosystem, which includes expert groups and standard-setting bodies

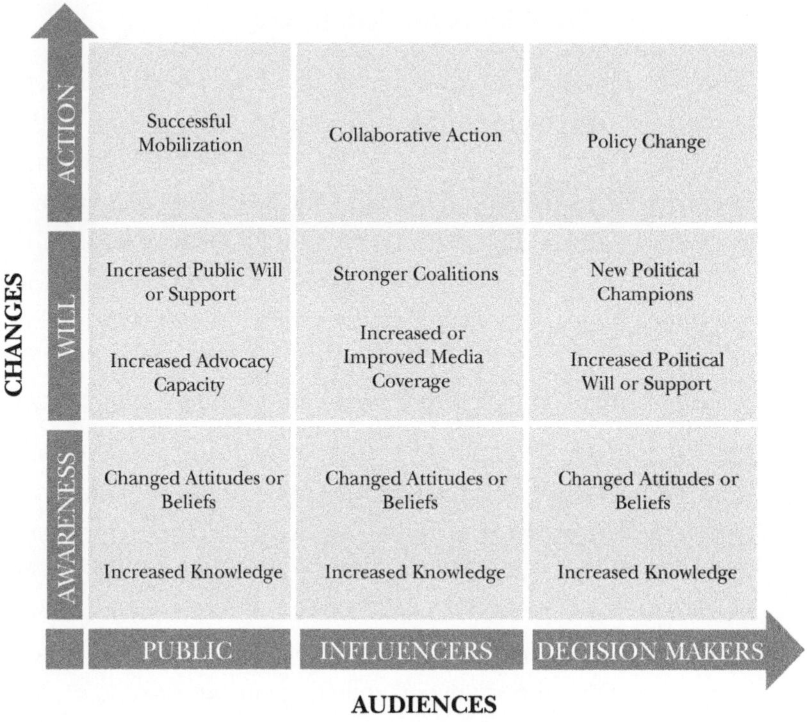

	PUBLIC	INFLUENCERS	DECISION MAKERS
ACTION	Successful Mobilization	Collaborative Action	Policy Change
WILL	Increased Public Will or Support Increased Advocacy Capacity	Stronger Coalitions Increased or Improved Media Coverage	New Political Champions Increased Political Will or Support
AWARENESS	Changed Attitudes or Beliefs Increased Knowledge	Changed Attitudes or Beliefs Increased Knowledge	Changed Attitudes or Beliefs Increased Knowledge

CHANGES (vertical axis) • AUDIENCES (horizontal axis)

FIGURE 4.5 Types of Interim Outcomes in Policy Advocacy
Source: Coffman and Beer (2015, 11). Reproduced with permission.

convened by the ILO. WIEGO rarely engages individual informal workers directly, working instead through their membership organizations. The changes that WIEGO seeks to achieve (the vertical axis) cut across all three levels: its statistics program increases knowledge about informal workers as a means to changing attitudes about them (awareness), while also building coalitions and political support both within and outside the ILO (will), in order to ultimately influence policies and standards (action).

On the second challenge of how to assess contribution, a growing literature on "contribution analysis" provides a systematic approach to evaluating complex interventions where causal attribution, particularly through experimental methods, is impractical or impossible (Kane et al. 2017; Lemire, Nielsen, and Dybdal 2012; Mayne 2001, 2008, 2012). Contribution analysis can be broken down into several main steps, which I describe only briefly here:[21]

- First, the organization or evaluator identifies possible *cause-effect relationships*, developing a theory of change that not only explicitly links interventions to results but also identifies assumptions and risks for each link in the chain. The process focuses attention on identifying interim outcomes over which the organization has some control (such as those in Table 4.1 for WIEGO's statistics program), rather than only final outcomes over which it has little control.

- Second, the organization or evaluator *gathers evidence* about actual results from a wide range of stakeholders, using a method such as outcome harvesting to retrospectively map outcome pathways (such as Figure 4.4). The evaluation literature emphasizes the retrospective nature of such analysis, conducted after some results can be observed, thus allowing for comparison between anticipated pathways and observed ones. In addition, the literature stresses the importance of soliciting various stakeholder perspectives in order to triangulate (cross-check) claims of influence. This step is critical to substantiating claims about the organization's contributions, and is enhanced by iterating at least once in order to refine the theory of change and to gather additional evidence.

- Finally, throughout the above process, the organization or evaluator explores rival explanations for both interim and final outcomes. This requires participants to consider alternative causal pathways and to search for evidence that challenges their own mental models of cause and effect.

In WIEGO's case, the first two steps of contribution analysis were carried out. It had a clear strategy for linking outputs to interim outcomes and a theory of change that plausibly linked interim outcomes to final outcomes. And, it used methods such as outcome harvesting to compile evidence about its contributions to several outcome chains. Moreover, outcome harvesting is now embedded into its culture. But the organization had not explored alternative explanations for its results (the third step above), at least not through a deliberate or systematic process.

The more general implication for organizations intervening in complex systems—where causal uncertainty is high and control over outcomes is low—is that it is nonetheless feasible to apply a degree of rigor and systematic analysis to identifying cause-effect pathways and for assessing performance. Accountability under these conditions is best focused on assessing interim rather than final outcomes and in identifying contributions to outcomes at a system level, rather than pursuing definitive cause-effect attribution. In Chapter 7, I revisit these methods from the perspective of funders in order to identify the conditions under which attribution-based versus contribution-based approaches are most appropriate.

Alignment: Linking Emergent Actions with Long-Term Goals

Finally, even when an organization has a clear framing of the system(s) in which it operates, and it has well-developed interim outcome targets, it still faces the problem of how to take action in a constantly changing environment. Many organizations engaged in advocacy have interim outcomes they wish to achieve, but their pathways cannot be fully or easily preplanned. For example, WIEGO's statistics program had a clear purpose—to integrate measurement of the informal economy into official national statistics—but the pathway and timeline for making progress were emergent:

> [M]ost of our projects are taking advantage of opportunities that [arise] because we wouldn't have the money to undertake massive statistical projects [on our own] as they are too costly. [W]e take advantage of a wide range of opportunities to improve these statistics. When a new opportunity arises, we discuss what it would mean for WIEGO, that is for what our members need or want and for the long-term impact on statistics on the informal economy. (Joann Vanek, September 12, 2015)

What kinds of systems or capabilities do organizations need in order to be able to take advantage of unexpected opportunities? How can they balance such emergent action with a focus on long-term objectives? In small organizations, such adaptation is typically achieved through ad hoc communication among team members, or what the management scholar Mintzberg (1983) has called "mutual adjustment." But as organizations like WIEGO grow and become globally dispersed, they require formal capacities both for seizing new opportunities and for integrating them with their long-term strategic goals.

Over time, WIEGO developed a repertoire of mechanisms for striking this balance that are summarized in Table 4.2. I distinguish between two broad sets of alignment mechanisms: those that enable the organization to identify and respond to new opportunities, and those that help it to maintain a long-term strategic focus.

The first set of mechanisms, *opportunity scanning and responding*, focus on scanning the environment for new opportunities, and acting quickly to take advantage of the most promising prospects as they emerge. In order to be aware of new opportunities, the organization needed to maintain regular contact with the actors it was trying to influence. The head of the organization's statistics program explained:

TABLE 4.2 Alignment Mechanisms within WIEGO

Opportunity Scanning and Responding	Strategy Creation and Coherence
Emerging opportunities are identified, shared, and screened through: *Ecosystem Scanning* Team members maintain lines of communication with key actors in their ecosystems, actively seeking out new opportunities. They also regularly participate in global, regional, and national events (such as the International Labour Conference or the UN's Habitat III Summit) to strengthen their networks and to identify emerging opportunities. *Opportunity Responding* Team members receive unanticipated invitations or intelligence from actors in their networks, responding quickly to take action on opportunities with high potential to advance their goals. *Rapid Response Consultations* The global leadership team and relevant program directors frequently convene on an ad hoc basis to assess unexpected opportunities. They assess alignment with program goals, and how to allocate scarce resources among emerging opportunities. *Quarterly Program Calls* Program directors share new developments and convey opportunities for partnering both with external actors and internally across programs. For example, multiple programs have worked together to facilitate delegations of informal workers to International Labour Conferences and other global events. *Ad Hoc Global, Regional, and National Meetings* Program teams regularly piggyback on external global, regional, or national events to hold face-to-face meetings with a subset of the organization's globally dispersed staff. About a dozen such opportunities arise in a given year, serving as a frequent vehicle for sharing new opportunities. *Program Advisory Committees* Each program convenes an external advisory group of key stakeholders (such as membership-based networks) that serves a dual function: to share information about potential opportunities for joint action across the networks; and to ensure goal alignment, solicit feedback on annual and five-year plans, and coordinate actions.	Long-term strategic focus is maintained through: *Five-Year Strategy Reviews* The entire organization undertakes a strategic review every five years. The board, global leadership team, and program directors develop a joint vision and program-specific targets aligned with that vision. Planning commences one year in advance of the end of the current strategy. *Cross-Functional Programming* Cross-cutting projects provide opportunities to integrate multiple programs at a single site or in "focal cities." Cross-functional support is provided to all programs in the areas of research, communications, policy analysis, and capacity building. *Semiannual Performance Reporting* Program teams report on progress towards their strategic goals on a semiannual basis, using logic models and outcome harvesting methods. The reporting formats are designed to help teams to clearly link their targets to organization-wide strategic goals. *Annual Retreats* All team members from around the world convene annually for a four-day retreat focused on building solidarity and strategic coherence. The agenda is highly orchestrated, consisting of results reporting and planning for the coming year, reinforcement of the organization's theory of change, anticipation of challenges on the horizon, and socialization of new staff into the organization's norms and culture. *Annual Learning Meetings* Each program team holds a two-day event to identify and distill key lessons learned. Members from other programs are invited in order to cross-fertilize lessons and to strategize future joint efforts. The meetings provide opportunities for midcourse correction and partnership across programs. In addition, all of the program directors convene once yearly; alongside a board meeting, in order to improve coherence across programs.

Given my background in the international statistical system, it is not difficult for me to maintain contact with ongoing efforts in the field and even to initiate activities with statisticians at the international level and in countries. (Joann Vanek, August 2, 2016)

In order to share new opportunities across the organization, and to determine which ones to pursue, WIEGO developed multiple ways of sharing intelligence internally. These mechanisms ranged from rapid response consultations, in which the relevant program director (such as the head of the statistics program) consulted with the global leadership team (which typically included the international coordinator and the directors of program support and operations) on a new opportunity. While such calls were conducted on an ad hoc basis, they were part of a standard protocol for identifying who to involve in the call, assessing the opportunity in light of program goals and costs, and how best to allocate scarce resources to the task. For decisions that could wait or that necessitated broader consultation across programs or with external partners, there were numerous additional mechanisms for sharing opportunities—such as quarterly calls among program directors, face-to-face meetings at national or global events, and meetings of program advisory committees. These mechanisms were especially important given the globally dispersed nature of the organization, where staff did not regularly encounter one another in an office. One program director who oversaw a team with members in Brazil, India, and South Africa, explained:

[E]very time we get together . . . [we ask] what have we learned since I saw you last? What has happened. . . ? What are the things that jump out? . . . So it's diffuse and constant, but not centralized. (Sally Roever, director of urban policies program, October 28, 2015)

The key pragmatic insight from WIEGO's experience is that the organization was deliberate in creating multiple contact points for its program staff and leadership to identify, share, and screen new opportunities. These mechanisms provided a structured basis for emergent action.

Second, WIEGO developed a series of *strategy creation and coherence* mechanisms for maintaining a clear, long-term focus. In contrast to opportunity scanning, these mechanisms were highly centralized with the objective of creating a global strategy and performance goals shared across the organization. For example, each staff member was engaged in developing strategy at both the organization and team levels, and in reporting performance on a semiannual basis. In addition, WIEGO created a set of program integration mechanisms that could help it to execute multiple interventions more coherently. For instance, it worked in a series of "focal cities" around the world where it sought to deliver several programs simultaneously (such as in statistics, capacity building of local membership-based organizations, urban policy development, and legal rights) with support from cross-functional and cross-program teams. Each program also held an annual learning meeting, typically held over two days, where staff from other programs were invited in order to cross-fertilize lessons and to develop joint strategy. These mechanisms were not unusual in and of themselves—strategy reviews, annual retreats and learning meetings, and performance reporting—but their power lay in creating multiple structured opportunities for clarifying and reinforcing long-term goals across the organization. And, in so doing, they provided each staff member with an understanding of how their individual tasks contributed to the larger purposes of the organization.

Taken together, these two broad types of alignment mechanisms enabled WIEGO to bring coherence to its otherwise decentralized efforts. They can be seen as building on one another—opportunity scanning and responding enables information to flow across the organization to take advantage of emerging opportunities, while strategy creation and coherence maintains a focus on longer-term objectives—thus enabling the organization to align emergent actions with long-term goals.

Conclusion: Performance Management for an Emergent Strategy

The purpose of this chapter has been to lay out the characteristics of a performance system useful for organizations with an emergent strategy. The defining conditions of an emergent strategy are high uncertainty about cause and effect coupled with low control over outcomes.

I chose the case of WIEGO's statistics program to illustrate the three components of a performance system useful under such conditions. The first is a *system framing* that helps the organization to identify targets for action in terms of key actors, their interactions, and their underlying structures. The second is a focus on *accountability for interim outcomes*, supported by an analysis of how those interim outcomes contribute to system-level outcomes. The third component is internal *alignment* mechanisms that link emergent opportunities with long-term strategic goals. Taken together, these three components form an adaptation system that enables the organization to identify new opportunities, and to take action on those most likely to contribute to long-term system-level change.

One does not have to look far to see the relevance of adaptation systems to other organizations with emergent strategies. In concluding this chapter, I briefly consider two very different examples: an advocacy effort to reduce teen pregnancy rates in the United States, and a leadership program to reduce long-term violent conflict in Burundi.

The National Campaign to Prevent Teen and Unplanned Pregnancy in the United States (National Campaign) is a national advocacy organization. When it was first established in 1996, the National Campaign set a clear long-term outcome goal: to reduce US teen pregnancy rates, which were among the highest in the industrialized world, by one-third by 2005 (from their 1996 levels). One of the organization's first actions was to map its system, that is, to identify key sets of actors and their interactions that would be central to shaping a solution. Its founders identified several types of actors who influenced teens: faith communities that exerted moral influence over teens and their families; popular media such as television networks that shaped cultural norms; local and state actors such as governments and nonprofits that were already providing youth programs and services; researchers that had studied teen pregnancy and had built an evidence base on program effectiveness; and, of course, the teens themselves, their peers, and their parents. Each of these actors were brought into task forces charged with both framing the problem and developing strategies for action at a national level.

Its next step was to identify a series of interim outcomes, supported by a theory of change that linked them to the long-term goal
of reduced teen pregnancy rates. Based on a review of the existing
research, the National Campaign identified three key levers for influencing teen sexual behavior: *information* regarding pregnancy and sex;
access to family planning and reproductive health services; and cultural
factors affecting the *motivation* of teens regarding sex and pregnancy.
Together, these three levers—all of which were interim outcomes—
could affect teen behavior by increasing either contraceptive use or
abstinence. Because many organizations in its ecosystem were already
working on the first two levers (information and access), the National
Campaign chose to focus on the third (motivation). It identified and
targeted key influencers—such as popular media, faith communities,
parents, and youth programs—to increase the motivation of teens to
avoid pregnancy.[22]

The National Campaign's strategy was necessarily emergent—requiring it to act quickly to take advantage of new opportunities as
they arose. For instance, the organization had difficulty gaining the
attention of policy makers in Washington but very quickly captured
the interest of executives in Hollywood. It jumped at the opportunity to influence the scripts of television programs watched by teens,
based on research suggesting that messaging through popular culture
could influence teen motivations regarding sex and pregnancy. Several
years later, it also launched a reality television series with MTV, *16 and
Pregnant*, that tracked the lives of teenagers navigating their lives after
pregnancy, showing the consequences, tradeoffs, and struggles of new
teenage parents.

The original goal of reducing teen pregnancy by one-third by
2005 was achieved, leading the organization to revise its target to reducing teen pregnancy rates by half by 2026. But the organization
faced the classic problem of attribution: the complexity of causal factors and actors, coupled with the lack of a counterfactual case (i.e.,
what would have happened in the absence of the National Campaign), made it very difficult to clearly attribute this decline to any
particular intervention. The organization thus focused its measure-

ment on interim outcomes—for example, assessing whether it was reaching teens with its media messaging (outputs), and whether teens reported any changes in motivations about pregnancy as a result of that messaging (interim outcomes). A study published by economists with the National Bureau of Economic Research found a correlation between the MTV show's premiere in 2009 and a decline in teen births by 5.7 percent in the eighteen months that followed (Kearney and Levine 2014). This effect was later disputed by other researchers who argued that it was most likely part of a broader set of forces contributing to a rapid decline in US teen pregnancy rates, notably the economic downturn following the financial crisis of 2008 (Jaeger, Joyce, and Kaestner 2016).

The broader lesson is that the National Campaign, like WIEGO, could at best make modest claims about interim outcomes (teen motivation as affected by media messaging) but could not directly attribute actual changes in behavior (use of contraception or abstinence) or outcomes (declines in teen pregnancy rates) to its work. As with WIEGO, it was best served by focusing on influencing key players in its system in order to shape interim outcomes, and by making reasonable claims based on the best available research about contribution rather than attribution.

The core components of an adaptation system highlighted in this chapter—system framing, alignment of emergent actions with a long-term goal, and assessment of interim outcomes—also apply to a radically different example. The Burundi Leadership Training Program (BLTP) was launched in 2003, just as the East African country was recovering from a violent ethnic civil conflict that had killed nearly 300,000 people.[23] Although a peace agreement had been signed in 2000 with the mediation of Nelson Mandela, it took three additional years for a ceasefire to be negotiated among warring factions. The BLTP was an effort to support Burundi's leadership in building stable institutions by providing training to key individuals in government who would play an important role in institutional reform.

Although the "system" targeted by the BLTP—Burundi's fledgling public sector leadership—was more tightly defined than the National

Campaign above, it was perhaps even more complex, divided along lines of ethnic and religious identity, socioeconomic status, political alliances, and civilian and military roles. Two scholars who evaluated the program remarked on the complexity of the challenge:

> Burundi's leaders were not a group of committed professionals negotiating to solve a difficult problem, but a group of distrustful, hurt, insecure, and often unrepresentative people who had used any tool, under conditions of near-Hobbesian institutional anarchy, to assure themselves of a seat at the table and a piece of an increasingly smaller pie. It is these leaders that the BLTP sought to assist in transforming Burundi. All of the program's efforts occurred against a backdrop of violence, unpredictability, profound institutional weakness, deep poverty and risk, and regional instability. (Campbell and Uvin 2015)

No doubt, even in the best of circumstances, this was a context of high causal uncertainty and low control over outcomes! Moreover, the BLTP was hardly the first training program attempted with the country's leadership. In the preceding decade, there had been at least thirty-six other efforts to implement some kind of conflict management program.

Yet, the BLTP made steady headway through a series of workshops over several years. Like the National Campaign, it focused on the interim outcomes of individual motivation and attitude. The first set of trainings, called the Ngozi workshops after the remote town in which they were held, provided small groups of thirty participants, selected to include all parties to the conflict, with skills of negotiation, visioning, and collaborative decision making while breaking down ethnic and political stereotypes. The initial content of these workshops was general, deliberately skirting contentious issues specific to the conflict. The evaluators found that "at the level of individual attitude change . . . the BLTP workshops did effect a personal transformation in the way people perceive themselves in relation to other participants. . . . [They] broke through some of the stereotypes that they may have carried for years." But they also noted that the BLTP missed two opportunities: "the workshop hardly dealt with the concrete issues in Burundi, and the tools taught in the workshop trainings were not modified for the Burundian context." In other words, the workshops were being delivered as part of a standardized system (like the niche and integrated strategies in chapters 2 and 3), despite the complexities of a context that required a more emergent strategy.

The real breakthrough came when prior workshop participants advocated for creating a steering committee to guide the direction of a new set of workshops. They wanted content that would be targeted to very specific challenges in Burundi. It was a moment of emergent action:

> The targeted workshops represent . . . a project's ability to respond flex- ibly to emerging opportunities and challenges while still maintaining a long-term vision. Although the targeted workshops were not part of the BLTP's original project proposal, they did fit the BLTP's vision, and the BLTP team was quick to respond when Ngozi participants requested them. They were also flexibly designed, allowing workshop content to be adapted to the new aims, and rapidly implemented, enabling them to respond while the need was still felt. With hindsight, they may well have been the BLTP's most influential activities. (Campbell and Uvin 2015)

Among the new workshops, one of the most successful targeted the Integrated Military Chiefs of Staff which, according to workshop participants and observers, broke through a core problem on "the sta- tus of enemy combatants" that had plagued the integration of the army. Military leaders were able to reach an agreement shortly after the workshop.

But even with such apparent success, the BLTP could hardly attri- bute success primarily to its intervention. A similar training provided to the Joint Ceasefire Commission, which was also charged with work- ing out key issues of military integration, failed to break a deadlock in negotiations. Evaluating the program ran into the classic problem of attribution versus contribution:

There is [a] risk of falling into the traps of either overattribution or cynicism. The BLTP did not build peace in Burundi. It did not transform all of Burundi's leaders into peace-loving, cooperative individuals. At the same time, it was not a waste of time and money. It helped several leaders build relationships and gain tools that, in conducive institutional and organizational contexts, helped to achieve significant breakthroughs and increase understanding and confidence. (Campbell and Uvin 2015)

In sum, the experiences of the BLTP, the National Campaign, and WIEGO all point to a shared set of insights concerning performance in complex contexts. Each organization or program understood the larger system in which it intervened—the key actors, their interactions, and the underlying structures that it sought to change. But each also recognized that it could, at best, produce interim outcomes such as changes in capabilities, motivations, or visibility among its target group. Any final outcomes—such as a lasting peace in Burundi, or reduced teen pregnancy rates in the United States, or improved conditions for informal workers around the world—could only be achieved through the collective actions of many actors at a system level. They could contribute to that change, but could not attribute it to their work. And finally, each recognized that it could not succeed with a preplanned strategy but instead had to seize unanticipated opportunities that were aligned with its long-term goals. In short, they needed an emergent strategy supported by a performance system that enabled adaptation.

Chapter 5

ECOSYSTEM STRATEGY

ecosystem: the complex of a community of organisms
and its environment functioning as an ecological unit.[1]

I]n the past, the homeless services system has been
kind of . . . "loosey-goosey" with how we operate. A
lot of providers [were] operating in their own silos,
they were housing people according to their own
application process, their own requirements, [and they]
weren't necessarily talking to other housing providers.
It just wasn't organized; it wasn't efficient. So [we
needed to] . . . all pull together and assess people
using a common assessment, so we're all speaking the
same language. And then create a system where we
can help walk people through the housing process.

EMILY BUZZELL, SENIOR CASE MANAGER,
MIRIAM'S KITCHEN

NESTLED AMID THE EDIFICES of global power—within walking distance
of the White House and the World Bank—sits a modest Presbyterian
church with a soup kitchen in its basement. Every weekday morning
at 6:30 a.m., the doors open to its guests: over two hundred homeless
men and women arriving for breakfast. These clients, invisible during
the day and night, fill the dining hall within minutes, a microcosm of
America's burgeoning underclass. They are served a meal of restau-
rant quality with a menu that, on a typical day, might include sautéed
kale, gravlax, scones, and fruit smoothies. This unusual attention to

high-quality and healthy meals drew a visit from former First Lady Michelle Obama who served Thanksgiving lunch to guests in 2009 (Brown 2009).

The organization serving these meals is Miriam's Kitchen, a secular nonprofit that operates on a small annual budget (under $5 million) but faces a demand for services that far exceeds its capacity. I first visited Miriam's in 2005. Accompanied by a research assistant, we entered through the church's underground garage, making our way to the kitchen where, with several other volunteers, we took our marching orders from the chef in preparing and serving breakfast to clients. A decade later, in 2015, I visited again with another research assistant. Everything seemed the same: the entryway, the buzz in the dining hall, the high-quality food, and the unrelenting demand for services. Considering that Washington, DC, has among the highest per capita rates of homelessness in the United States, Miriam's services seemed like a band-aid on an open wound.

But appearances can be deceptive. During the intervening decade, Miriam's Kitchen had undergone a transformation in its strategy for addressing homelessness. In the language of this book, the organization had shifted from a *niche* to an *ecosystem* strategy. It had moved from being an isolated provider of basic services (such as meals, clothing, counseling, case management) to becoming an "orchestrator" in a community of over one hundred organizations serving the homeless. This organizational ecosystem had a unifying goal: to end chronic homelessness in the city in less than a decade. Miriam's Kitchen developed an ecosystem strategy that sought to increase control over outcomes through coordination and restructuring of highly interdependent interventions and actors.

What's fascinating about organizational ecosystems is that outcomes, such as rates of poverty and homelessness, are usually not terribly difficult to measure. What's difficult is figuring out the pathways for getting to outcomes. Our usual method for uncovering those pathways typically involves examining each intervention in isolation from the others. But in an ecosystem involving many nonlinear interactions among interventions—such as between emergency shelter provision, food services, mental and physical health services, substance abuse counseling, housing provision, and so on—such an approach is both unhelpful and impractical.

What if we could examine the effects of many interventions together, as a constellation, rather than obsessing about the effects of each one separately? Could this help move the needle on a complex social problem? In this chapter, I consider just such an approach to addressing chronic homelessness, known as permanent supportive housing (PSH). There is compelling evidence that permanent housing, when combined with a series of support services, leads to a decline in chronic homelessness. We have a fairly good understanding of the package of interventions that can address the social problem, but it is difficult to attribute those effects to any specific intervention, or to assign weights to each intervention. In other words, causal uncertainty may be high for each intervention in isolation, but it is low for them in combination. The effective delivery of these interventions thus requires a process for coordinating among many specialized actors. This is what it means to be an organizational ecosystem—a complex community of organizations functioning as a cohesive unit.

What does a performance system look like in an organizational ecosystem? In this chapter, I elaborate four key components:

- a system framing of the social problem
- an interdependent social change model
- accountability for collective outcomes
- capacities for coordinated action and advocacy

I use the example of Miriam's Kitchen's work in Washington to explore these challenges. (I also draw on the insights and tools discussed in Chapter 4, particularly on system framing and measuring contribution rather than attribution to outcomes.) Miriam's is not alone, or even particularly unique, among homeless-serving organizations in its shift to an ecosystem strategy. It is part of an initiative underway in over twenty-five cities across the United States to develop a more coordinated approach to ending chronic homelessness. As such, it is not an isolated aberration but an illustration of a replicable model of ecosystem-level social change.

From a Niche to an Ecosystem Strategy

Efforts to measure and address the problem of homelessness run into two features of the existing system: a highly mobile client population and a lack of data sharing among service providers. By definition, homelessness is a condition where individuals or families lack a "fixed, regular, and adequate nighttime residence" (HEARTH Act 2009). A client may have breakfast at Miriam's Kitchen, lunch at another organization, and sleep in a shelter run by a third provider. This mobility of the population, combined with the fact that service providers generally do not share information with one another on their clients, makes it difficult to track and coordinate clients and their needs over time.

In tracking the number of homeless in a city or country, most US figures rely on a "point-in-time" estimate, taken on a single night in January of every year, in which volunteer enumerators scour the streets to count homeless individuals. The point-in-time data also include individuals sleeping in emergency shelters or in transitional housing on the night of the count. Table 5.1 provides estimates in 2016 for ten US cities with the largest total number of homeless people, broken down into various subpopulations. Across the United States, nearly 550,000 people were estimated to be homeless in 2016, with just over two-thirds staying in emergency shelters or other forms of temporary housing, and the remaining one-third living in unsheltered locations. Approximately two-thirds of these homeless people were individuals, and the remaining third were families, with an estimated one-fifth of the total being children. These figures likely substantially underestimate the number of people facing an episode of homelessness during the year—due to the mobile nature of the population and the fact that not all individuals are homeless at a single point in time (Department of Housing and Urban Development 2016).[2]

In this chapter, I focus on efforts to address homelessness among two particularly vulnerable subsets of this population: chronically

TABLE 5.1 Homeless Point-in-Time Estimates, Ten U.S. cities, 2016

	Total Homeless	Homeless Individuals	Homeless People in Families	Chronically Homeless Individuals	Homeless Veterans
New York City	73,523	28,965	44,558	3,230	559
Los Angeles City & County	43,854	37,726	6,128	12,970	2,728
Seattle/King County	10,730	7,748	2,982	785	656
San Diego City and County	8,669	6,955	1,714	1,345	1,156
District of Columbia	8,350	3,683	4,667	1,501	350
San Francisco	6,996	6,309	687	1,805	580
San Jose/Santa Clara City & County	6,524	5,585	939	2,095	701
Boston	6,240	2,485	3,755	605	222
Las Vegas/Clark County	6,208	5,851	357	285	730
Philadelphia	6,112	3,430	2,682	774	293
Chicago	5,889	3,721	2,168	334	601
USA Total	**549,928**	**355,212**	**194,716**	**77,486**	**39,471**

Source: 2016 Annual Homeless Assessment Report (AHAR) to Congress, November 2016, U.S. Department of Housing and Urban Development, Office of Community Planning and Development; https://www.hudex change.info/resource/3031/pit-and-hic-data-since-2007/ (accessed December 14, 2016).

homeless individuals and military veterans, respectively accounting for 14 percent and 7 percent of the total numbers of the homeless nationwide. Chronic homelessness is a condition where an individual has been continuously homeless for a year or more, or has had at least four episodes of homelessness in the past three years (Department of Housing and Urban Development 2015). The chronically homeless are generally considered to be the most difficult population to assist as they typically experience a combination of challenges with substance abuse, mental health, and unemployment.

In addition to the problem of a mobile population, the ecosystem of social service providers is diverse and fragmented. There are providers of various types of shelter (emergency, transitional, and permanent housing), food services (food banks, soup kitchens), substance abuse services (treatment, counseling), AIDS/HIV services, employment support, financial and legal assistance, and antipoverty advocacy organizations. The service providers are also segmented by the type of population they serve. Miriam's Kitchen, for example, primarily serves homeless men, while other organizations focus on families, women, or youth. This fragmentation is exacerbated by a competitive funding environment, with limited financial incentives for collaboration among providers. Policy makers, funders, and the public typically want to know how many people have been "moved off the streets" and into housing as their primary outcome metric. But an exclusive focus on such a measure undervalues the work of organizations that are not primarily engaged in the provision of housing but that nonetheless provide other crucial services to the homeless (Benjamin 2012). In addition, long-term outcomes such as movement of clients into permanent housing, stable health, and employment are beyond the services that a single organization can reasonably provide.

In short, the homeless services sector is characterized by a mobile client population, fragmentation and lack of data sharing among service providers, and a funding environment that disincentivizes collaboration. The result is a collection of niche services that lack coherence. Yet, as the case of Miriam's Kitchen and dozens of communities across the United States show, it is possible to shift from a fragmented system to a cohesive one. At the heart of this shift lies an interdependent social change model that focuses attention on collective outcomes.

Building an Interdependent Social Change Model with Accountability for Outcomes

Founded in 1983, Miriam's Kitchen focused primarily on providing direct services to homeless clients in the form of meals, clothing, therapy, and counseling. In 2005, when I first visited the organization, it operated three main services: (1) a *meals program* that provided clients with nutritious and restaurant-quality meals every weekday (primarily breakfast, with dinner being added a few years later), typically feeding about two hundred guests per day; (2) *Miriam's Studio*, a nontraditional therapeutic program that engaged clients in a variety of art projects while also building relationships and trust with case managers, typically reaching 10 to 20 percent of its breakfast guests; and (3) *case management*, to support clients in identifying needs, setting goals, and linking them to services offered by other nonprofit and public sector agencies such as health care, counseling, financial support, and housing. About 1,300 unique clients sought case management services in 2005.

Given that DC's homeless population was estimated to be about 6,000 individuals at the time, Miriam's meals program served only a small part of this population, whereas its case management program reached over one-fifth of it. As the organization's capacity grew, so did demand for its programs. By 2015, it was serving about 350 meals per day, still a drop in the bucket, but had grown its case management services sixfold to nearly 6,000 unique clients over the course of the year, in an estimated homeless population of about 8,350. On the face of it, although Miriam's was reaching a substantial proportion of the city's homeless population, its basic services were merely keeping pace with the effects of homelessness rather than finding ways to reduce it.

A turning point came in 2010 when Miriam's Kitchen adopted a new model for addressing chronic homelessness—PSH or "housing first"—that was gaining national attention for its effectiveness. Traditional approaches to addressing homelessness, often called a "linear continuum model" or a "linear residential" model, typically required individuals to first satisfy a series of conditions, such as sobriety or substance abuse treatment, before they could be considered for housing. The PSH model turned this conventional wisdom on its head by *first* getting vulnerable people into housing and then providing them with a series of supportive services that would enable them to stay in housing, such as mental and physical health care, substance abuse treatment and counseling, and education and employment services.[3]

There was growing evidence that the PSH model worked not only in getting people housed but, more importantly, in increasing housing retention and thereby reducing chronic (repeated) homelessness. For example, one of the earliest studies compared 242 individuals housed using the PSH model to 1,600 people housed with the linear residential model in New York City, controlling for client characteristics. The research documented a housing retention rate for PSH clients of 88 percent, as compared to 47 percent for the linear residential model, despite the fact that the PSH sample had a greater percentage of individuals with diagnoses for substance abuse and schizophrenia (Tsemberis and Eisenberg 2000). In the ensuing decade, a number of other studies documented the effectiveness of a PSH model for helping the chronically homeless (Mares and Rosenheck 2010; Padgett, Henwood, and Stanhope 2007; Rosenheck et al. 2003) and its significance for reshaping public policy (Burt 2003; Culhane and Byrne 2010).

The PSH model was especially cost effective for the worst off—the roughly 10 percent of the homeless who were chronically on the streets and thus cost the most in terms of emergency public services. The organization that pioneered PSH in New York City, Pathways to Housing, put its program costs at about $21,000 per client per year, as compared to $27,000 for emergency shelter, $60,000 for prison, and $170,000 for placement in a state psychiatric hospital (as noted in Padgett et al. 2007). At about the same time, a *New Yorker* essay by Malcolm Gladwell, "Million-Dollar Murray" (Gladwell 2006), caught the attention of policy makers by articulating the disproportionately high public costs of emergency services to the chronically homeless. Other studies placed the public costs of supporting a chronically homeless person at $35,000–70,000 annually using the existing patchwork system, based on a combination of stays in shelters and prison, along with emergency medical costs, and mental health and detoxification services—approximately two to five times higher than a supportive housing-based approach (Culhane and Byrne 2010; Culhane, Metraux, and Hadley 2002; Economic Roundtable 2009). An analysis conducted for Miriam's Kitchen similarly estimated that the most vulnerable homeless individuals, typically the chronically homeless, cost an average of $41,000 per person in emergency services per year, while PSH would cost about $22,000 per person annually (Advisory Board Company 2015).

Thus by the time Miriam's Kitchen began to consider PSH, momentum for the approach was on the upswing across the country. Federal policy had already begun to recognize PSH, setting aside funds at the Department of Housing and Urban Development (HUD) for this purpose. A public agency—the US Interagency Council on Homelessness (USICH)—was tasked specifically with coordinating the efforts of other public agencies and prepared the country's first strategic plan to prevent and end homelessness (USICH 2010).[4] USICH also worked with a national nonprofit group, the National Alliance to End Homelessness, to encourage states and localities to create ten-year plans for ending homelessness using PSH as a key pillar of the solution.

It was this growing momentum, and the evidence base behind it, that convinced Miriam's Kitchen's leadership to rethink its own work—and ultimately to shift from a niche to an ecosystem strategy. The most profound aspect of this shift lay in how the ecosystem and its possibilities were perceived. The organization's head of programs explained:

> [H]ow do you start seeing yourself as an agency that's not just the programs that we've always done but this bigger vision about ending a social problem? . . . The first barrier, we've learned, is whether people can believe that it's possible. A lot of times people's first reaction to that bigger vision is "You know we've heard so many of those plans about ending homelessness, but nothing changes." (Adam Rocap, deputy director, March 26, 2015)

Miriam's chief executive was one of the initial skeptics:

> Frankly . . . I had to be convinced of it as well. Adam and Catherine [on the leadership team] came and said, hey this is what we're reading and this is what we're seeing. Miriam's should really start adopting this approach [to PSH]. . . . I didn't want to go down that road and potentially [open up a] credibility gap. But once we started really talking about it, I recognized that actually this was the intervention that had nationally . . . close to a 90 percent success rate. . . . Success being

you don't relapse into homelessness. (Scott Schenkelberg, president and CEO, March 26, 2015)

Over the next two years, Miriam's Kitchen rethought its role in the homelessness ecosystem—developing a new mission statement, a new theory of change, a new strategy, and building new capacities to execute these changes. The previous mission statement had been a catch-all: "To provide individualized services that address the causes and consequences of homelessness in an atmosphere of dignity and respect both directly and through facilitating connections in the Washington, DC community." In contrast, the new mission was concise, measurable, and motivating: "To end chronic homelessness in Washington, DC."

The organization was also more clear about its strategy: "We advocate for permanent supportive housing as a long-term solution, while meeting short-term needs by providing healthy meals and high-quality social services to the chronically homeless." In other words, Miriam's Kitchen continued to provide its basic services in meals and case management (a niche role), but it now also engaged in advocacy work and coalition building to advance PSH (an ecosystem-building role). This combination of both a niche and ecosystem strategy required substantial new leadership skills and capacities:

> [O]ur value proposition has changed. So to that end, we had to reshape our leadership and reshape our management team, in addition to adding the advocacy piece so that our leadership would have more of an external kind of system perspective. (Scott Schenkelberg, March 26, 2015)

The organization added two new programs. The first and most ambitious was an advocacy program designed to serve a dual purpose: to engage with other nonprofits and public agencies in the District of Columbia to advance PSH; and to build grassroots capacity and agency among homeless individuals to advocate for their own needs. The second new program, PSH services, worked with local public agencies to provide case management to individuals placed in permanent supportive housing. Rather than expecting newly housed individuals to come to Miriam's for support, the organization's case managers would go to them in order to provide customized services (in physical and mental health, life skills coaching, employment support, and so on), thereby reducing the likelihood of returning to homelessness.

Notably, the organization also began to get clarity on what it would *not* do. It would not build or provide housing itself—terminating a small transitional housing facility it had recently started—but would work with others to advocate for more permanent housing and to develop a coordinated citywide housing placement system.

Figure 5.1 captures Miriam's Kitchen's new social change model, using a logic model format. A more generalized version of this figure was introduced in the opening chapter (Figure 1.1). The dashed line cutting across the figure depicts the organizational boundary separating Miriam's from its ecosystem. Actions and results below this line are largely within the control of Miriam's Kitchen (a strategy map), whereas those above the line are interdependent with the ecosystem of stakeholders (an impact map).

At the top of the figure is the end outcome: no chronically homeless individuals in Washington, DC. At the bottom of the figure are five components of Miriam's strategy. Strategy 1 retained the organization's historical strengths in meals and case management. These services, which were previously niche interventions, were now seen as a basis for establishing trusted relationships with clients to nudge them towards permanent supportive housing. The other four strategies embedded Miriam's work within a larger ecosystem of actors and interventions. Strategy 2 was Miriam's new program of providing services to clients who were placed in permanent supportive housing. And strategies 3 to 5 all focused on new efforts related to policy advocacy that included educating its donor and volunteer base, engaging with partners in the ecosystem on policy issues, and aligning their collective efforts.

As a result of its new strategy, Miriam's Kitchen now set its sights on *accountability for outcomes*—as measured by reductions in chronic and

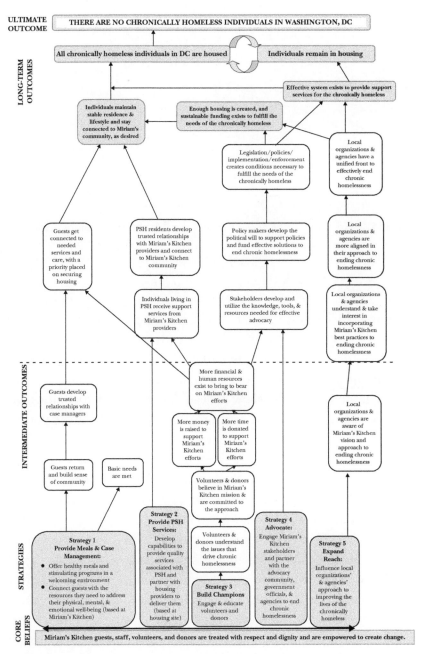

FIGURE 5.1 Social Change Model, Miriam's Kitchen

Source: Adapted from Adam Rocap, Miriam's Kitchen, 2015. Reproduced with permission.

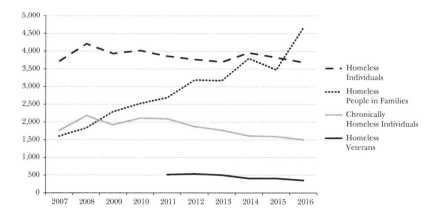

FIGURE 5.2   Homeless Point-in-Time Estimates, District of Columbia, 2007–2016
Source: Based on data from Department of Housing and Urban Development (2016).

veteran homelessness—rather than merely the number of people or meals it served. Figure 5.2 shows the trends for homeless populations in the District of Columbia from 2007 to 2016. The focal populations for Miriam's work, the chronically homeless and veterans (the two solid lines in the graph), show a steady decline since 2010, the year in which Miriam's Kitchen began to push for permanent supportive housing solutions for these two particularly vulnerable groups. Based on city estimates, Miriam's put the number of chronically homeless at approximately 1,500 individuals in late 2016, down from a peak of 2,200 in 2008. The number of homeless veterans had declined from 530 individuals in 2012 to about 350 in 2016.[5]

But correlation does not imply causality. As I elaborate below, progress among chronically homeless individuals and veterans could hardly be attributed to Miriam's Kitchen alone, but was the product of the joint efforts of numerous actors organized through a formally coordinated process. Moreover, despite initial progress in both housing placement and housing retention, there remained a long way to go. The initial target date for ending chronic homelessness in the District of Columbia, as laid out in a citywide strategic plan, was the year 2017 (DCICH 2015). But by 2015, it was obvious that this target was far from being achieved. The challenges facing Miriam's Kitchen and its partners lay in building common cause with other actors in the ecosystem and in securing resources and cooperation at a citywide level. It is to these orchestration challenges that I now turn.

Designing a Performance System: Orchestration

In the process of developing an ecosystem strategy, Miriam's Kitchen underwent a shift in perception about its own role. It began to see itself as an "orchestrator" of social change responsible for "coordinat[ing] action across groups, organizations, and sectors to scale the proposed solution" (Battilana and Kimsey 2017). Miriam's was committed to PSH as a feasible and evidence-based solution to chronic homelessness, but it needed a new way of framing its relationship with other actors in its ecosystem, and it needed new capacities for coordinating with those actors in order to design and execute the PSH model. I discuss each of these challenges—system framing and building new capacities—in turn below.

System Framing: Seeing Interdependence

In shifting from its traditional niche role as a service provider to that of an orchestrator in an ecosystem, Miriam's Kitchen needed to develop a deeper understanding of its position and leverage within its ecosystem. Figure 5.3 is its mapping of that ecosystem. Two features of this map stand out. First, Miriam's Kitchen now saw its own role (depicted by dashed boxes and arrows) in interdependent terms. Rather than operating in isolation from others, Miriam's saw itself as playing a number of important connective roles: its historical niche function as a provider of basic assistance to the homeless, and in connecting clients to services provided by others; a growing role in supporting permanent housing efforts, both through direct services to clients once they are housed and coordinating with other service providers; and its newest roles in coordinating local efforts on PSH and in policy advocacy.

The second important feature of the mapping is the articulation of three distinct backbone functions played by different sets of actors in

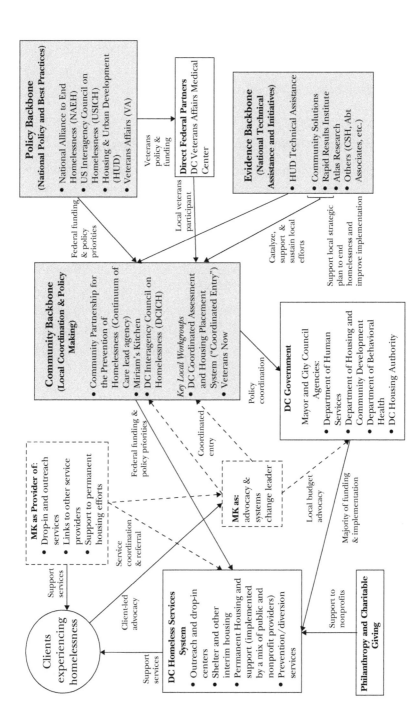

FIGURE 5.3 Ecosystem Map for Ending Veteran and Chronic Homelessness in Washington, DC Adapted from Adam Rocap, Miriam's Kitchen, 2018.

the ecosystem (shaded in gray in the figure). My use of the term *back-bone* draws on a body of work on "collective impact" that suggests that coordination is best undertaken by a dedicated support organization that "can plan, manage, and support the initiative through ongoing facilitation, technology and communications support, data collection and reporting, and handling the myriad logistical and administrative details needed for the initiative to function smoothly" (Hanleybrown, Kania, and Kramer 2012; Kania and Kramer 2011, 40). Miriam's Kitchen found, however, that many different actors could be mobilized to serve various types of backbone support functions.

Policy backbone

Four national-level actors provided guidance on policies and best practices to cities on how to address homelessness. Miriam's originally tapped into the policy research, advocacy resources, and networks of a national nonprofit, the National Alliance to End Homelessness, as it began its shift to an ecosystem strategy. Miriam's was also linked to a national initiative, the 25 Cities Initiative,[6] that assisted cities in developing a coherent approach to addressing chronic homelessness particularly for veterans. This support role was played by Community Solutions, a national nonprofit, and by several government agencies including the US Department of Veterans Affairs in partnership with HUD and the USICH.

Evidence backbone

Several organizations played key roles in providing research and technical assistance for executing coordinated efforts: Community Solutions, a national nonprofit organization, provided support with data dashboards and survey instruments for assessing homeless clients in order to match clients to appropriate housing, while also leading two national campaigns to end chronic and veteran homelessness (Built for Zero, and the 100,000 Homes Campaign, involving over seventy cities and communities);[7] Rapid Results Institute supported a process for mobilizing communities to target and report results in "100-day" periods, thereby inspiring intensive bursts of innovation and collaboration among partners; and Atlas Research provided assistance on measurement, research, and evaluation. The training, how-to manuals, data dashboards, and data aggregation provided by these three organizations, among others, enabled consistency in execution and comparability in results across various cities. Federal agencies (such as HUD) played an important role in providing funding to these technical assistance providers.

Community backbone

Execution ultimately relied on action at the city level, where leadership staff from local community-based organizations took on the tasks of developing shared goals, implementing a common system to assess and match homeless clients to housing, coordinating support services among one another, gathering citywide data, and collectively lobbying city government for changes in policy and budgets. In Washington, DC, Miriam's Kitchen played a central orchestrating role in this process, along with the Community Partnership for the Prevention of Homelessness, and with the support of three other partners: Community Connections, Friendship Place, and Pathways. Together, they mobilized the government's coordinating agency, the DC Interagency Council on Homelessness (DCICH), along with 102 service providers in DC to develop a coordinated approach to addressing chronic homelessness. Miriam's Kitchen was also active on two local working groups that were central to this task of coordination.

The execution of an ecosystem strategy among the dozens of players in the Washington, DC, region—including the three types of backbones above—required Miriam's Kitchen to develop new types of organizing capacities: a capacity for coordinating the actions of service providers in its ecosystem, and a capacity for policy advocacy to address city-level bottlenecks in the ecosystem.

Building a Capacity for Coordination

To execute the new social change model of PSH across the entire city, Miriam's Kitchen and its partners needed to develop an evidence-based process for answering some fundamental questions: How should they assess which clients were most vulnerable and thus should be prioritized for PSH (as compared to other less comprehensive services)? Once clients were assessed, how could they match them to housing and support services?

In early 2014, Miriam's Kitchen began working with several other service-providing organizations to pilot a coordinated process. A senior case manager at Miriam's Kitchen, Emily Buzzell, took on the lead role in developing this process. She described its purpose:

> [W]e want to make sure that we're matching the right type of people with the right type of housing, but also identifying the people who are at high risk of dying on the streets to prioritize them for housing sooner rather than later. So it's an effort to . . . right-size our system, assess the needs of the population, be able to implement housing interventions to meet those needs, and then coordinate everything as efficiently as possible. (March 26, 2015)

The resulting "coordinated entry" process consisted of three main steps: client assessment, housing navigation, and housing match. It lay at the heart of the local workgroup efforts in the middle of Figure 5.3.

The first step was to identify a reliable method for assessing homeless clients that could be used by all service providers. Miriam's sought the help of the technical backbone organizations supported by the federal government. One of these organizations, Community Solutions, had developed an assessment instrument known as the Vulnerability Index-Service Prioritization Decision Assistance Tool (VI-SPDAT) that used an interview survey to assess various risk factors for homelessness.[8] These factors included, for instance, the client's history of homelessness, interactions with the police and emergency services, mental and physical health, substance abuse, money management abilities, social networks, and several other categories. Responses to the survey generated a numerical score (from 0 to 17) indicating the degree to which an individual was considered at risk of remaining chronically homeless and of dying on the streets. The higher the score, the greater the vulnerability and needs of the client (see also Cels et al. 2012).

The score provided a basis for segmenting the market, that is, for sorting individuals to prioritize the type of interventions best suited to their needs. Figure 5.4 illustrates the coordinated entry model, and how the vulnerability assessment segmented the homeless population into three different tracks: the most vulnerable clients, typically the chronically homeless, would be prioritized for permanent supportive housing; a second group would receive support to get rapidly re-housed, often with a subsidy but without other social services; and, a third group, considered at low risk, would receive other kinds of temporary assistance rather than housing, such as help in searching for housing, applying for public support, or making a rental deposit.

As a result of the efforts of Miriam's Kitchen and its local partners, over 12,000 VI-SPDAT assessments were conducted within a three-year period in the Washington, DC, area. The point-in-time estimate of the District's homeless population was 8,350 in 2016, suggesting that the actual numbers of homeless during the year were at least 50 percent larger, and quite possible double, that single-night estimate. Figure 5.5 provides a snapshot of the resulting segmentation. Individuals scoring 8 or above were prioritized for permanent supportive

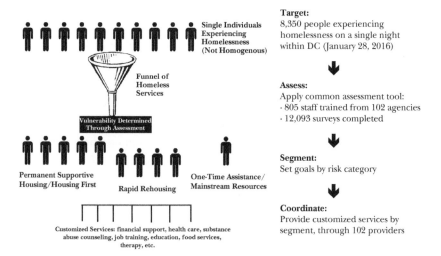

FIGURE 5.4 Coordinated Entry Model
Source: www.CoordinatedEntry.com. Reproduced with permission.

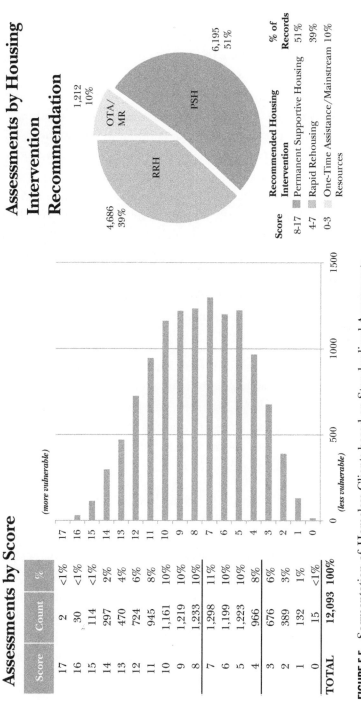

Assessments by Score

Score	Count	%
17	2	<1%
16	30	<1%
15	114	<1%
14	297	2%
13	470	4%
12	724	6%
11	945	8%
10	1,161	10%
9	1,219	10%
8	1,233	10%
7	1,298	11%
6	1,199	10%
5	1,223	10%
4	966	8%
3	676	6%
2	389	3%
1	132	1%
0	15	<1%
TOTAL	**12,093**	**100%**

Assessments by Housing Intervention Recommendation

Score	Recommended Housing Intervention	% of Records
8-17	Permanent Supportive Housing	51%
4-7	Rapid Rehousing	39%
0-3	One-Time Assistance/Mainstream Resources	10%

FIGURE 5.5 Segmentation of Homeless Clients based on Standardized Assessments.
Source: www.CoordinatedEntry.com. Based on all assessments conducted as of October 1, 2016, Washington, D.C. Reproduced with permission.

housing, those scoring 4 to 7 for rapid rehousing, and those at 3 or below for one-time assistance. The pie chart shows that about half of the clients were prioritized for PSH at the time, an intervention best suited to the chronically homeless.

Although the assessment process may seem fairly straightforward, its execution required an enormous amount of local coordination and training. This was the role of the community backbone, led by Miriam's Kitchen and Community Partnership. They took on the task of reaching out to other service providers in the region to get them to agree to using the VI-SPDAT as a common assessment tool, providing training on using the tool (with support from the evidence backbone organizations), and setting up a coordinating committee of five local organizations to support the process and address hurdles. Within a three-year period, they succeeded in securing the cooperation of 102 local service providers and trained 805 staff within these organizations to conduct the VI-SPDAT assessment (Coordinated Entry 2016). The efficiency gains were notable:

> Someone can go to Miriam's Kitchen, they can go to Bread for the City, they can go to Pathways to Housing, they can go to any of these agencies in DC and take *one* assessment. And they don't have to repeat their story over and over and over again and go to a million different places just to be put on a million different waiting lists. (Emily Buzzell, senior case manager, March 26, 2015)

The data on clients gathered through the common assessment tool were entered into a publicly funded web-based system, the Homeless Management Information System (HMIS), enabling key information about each client to be shared across executing agencies as needed. Each homeless individual was provided a unique identifier. The DC backbone organizations, like their counterparts in other cities, sought to have a comprehensive database, aiming to get every homeless client entered in the system with a completed VI-SPDAT. Doing so would not only enable better coordination in providing services to homeless clients, but would also enable longitudinal outcome tracking by repeating the VI-SPDAT with clients over time.

Clients were generally willing to provide their data for entry into the HMIS. But this had not always been the case. A prior iteration of the database, introduced more than a decade earlier, had been resisted by many homeless individuals who were concerned about providing their personal information to the government out of fear that "Big Brother" was following them. Miriam's CEO explained the shift from paranoia about the database to active interest in using it:

> [W]hat's different is *how* it's being used. [B]efore it was just "Oh we're collecting all this data from you and it's just going to sit in some database somewhere." [But] now we need this data because actually you could get into housing. . . . [Clients] now see, wow, this person got their own apartment. Wow, this person actually has some income now. . . . [T]here is enough of the success narrative that people are like "Oh I want that." And the gateway to doing that is this assessment tool. (Scott Schenkelberg, March 26, 2015)

Once clients had been assessed and prioritized for housing, they could proceed to the next step, housing navigation. They needed support in securing key documents, applying for, and finding housing:

> [We are] basically plugging people into the right resources so they can navigate the housing process. They can get their documents. They can communicate with the housing provider. They can apply for a voucher, view apartments, select an apartment, [and] ultimately lease up. [G]etting identification documents . . . is real hard for this population. They lose their stuff. Their stuff gets stolen. If you don't have an address, how do you verify your residency to the DMV [Department of Motor Vehicles]? You know, we've had to do a lot of work with this housing navigation component to try to make it efficient. (Emily Buzzell, senior case manager, March 26, 2015)

And finally, the third step was the housing match. This required other parts of the ecosystem to act in concert. Most critically, it was necessary to get housing providers to agree to prioritize clients based on the VI-SPDAT. Many providers had their own application process, assessment criteria, and priority lists. The coordinated entry process sought to overhaul this fragmented process by getting providers to agree to a single registry, based on the vulnerability assessment, for prioritizing housing across the city. But success was proving elusive. Miriam's CEO explained:

> Right now we have a [part of the] housing inventory that doesn't use this assessment tool at all. [Y]ou show up in their line for housing and, depending on when your number comes up in their line, you get housing. . . . So it's great to have this common assessment tool but if you don't have the resources lined up behind [it], then all you're doing is creating a new line for people. . . . [If] you don't have the housing stock available, what difference does it make? (Scott Schenkelberg, March 26, 2015)

A second bottleneck was finding and paying for housing. Housing units for the chronically homeless were paid for through vouchers funded by the city government (with each voucher being worth approximately $1,200 per month in 2016). It fell to Miriam's Kitchen staff to find private landlords who would accept the vouchers:

> We [spend] staff time scouring neighborhoods, finding landlords, engaging landlords in a conversation about why they should take the vouchers. . . . [P]eople who are chronically homeless have horrible or no credit history, [so] it's also a bit of a sales job to be able to get people to take that voucher. . . . There are neighborhoods we cannot find units in because of the price. There are areas of the city that will always be out of reach. (Scott Schenkelberg, November 18, 2016)

Housing inventory remained an ongoing systemic concern, as it depended not only on convincing housing providers to allocate units to the homeless but also on lobbying city government to allocate adequate funding for housing vouchers and housing development. But doing so required having reliable and transparent data on housing placement and need. To track progress on housing placements, data from housing providers were aggregated and updated monthly (on an internal *Built for Zero* campaign website managed by Community Solutions, an evidence backbone organization) for all participating organizations to see.[9]

There was no way to pad the results. By early 2016, the monthly and aggregate data showed that DC was making substantial progress towards ending veteran homelessness but was falling substantially short on housing the chronically homelessness. Miriam's Kitchen was transparent about this shortfall, posting a quarterly performance report card on its website. At the top of the card, text in bold purple print showed the stark gap between ambition and reality: only 14 percent of the city's goal of housing chronically homeless individuals had been achieved by the second quarter of the fiscal year (i.e., 217 people housed out of a goal of 1,502 for that point in time) (Miriam's Kitchen 2016).

This transparency with outcome data enabled Miriam's Kitchen to highlight the key bottlenecks: gaps in uptake of the single housing registry, insufficient funding for vouchers, and an inadequate future housing supply. At the heart of these bottlenecks was an ecosystem problem: lack of alignment between city government and housing providers. Simply having the common assessment tool (VI-SPDAT) and a common registry for matching clients to housing was not enough. The technical work of assessment and matching needed to be complemented by the political work of strengthening relationships with city government and housing providers as part of a coherent ecosystem strategy.

Building a Capacity for Advocacy

Miriam's leadership recognized that addressing homelessness at a citywide level required it to engage in the political work of influencing public policy and budgets. Having been a social service organization for over two decades, the shift required new ways of working and thinking. One of the organization's key strengths as a service delivery organization was its relationships with homeless clients. Its initial advocacy efforts thus built on these relationships, working with the clients in its breakfast and case management programs to facilitate the creation of a client-led advocacy group, the People for Fairness Coalition (PFFC). This group aimed to build the leadership skills and agency of homeless individuals so that they could advocate for their own interests.

Together, PFFC members and Miriam's staff began to participate in meetings of public agencies. A key player was the DCICH, a group of public agency heads, nonprofit leaders, advocates, and homeless representatives tasked with guiding the city's strategy on addressing homelessness.[10] Over time, the Miriam's Kitchen advocacy program built a strong working relationship with the DCICH and identified three main policy targets at City Hall: (1) full funding for a citywide plan to create new permanent supportive housing units; (2) adoption of the coordinated entry process for all publicly supported housing (i.e., use of a common assessment tool *and* a single housing registry); and, (3) adequate staffing and resources for the DCICH to coordinate the city's collective efforts.

Miriam's advocacy program became increasingly focused on raising awareness and urgency among city leaders about homelessness and its solutions, particularly in the mayor's office and city council (not unlike WIEGO's advocacy at the ILO, discussed in the previous chapter). Miriam's engaged directly with the mayor, deputy mayor, budget director, city council members, and their staff to promote budget and policy priorities for ending chronic homelessness. It also served as a provider of expertise, leading presentations and workshops on coordinated entry at DCICH meetings, helping develop a permanent supportive housing inventory, participating in DCICH executive and strategic planning committees, and providing testimony at public hearings of various city government agencies.

These efforts in policy advocacy were a radical departure from Miriam's service delivery work and required entirely new approaches to assessing and improving performance. The organization thus developed two ways of measuring the performance of its advocacy. The first measured progress towards ecosystem-level advocacy goals that were beyond Miriam's direct control: Were the three advocacy targets—full funding for PSH, adoption of coordinated entry, and adequate resources for DCICH—being achieved? The organization reported progress on these targets in an end-of-year advocacy report and in a quarterly scorecard. For example, it reported that permanent supportive housing was fully funded in 2015, with a new injection of resources in the DC budget of $12.25 million for PSH, rapid rehousing, affordable housing, and coordinated entry. This momentum was not sustained in 2016, with the mayor proposing only $6 million in new funding, a figure that Miriam's estimated was only 18 percent of the total funding needed to end chronic homelessness (Miriam's Kitchen 2016). However, near the end of that year, the mayor's office announced a major $106 million initiative to rehabilitate or build affordable housing, of which about $8.8 million would be allocated for PSH (O'Connell 2016). Although Miriam's Kitchen itself could take little direct credit for the success of such a collective advocacy effort, what mattered was that there was progress towards a set of clearly specified advocacy goals.

The second way in which Miriam's measured the performance of its advocacy work was by assessing improvements in its own advocacy capacity. As discussed in the previous chapter, this was an *interim* outcome that lay within the control of the organization. Adam Rocap, who had led the early development of the organization's advocacy program, elaborated:

> It's not just about the policy wins or the budget wins. It's also about the advocacy capacity that you're building . . . because that's an outcome in itself in many ways. . . . [W]e try to do a self-assessment once a year to try to see whether we're building our own capacity over time. We also believe in building the capacity of people with lived experience of homelessness to have leadership in ending homelessness. (Adam Rocap, deputy director, March 26, 2015)

Advocacy capacity, as described by Rocap, was not merely a means of achieving policy goals but could be seen as an important result in itself—as a measure of the strength of civil society, of the voice and agency of a collective.[11] To assess its advocacy capacity, Miriam's Kitchen used an off-the-shelf tool developed by the Alliance for Justice, a national advocacy membership association.[12] This online instrument enabled Miriam's to self-assess its advocacy capacity on an annual basis, using a series of indicators in four main categories: (1) developing advocacy goals, plans, and strategies; (2) capacities for conducting advocacy; (3) making use of various advocacy avenues (such as administrative, legislative, electoral, or litigation); and (4) sustaining advocacy within the organization. The survey tool provided a tally of scores under each category, highlighting areas for improvement. The process of completing the survey provided a structured basis for the advocacy team to reflect on its own strengths and weaknesses. (Links to these resources are provided in the Appendix to this book.)

An iteration of the survey taken in 2013, for example, showed that Miriam's Kitchen was adept at developing advocacy plans and building partnerships. But there was much room for improvement in execution, particularly in terms of understanding how to influence decision makers and exploring a wider range of avenues for advocating its interests. In an email communication, Miriam's chief program officer reflected on some of the organizational learning that arose from the assessment:

> You can see in our [July] 2013 advocacy self-evaluation that we saw that having direct conversations with DC council staff members at the right time had a big impact in getting some of our advocacy priorities in the budget that year. Since that summer, we've invested more time in building direct relationships with city council members and their staff members (rather than just working through public hearings, coalitions, and other policy-making groups) . . . . We also realized we did not have many direct relationships with key staff in the executive branch, so we've also put a lot more time into building working relationships with executive branch staff, particularly staff in the deputy mayor's office.
>
> We've also learned that we can have the biggest impact in budget advocacy if we can influence the mayor's budget (rather than just focusing on council's approval of the budget), so over the years we've

moved our major events and advocacy actions earlier in the year . . . to maximize possible impact on influencing the mayor's budget. (Adam Rocap, deputy director, e-mail communication, April 1, 2015)

In sum, Miriam's Kitchen's role as an orchestrator had required it to develop two new capacities—for policy advocacy and for coordinating the efforts of service providers. On its own, Miriam's could take little credit for outcomes such as reductions in chronic homelessness or even for interim outcomes such as improvements in city policy and budgets. But as an orchestrator in an ecosystem, it had to stay focused on those outcomes and hold itself accountable for them.

Conclusions: Performance Management for an Ecosystem Strategy

I began this chapter by describing the shift in Miriam's Kitchen from a niche to an ecosystem strategy. This shift involved a fundamental change in the value proposition and social change model of the organization—from being an isolated actor operating under conditions beyond its control to a strategic player in an ecosystem where control over outcomes could be achieved through joint goals and coordinated action with others. This required joining forces with a diverse range of actors including national nonprofit organizations and federal agencies, city hall and numerous municipal government departments, and dozens of local service providers.[13] Historically, most local social service providers that serve the homeless have tended to operate in isolation, each occupying a niche in a fragmented landscape.

The experience of Miriam's Kitchen over the past decade, and of similar efforts underway in many cities across the United States, offers several broader insights on the measurement and management systems needed for building an ecosystem strategy. Miriam's performance system consisted of four core components summarized below—a system-level framing of the problem and its actors, an interdependent social change model, accountability for collective outcomes, and a capacity for organizing the ecosystem. Together, these components constitute an orchestration system that aligns the niches in the ecosystem in order to deliver outcomes.

System Framing

An ecosystem strategy requires a system perspective on a social problem. For the problem of chronic homelessness, Miriam's Kitchen identified over one hundred key actors working on some aspect of the problem in its city, the interactions among them, and the policy and funding structures in which they were embedded. Miriam's mapped out these relationships in order to better understand the interdependent nature of the system and to identify its own points of leverage within this larger landscape (see Figure 5.3). At the heart of this reframing was a new value proposition—ending chronic homelessness in Washington, DC—that could help pull together the work of the fragmented actors in the system. This value proposition not only provided a measurable system-level outcome, but it also emphasized the need for coordinated action.

Interdependent Social Change Model

Delivering system-level outcomes requires a social change model that restructures relationships among key actors in the system. In this case, there was growing convergence nationally around the model of PSH. It is important to note that PSH is not a single intervention but a reorganizing of many interventions: housing coupled with a range of supportive services (health care, substance abuse treatment, mental health counseling, food services, job training, and so on) that do not follow a linear formula but are customized to the needs of individual clients.[14] Notably, causal uncertainty is high for each intervention in isolation, but not for the constellation of interventions as a whole. The strategic task thus lay in coordinating these multiple interventions in order to deliver on the system-level goal.

Accountability for Collective Outcomes

While outcomes in an ecosystem are often measurable, they cannot be easily attributed to any single intervention or pathway. In the case of chronic homelessness, the outcomes (e.g., reductions in the numbers of chronically homeless individuals, numbers placed in permanent supportive housing, and rates of recidivism) are a product of dozens of actors contributing to the solution of permanent supportive housing. For an ecosystem strategy, it may be more feasible to track whether a constellation of interventions collectively moves the needle on an outcome (contribution), rather than trying to parse out the role of each intervention separately (attribution). Measurement focused primarily on attribution can undermine the collective efforts of actors in an ecosystem when it incentivizes them to seek credit and funding for individual behavior (a zero-sum game) rather than to produce interdependent results (a mutual-gains game).[15]

Capacities for Organizing

Perhaps most critically, an ecosystem strategy hinges on building two types of organizing capacities: for coordinating the actions of multiple actors in the system and for joint advocacy. For instance, Miriam's Kitchen played a key role in creating a "coordinated entry" process for assessing the vulnerability of clients and then matching them to appropriate services in the ecosystem. This coordination capacity was the result of a working group of local actors (a community backbone), and was supported by national policy players (a policy backbone) and several data and technical assistance providers (an evidence backbone). The second type of capacity, advocacy, was built by creating an entirely new team within the organization whose purpose was to work with other local organizations, coalitions, and client groups to build relationships with city government in order to influence budget and policy priorities.

These core components of an orchestration system are not limited to addressing urban homelessness but are relevant to a range of other social problems and contexts. Consider a brief illustration from the experience of the United Way (UW) of America, a vast organization comprising approximately 1,300 local chapters across the United States.[16] Historically, these local chapters were known for conducting annual "workplace giving" drives that raised money for local nonprofit organizations that served community health and human service needs. Together, these local UWs were thus seen as a community fund that raised billions of dollars per year to distribute to nonprofits. This was a niche role in a complex ecosystem. But in the early 2000s, under new leadership, the organization began to rethink this role, shifting away from being primarily a fundraising organization and towards taking on a "community impact" role. Its new strategy was to leverage its central community role by bringing together local stakeholders to identify key social challenges in their communities, identify their root causes, and then to develop a collective strategy for addressing those problems. In other words, the UW chose to become an orchestrator that sought to convene local actors to develop an interdependent social change model and deliver collective outcomes.

For instance, the local UW of Dane County, Wisconsin, convened community stakeholders around the problem of a racial achievement gap in third-grade reading, particularly among African American, Hispanic, and Southeast Asian students. Working together with local schools, nonprofits, citizen groups, government, academic researchers, and the media, the local UW chapter was able to galvanize actions that closed this reading gap within nine years. To be sure, the local chapter still functioned as a fund raiser, but it was no longer merely a conduit for funds. Instead, it was an orchestrator: it framed the racial achievement gap as a system-level problem, developed a model of social change that required joint actions, focused accountability on outcomes, and provided much-needed capacity for coordinated action, measurement, and policy research. Similarly, the United Way of Greater Los Angeles identified urban poverty as its core issue, developing ten measurable outcome goals (such as ensuring that 100 percent children have health insurance and increasing high school graduation rates to 75 percent). It saw itself as a "mobilizer" working with key stakeholders in the ecosystem to coordinate their interventions, make grants focused on outcomes, provide expertise on poverty issues, and play a leading role in local policy advocacy.

Like Miriam's Kitchen, these local UW chapters shifted from a niche to an ecosystem strategy. Their performance challenge lay in bringing coherence to series of fragmented but interdependent interventions in order to generate long-term outcomes. That is both the paradox and beauty of ecosystem orchestration: to focus the entire system on accountability for outcomes while taking little individual credit for the results.

Chapter 6

DESIGNING SOCIAL PERFORMANCE SYSTEMS

I will introduce you to a systems zoo—a collection
of some common and interesting types of systems.
You'll see how a few of these creatures behave and
why and where they can be found. You'll recognize
them; they're all around you and even within you.

DONELLA H. MEADOWS, *THINKING IN SYSTEMS* (2008, 5)

HAVING EXAMINED FOUR DIFFERENT TYPES of organizational creatures in
the preceding chapters, it is now time to bring them together. In my
conversations with social sector leaders during this research and in my
teaching, a recurrent theme has been the search for a "fit" between
their strategies for social change and their systems of performance
management. On one hand, they were looking for a generalizable approach to measuring and improving social performance. On the other,
they expressed a need for performance systems that could recognize
and accommodate the complex contingencies of their work. This
chapter attempts to provide both a general model of the core components of a social performance system and a contingency framework
for different types of performance systems.

In doing so, I revisit the two frameworks introduced in the opening
chapter—on the core components of social performance (Figure 1.2)
and the contingency framework (Figure 1.3) that have provided the
structure for this book—and I revise them based on the insights from
our cases. I provide a side-by-side comparison of the cases, identify-

ing not only what they have in common but also how they differ in fundamental ways. I close the chapter with several broader reflections on the implications of a contingency framing for the design of social performance systems.

A General Model of Social Performance

Figure 6.1 provides a general model of a social performance management system. It consists of four core components: an organization's purpose (value proposition), how it aims to bring about change (social change model), how it holds its own feet to the fire (accountability), and the capacities it needs in order to deliver results (performance system). The first three of these components were elaborated in Chapter 1, so I do not discuss them further here.

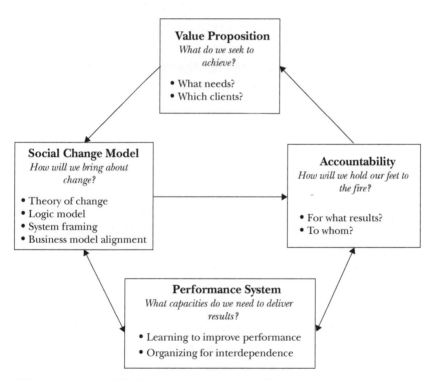

FIGURE 6.1   A Social Performance Management System

The new addition to the figure, performance systems, is at the heart of the case studies in this book. The cases highlight two distinct sets of capacities essential to any performance system. The first *is a capacity for learning to improve performance.* This includes the codification of existing know-how in the organization through the standardization of tasks and procedures, quality control processes, and monitoring and assessing performance. It also includes the development of new knowledge, particularly under conditions of high causal uncertainty, which requires taking advantage of new opportunities, hypothesizing cause-effect pathways, and adapting to changes in one's environment. These two types of learning—*standardization* and *adaptation*—have long been studied in the organizational learning literature, sometimes being called *exploitation* and *exploration* (March 1991).

What is often overlooked, however, is the second type of capacity apparent in the cases, a *capacity for organizing interdependence.* Given that social change can rarely be achieved alone, this capacity is about aligning multiple interventions, inside or outside the organization, in order to produce interdependent results. The cases illustrate two general mechanisms for organizing interdependence. The first is coordination, which involves prioritizing and sequencing multiple activities, as on a conveyor belt or a vertically integrated pipeline of services where there is a handoff from one intervention to the next. The second mechanism, orchestration, involves fundamentally restructuring the relationships among multiple actors towards a system-level goal. Such orchestration necessitates that key actors adopt not only shared (supraorganizational) outcome measures, but also that they develop joint decision-making processes and sometimes even engage in joint advocacy. The external incentives for building these organizing capacities are few; funding for such backbone work remains rare, and it is difficult to attribute results directly to such work. The primary incentives are internal: an organization's own commitment to addressing interdependent social problems, as embodied in its value proposition.

The relationship between an organization's performance system and its social change model is iterative (as indicated by the bidirectional arrows in the figure). The capacities an organization needs are informed by its theory of change, and those capacities in turn generate information for refining the theory of change. The relationship with accountability is similarly reciprocal. A performance system aims to produce results for which the organization is accountable. But the organization's key stakeholders, to whom it is accountable, provide feedback that informs its learning.

The general model depicted in Figure 6.1 is intended to assist managers in identifying their high-level needs as they build their performance management systems. A general model does not, of course, mean that all performance systems should end up looking alike. On the contrary, organizations may choose to emphasize some capacities over others, depending on their strategic needs. It is to these contingencies that I now turn, summarizing the distinct features of four types of performance systems—standardization, coordination, adaptation, and orchestration.

Four Types of Performance Systems

The central message of the four cases in this book is captured in Figure 6.2. The primary question addressed by the figure is: What kind of performance measurement and management system best fits each type of social change strategy? The core conclusions are:

- A niche strategy requires *standardization* to produce outputs of reliable quality.

- An integrated strategy requires *coordination* to produce, prioritize, and sequence outputs that generate interdependent outcomes.

- An emergent strategy requires *adaptation* to influence key actors in a complex system in order to produce interim outcomes.

- An ecosystem strategy requires *orchestration* to restructure relationships among actors in a complex system in order to generate interdependent outcomes.

I briefly discuss the key features of each of these four types of performance systems and their strategies below. Table 6.1 provides a summary.

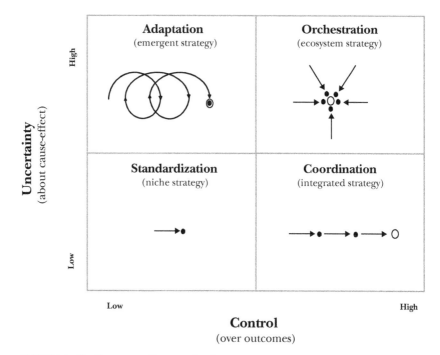

FIGURE 6.2 Performance Systems by Strategy

Standardization

A standardization system is necessary for supporting a niche strategy, where the performance goal is to address a highly focused social need. This goal is accomplished by producing outputs of reliable quality.

Chapter 2 illustrated one such example, Ziqitza Health Care Limited, an emergency medical response service. ZHL's performance system relied on outputs as the primary measures of performance (such as emergency response time and proportion of patients reached in base of pyramid markets) and quality controls for ensuring consistent delivery of outputs. ZHL's performance system consisted of three main components. The first was a standardization of work tasks. Every stage of operations—call handling and dispatch, patient transport and delivery, vehicle maintenance, and patient follow up—had clearly defined roles, responsibilities, performance indicators, and quality standards.

TABLE 6.1 Four Strategies and their Performance Systems

Strategy	Niche	Integrated	Emergent	Ecosystem
Value proposition	address a highly focused social need	address a social need that has multiple related parts	influence key actors within a complex system	reorganize a complex system around a common goal
Social change model	produce outputs of reliable quality	produce and combine multiple outputs to generate interdependent outcomes	produce interim outcomes that "contribute" to long-term outcomes	restructure relationships among multiple actors to generate interdependent outcomes
Accountability	outputs	outputs + outcomes	influence (interim outcomes)	outcomes (individual + societal)
Performance System	Standardization	Coordination	Adaptation	Orchestration
Capacity for improving performance	• standardize work tasks • quality control • assess outputs	• standardize output delivery • assess outputs and interdependent outcomes	• system framing; identify key actors, interactions, and structures • assess interim outcomes and contribution to system outcomes	• system framing; identify key actors, interactions, and structures • develop an interdependent social change model • assess collective outcomes
Capacity for organizing interdependence	• handoff clients to next niche in ecosystem	• combine multiple outputs in a systematic way—prioritize sequence, execute, and manage	• scan for, and respond to, opportunities to influence key actors; align emergent actions with long-term goals	• structure and coordinate action and advocacy among multiple actors
Case examples	Emergency medical services (Ziqitza Health Care Limited, Chapter 2)	Agricultural and natural resource management (Aga Khan Rural Support Programme India, Chapter 3)	Global standards on labor statistics (Women in Informal Employment: Globalizing & Organizing, Chapter 4)	Chronic homelessness (Miriam's Kitchen, Chapter 5)

Second, these standardized tasks were supported by intensive quality control processes. A set of standard procedures were combined with continuous internal feedback (learning) in order to improve performance. For example, call center agents received on-site supervision, one-on-one coaching, and group analysis. Ambulance teams received regular training to meet certification standards, supported by on-call doctors. Quality control was further supported by a range of accountability mechanisms such as surprise audits by internal quality teams and external experts.

And finally, the organization focused its measurement on output assessment, with its key performance indicators being emergency response time and the proportion of patients it was serving in low-income markets. Client feedback mechanisms were critical to gathering reliable output data. For example, follow-up calls with patients systematically gathered data on their experience, with special attention to the timeliness and quality of service. In addition, the organization worked with third parties such as the Grameen Foundation to gather robust data on the socioeconomic profile of its customers and to help it identify how to better reach and serve its target clients.

The core features of this system—standardized work tasks, quality control, and output assessment—are relevant to other niche strategies. Notably, ZHL did not require strong capacities for organizing interdependence, that is, for aligning its activities with other actors in its ecosystem. This is because it could hand off patients to the next niche in the ecosystem, the hospital. While ZHL needed to build relationships with hospitals in order to access their emergency bays, it operated in an ecosystem where such a handoff process was possible. There are many other examples of niche strategies where the ecosystem is sufficiently developed to enable a handoff to the next niche. For instance, most educational systems are designed to enable a handoff from one niche to another, as children move from primary to middle to secondary schools. But in settings where there is no actor to fill the next niche, or when there is no established process for enabling a handoff, organizations may need to build new organizing capacities and thus expand beyond a niche strategy to an integrated one.

In sum, a niche strategy is best supported by standardization system that enables it to deliver a highly focused output(s). This standardization system is depicted in Figure 6.2 by a single arrow representing the core intervention that is delivered through a standardized process, which then results in a key output (the shaded circle). A niche strategy is appropriate where the output is valuable in and of itself, such as in emergency response to a health crisis or to a natural disaster such as an earthquake. In such instances, there is no expectation that the outputs (such as providing temporary shelter, clean water, and food) will address the root causes of the problem. In other instances, such as in the provision of medical immunizations, a niche strategy requires well-established research linking the output (vaccination) to an outcome (prevention of measles), such that measures of the output can serve as a reasonable proxy for outcomes. Many organizations that provide emergency services are engaged in a niche strategy including, for instance, Doctors Without Borders, the Red Cross, and food banks.

Coordination

In comparison, organizations with an integrated strategy face a more complicated value proposition, where addressing a social need requires combining multiple related parts. Or, in the language of this book, multiple outputs must be combined in order produce interdependent outcomes. To do so, they require not only attention to standardization and quality control for each output (as in a niche strategy), but also figuring out how to sequence or combine those outputs in a systematic way. Such a system is illustrated in Figure 6.2 by a series of interventions (arrows) producing separate outputs (shaded circles) that, when coordinated, produce an outcome (open circle). Coordination is especially critical under conditions of interdependence, that is, "whenever one actor does not entirely control all of the conditions necessary for the achievement of an action or for obtaining the outcome desired from the action" (Pfeffer and Salancik 1978, 40).

Chapter 3 provided the case of a rural development organization, the Aga Khan Rural Support Programme India. This organization

produces a series of outputs—soil and water conservation technologies, check dams and other water harvesting infrastructure, agricultural credit and input supply, farmer training, access to markets for
crops, and so on—that in combination increase farmer incomes in
a sustainable manner. Rather than delivering each intervention as a
separate output, AKRSP's primary innovation lay in delivering them
in a coordinated manner.

The underlying logic of an integrated strategy is that a carefully
combined set of outputs can produce outcomes that are greater than
the sum of their parts. But the challenge lies in finding a systematic
and replicable means of integration. The coordinated pipeline developed by AKRSP had three main parts. The first, as with a niche
strategy, was the standardized delivery of outputs. Each department
within the organization established a process for creating outputs
of consistent quality, while also setting multiyear targets and building tracking systems for delivering those outputs. Output targets were
laid out in annual work plans that were tracked by a monitoring and
evaluation department.

Second, AKRSP assessed both the outputs of each department
(such as water resources development, watershed development, and
agriculture) and their interdependent outcomes—such as increased
household incomes, improved land productivity, and reduced seasonal
out-migration in search of work. Assessing these outcomes was beyond the organization's capacity, as it required social science expertise
for gathering baseline data, identifying control groups, and measuring
outcomes over time. While it was able to develop some internal capacity for doing so, such long-term outcome assessment was generally
contracted out to external consultants and local academic institutions.

The third component of AKRSP's performance system was the
combining of interventions in a systematic way. Rather than delivering outputs in isolation from one another, the organization needed a
way to prioritize, sequence, execute, and manage multiple interventions at a community level. This required it to develop a capacity for
organizing interdependence, both internally and externally. Inter-

nally, it developed a vertically integrated model to align its core interventions. Externally, it established local community institutions that played a central role in prioritizing and managing the interventions in their communities. Some of these community institutions focused on managing a specific resource (such as irrigation or drinking water) while others were pan-village entities responsible for managing natural resources across the community. Their roles also included managing conflict and allocating benefits in an equitable manner to their members. In order to better support these community institutions, AKRSP developed ratings tools to assess their quality to identify areas of improvement.

These three components of a coordination system—standardizing output delivery, assessing both outputs and interdependent outcomes, and combining interventions in a systematic way—are not unique to AKRSP, but are also apparent in the work of other organizations such as the Harlem Children's Zone in New York and BRAC in Bangladesh. All three have integrated strategies that require coordination systems for combining multiple outputs to reliably produce outcomes.

Adaptation

Organizations with an emergent strategy face the complex challenge of high uncertainty about cause and effect, coupled with little control over long-term outcomes. They are best served by an adaptation system that enables them to influence key actors or levers in a complex system. This system is visualized in Figure 6.2 by a series of iterative loops that eventually lead to an interim outcome (a shaded circle nested in an open circle).

Chapter 4 considered the experience of such an organization—Women in Informal Employment: Globalizing and Organizing—as it sought to influence policy making and standard setting at the International Labour Organization. The chapter examined WIEGO's statistics program, whose advocacy goal was to integrate measurement of the informal sector into official national labor statistics. In order to influence the key actors responsible for setting these standards and guidelines (an interim outcome), WIEGO developed a performance system made up of three main parts: (1) a system framing to help it understand how best to intervene in a complex ecosystem; (2) performance assessment focused on interim outcomes; and (3) a process of scanning for, and responding to, new opportunities to influence key actors while staying focused on its long-term goals.

First, the organization developed an understanding of its social system—by identifying the main actors, the interactions among them, and the underlying norms and structures that shaped their interactions. The key actor at the heart of the employment statistics system was the ILO, which developed standards and guidelines on labor statistics. WIEGO's efforts thus focused on building and maintaining relationships with the ILO, getting access to key meetings and advisory bodies where labor statisticians interacted, and providing expert input to standards development.

Second, the organization focused on assessing interim outcomes such as its influence on standard-setting decisions at the ILO. Organizations operating under high causal uncertainty and low control over outcomes—which is typical of policy advocacy work—can rarely attribute outcomes solely, or even primarily, to their work. However, WIEGO was able to use methods of contribution analysis such as outcome harvesting (rather than attribution-based methods) to make a credible case for how its work influenced policy decisions. Recent advances in the field of evaluation research provide insights on both how to identify what interim outcomes to measure and how to assess contribution to a set of system-level outcomes (see Chapter 7 and the Resource Appendix).

And finally, in order to intervene within this system, the organization learned to scan for new opportunities to influence policy actors and to align such emergent action with its long-term goals. This challenge is common among advocacy organizations because they do not control the policy-making process and cannot easily anticipate when new policy windows might open up. WIEGO thus learned to respond quickly to new opportunities and to share that information across the organization, while also being clear about its own long-term goals when selecting which opportunities to pursue.

In sum, the purpose of an adaptation system is to channel emergent action towards focused long-term goals (as illustrated by the loops in Figure 6.2). WIEGO is not unique in this respect. A wide range of organizations seek to change societal norms and policies—such as global campaigns to promote human rights, or national campaigns to prevent teen and unplanned pregnancies. They all operate in rapidly changing and highly politicized settings that require them to take advantage of new opportunities as they arise. Such organizations are best served by performance systems that help them to identify key actors in a complex system, to specify their interim outcome goals, and to take advantage of unexpected opportunities for achieving those goals.

Orchestration

An ecosystem strategy aims to reorganize a complex system in order to generate interdependent outcomes. It is different from an emergent strategy that seeks to influence actors within an existing system without fundamentally altering how that system is organized. An ecosystem strategy requires orchestration, that is, a set of capacities for fundamentally restructuring the relationships among multiple actors. Figure 6.2 illustrates an orchestration system, in which the interventions produced by many actors (arrows) produce outputs (shaded circles) that must be aligned in order to generate an interdependent outcome (open circle). Research on complex organizational collaborations suggests that such joint action is enhanced by galvanizing commitment to shared system-level goals (Brown, Ebrahim, and Batliwala 2012; Gulati, Puranam, and Tushman 2012; Ostrom 2010; Tuertscher, Garud, and Kumaraswamy 2014).

Chapter 5 provided the example of Miriam's Kitchen, an organization that has played a pivotal role in reshaping the organizational ecosystem for addressing chronic homelessness in Washington, DC. Efforts to address homelessness in American cities have tended to be highly fragmented, with numerous organizations typically acting in isolation from one another in providing a range of services to homeless clients (such as shelter, food assistance, substance abuse counseling, health services, employment support, financial and legal assistance, and so on). This is a system characterized by small actors, few interactions or relationships among them, and a lack of formal structures to facilitate joint action. Miriam's Kitchen has been part of a movement in many cities across the United States to restructure this system in order to better achieve the outcome of ending chronic homelessness.

An orchestration system consists of four main parts. The first is developing a perspective on the larger social system by mapping it and identifying opportunities for intervening in it. Miriam's Kitchen saw that the homelessness services ecosystem was highly fragmented with little coordination among service providers. It also saw that ending chronic homelessness could only be achieved by better aligning the efforts of over one hundred nonprofit and public sector actors in the ecosystem.

The second key component of an orchestration system is developing an interdependent social change model. For the case of chronic homelessness, this was the model of "permanent supportive housing." PSH was not a single intervention but a reorganizing of many interventions in a more effective way. Clients were prioritized for housing and then provided with a range of "wrap-around" supportive services customized to their individual needs and circumstances. The power of the model lay in its restructuring of relationships within the ecosystem, and in customizing the pathways for clients, in order to deliver outcomes. This brings us to the third feature of the system, which was a clear collective outcome goal—to end chronic homelessness in the city. This goal possessed a number of important characteristics: it was a powerful expression of values that could motivate joint action among diverse actors; it could only be achieved through joint action across the system; and it was readily measurable, such that progress could be transparently assessed.

And finally, an orchestration system requires substantial investment in capacities for coordinating tasks and decision making among multiple actors, including joint policy advocacy. In the case of chronic homelessness in Washington, DC, such coordination was undertaken by a working group of local actors (a community backbone) that developed a "coordinated entry" process for assessing clients and assigning them to housing while investing in advocacy capacity to lobby city hall. They were supported by several data and technical assistance providers (an evidence backbone) and national actors engaged in policy issues (a policy backbone).

In short, the purpose of an orchestration system is to align a fragmented set of interventions around a common performance goal. The four components listed above are not unique to addressing chronic homelessness, but cut across many types of social problems. A growing body of work on "collective impact" has demonstrated the importance of a system framing, shared outcomes, and backbone capacity for delivering system-level results in sectors as diverse as health care, livelihood development, and education.

Conclusions: Four Strategies and their Performance Systems

The four types of performance systems discussed above are visualized in Figure 6.2, which positions them along the two contingencies of uncertainty about cause-effect and control over outcomes. The figure offers three concluding messages. The first is that the "right" performance system for any organization is contingent on its strategy. It does not make sense for all organizations to build capacities for outcome measurement when they might be better off focusing on output measurement and quality control. The contingency framework used in this book provides a simple device for clarifying one's strategy and thus for designing appropriate performance systems.

Second, organizations operating under conditions of high causal uncertainty (the upper half of the figure) need systems that nurture nonlinear pathways to solving social problems. These are systems of adaptation that enable organizations to take advantage of new opportunities as they emerge, or systems of orchestration that fundamentally reorganize the way things are done. In contrast, organizations operating under conditions of low causal uncertainty (the bottom half of the figure) benefit from systems that help them to better exploit the knowledge they already have, either by standardizing what they do or by coordinating what they do in a systematic way.

Third, an organization's control over outcomes (the horizontal axis of the figure) can be increased by building its systems for coordination or orchestration. Some organizations can hand off their clients to the next niche in the ecosystem (like ZHL's ambulance service that delivers patients to a hospital) and therefore do not need to invest heavily in systems that increase their control over outcomes. But such a handoff is not possible where the ecosystem is underdeveloped. In such instances, organizations may need to provide the necessary sequence of interventions themselves, supported by coordination systems (like AKRSP's vertical integration of agricultural services), or to orchestrate the actions of many players in their ecosystem (like Miriam's Kitchen's coordinated entry process and advocacy for permanent supportive housing). Classic scholarship in administrative theory has characterized these various types to interdependence as *pooled*, *sequential*, or *reciprocal*, depending on the mechanisms required for organizing action (Thompson 1967, 54–56).

Finally, a couple of caveats are in order. Most important, each quadrant in the figure represents an "ideal type" of relationship between a performance system and a strategy. In reality, of course, an organization may deploy multiple strategies simultaneously. As a result, these four performance systems—standardization, coordination, adaptation, and orchestration—should not be seen as mutually exclusive. For example, AKRSP's integrated strategy requires that it build a coordination system; without such a system, its outputs will fail to produce interdependent outcomes. But at the same time, each output (such as a check dam or irrigation system) also requires systems of standardization and quality control. Or consider the case of WIEGO, which has developed a system of adaptation to take advantage of opportunities to influence policy making at the ILO. Yet, not everything the organization does needs to be adaptive; part of its challenge is to identify what work tasks can be formalized into standard operating procedures, particularly as the organization grows. More generally, the task for managers is to identify which capacities are most important for supporting their primary strategy, and then to focus on building those capabilities and systems.

The four cases in this book were selected on conceptual grounds—as a vehicle for exploring how performance systems vary with different kinds of strategy. My interest was in going deep rather than wide. The result is a series of insights about performance systems that should be treated as hypotheses for further development in a larger sample of organizations and contexts. I hope I have provided readers with a means of better understanding their own strategies for social change and the kinds of performance systems that might best fit their needs. My normative aim is to push back on the growing and largely unquestioned demands for outcome measurement in the sector, and to provide a more realistic and deliberate means for social sector leaders to set their own terms of accountability.

In the end, it falls upon managers to design the performance systems best suited to their strategies for social change. This task is complicated by the demands of the funding environment, where the expectations of donors or investors can often be at odds with those of the organization and its clients or beneficiaries. Funders occupy a position in the organizational ecosystem that can be enormously helpful, or harmful, to building useful performance systems. It is to these concerns that I turn in the final chapter.

Chapter 7

ROLES OF FUNDERS

IN THIS FINAL CHAPTER, I turn to the roles of funders—impact investors, philanthropic foundations, and governmental agencies—in supporting performance measurement in the social sector.[1] Funders have the potential to help or hinder the organizations they support. They are able to enhance performance measurement by providing resources to their investees for building data and learning systems, working with them to clarify and test their theories of change, supporting research that addresses key gaps in knowledge and develops new methodologies of measurement, and investing in backbone organizations dedicated to rigorous data collection and analysis.

But funders that provide such support remain the exception, not the norm.[2] The litany of complaints from investees is familiar to anyone who has been on the receiving end of funding: reporting requirements that take precious time away from the "real work" of the organization, unrealistic expectations of performance that incentivize an overstating of accomplishments, expectations of rigorous monitoring and evaluation but an unwillingness to pay for such "overhead" costs, and demands for accountability that are sometimes in conflict with those of beneficiaries or clients. The list goes on.

How can funders add the greatest value, in terms of performance measurement and management, to the enterprises they support? To unpack this question, I look at what three innovative funders are doing in measuring and supporting the performance of their investees. All three are considered to be at the vanguard of performance measurement. Acumen is an impact investor that works with early-stage social enterprises in Africa, Asia, Latin America, and the US; Robin Hood Foundation is a philanthropic grant maker created by hedge fund managers to fight poverty in New York City; and Millennium Challenge Corporation (MCC) is a development finance institution of the US government that seeks to reduce poverty through economic growth in developing countries. What do these organizations seek to measure? What kinds of measurement methods and capacities do they find useful? How do they support measurement in their investees?[3]

The experiences of these pioneers offer a number of general insights that I highlight throughout the chapter. First, they show that different stages of investment decision making require different measurement toolkits. I outline below four stages—search, diligence, improvement, and evaluation—and identify the measurement methods best suited to each one. For example, despite the fact that randomized control trials are often hailed as the "gold standard" for assessing impact, it turns out they are best suited to only one of the four stages and under a fairly specific set of circumstances.

Second, these innovators demonstrate how measurement can be designed to close the gap between upward accountability to funders and downward accountability to clients. Funders are paying growing attention to getting feedback directly from customers or beneficiaries—in order to serve them better—and to supporting their investees in gathering and using such data in decision making.

Third, a key strategic challenge for funders lies in holding themselves accountable for the performance of a portfolio of investments rather than just the performance of individual investments. Do they have a theory of change for their portfolios? Do they have impact goals against which they measure their own performance? How funders view their own accountability is partly shaped by the expectations of their principals, that is, those who provide them with capital. Acumen and Robin Hood receive their capital from many philanthropic donors, whereas MCC receives appropriations from the US Congress. But regardless of their sources of capital, a critical challenge for funders lies in designing portfolios of investments that, in combination, can generate deeper societal impacts than each investment alone. As we have seen throughout this book, societal outcomes are rarely achieved by isolated interventions, but rather by multiple, interdependent interventions.

Practical resources for many of the methods and tools outlined in this chapter can be found in the appendix to this book.

Performance Measurement by Funding Stage

The process of allocating funding and assessing performance typically unfolds through multiple stages of decision making. For most funders, this process can be broken down into four main stages:

- *Search* for investment opportunities
- *Diligence* to assess the potential for success
- *Improvement* to identify midcourse changes
- *Evaluation* to assess performance

Table 7.1 lists these stages and identifies a range of performance measurement methods suited to each.[4] The first two stages typically occur prior to making an investment, while the latter two are postinvestment. Below, I discuss each stage and its implications for assessing the performance of an investment, drawing on the experiences of Acumen, Robin Hood, and MCC to provide greater depth.

Search

Search refers to the efforts by a funder to identify potential investment opportunities. The initial scanning for opportunities, be it through a request for proposals or personal networks, is not a performance measurement activity per se. But the screening process that follows typically requires the funder to establish a set of assessment criteria.

TABLE 7.1 Performance Measurement by Investment Decision Stage*

Stage	Search	Diligence	Improvement	Evaluation
Purpose	*Identify opportunities*	*Assess performance potential*	*Improve performance*	*Assess performance*
	Is there a potential match?	What might success look like?	What midcourse changes are needed?	What was achieved?
Investment Performance	Screens to clarify: • Investor objectives • Investee readiness	Social change models: • Theory of change • Logic model • System framing • Business model alignment Accountability for results: • Metrics are contingent on strategy (niche, integrated, emergent, ecosystem) • Metrics tap scientific knowledge (scholarly literature, systematic reviews) Capacity assessments: • Organization-wide assessments • Intervention-specific assessments Cost-effectiveness comparisons: • SROI, BCR, ERR	Monitoring: • Baseline assessments • Work plans & targets • Scorecards (financial, operational, and social performance indicators) Impact management: • Systems are contingent on strategy (standardization, coordination, adaptation, orchestration) Feedback: • Participatory Rural Appraisal • Participatory poverty assessment • Constituent voice/beneficiary feedback • Grantee perception reports • Developmental evaluation • Lean Data	Attribution-based methods: • Experimental methods, e.g., randomized control trials • Quasi-experimental methods, e.g., pre/posttests, regression discontinuity design, difference in differences comparison Contribution-based methods: • Outcome harvesting • Contribution/process tracing • Qualitative impact assessment protocol • Outcome mapping • Most significant changes
Portfolio Performance	What is the larger system in which this investment sits? • System framing for a portfolio	What changes would this investment make in the larger system? • Theory of change at a portfolio level	How can this investment perform better as part of a portfolio? • Identify portfolio performance targets, and mechanisms for coordination across a portfolio	Were system-level goals achieved? How did this investment contribute? • Attribution- and contribution-based methods applied to a portfolio

* See the Appendix for resources on many of the performance measurement methods and tools identified in this table.

TABLE 7.2 Screening Criteria, Acumen (excerpt)

	Subcategories	1	2	3	4
Commitment to Acumen Mission	Commitment to Base of Pyramid (BoP)	Has demonstrated little commitment to serving BoP customers	Some stated interest in BoP markets, but little actual experience to date	Stated interest and tentative BoP explorations into BoP starting to generate lessons learned	Strong stated commitment to BoP markets and significant experience to date
	Commitment to market solutions	Believes charity or government aid is the best approach to supporting BoP	Believes subsidies or government contracts are required to make markets effective	Believes in using subsidies or government to stimulate private markets	Firm commitment to finding market-based solutions to delivering critical goods and services to the poor
Financial Sustainability	Cost recovery	Recovers less than 10% of its costs	Recovers 10%–50% of its costs	Recovers 50%–100% of its costs	Recovers over 100% of its costs
	Financial plan	Poor financial plan in place, lacking adequate controls	Financial plan in place, but disconnected from organization's operations (good accounting but not good planning)	Financial plan is an operational tool with clear targets; some weak assumptions, but otherwise fundamentally sound	Financial plan fully integrated into operations and strategy; well crafted and carefully designed
	Timeline for sustainability	Not seeking financial sustainability; or just starting to discuss options, but no real business model in place	Taking steps toward sustainability, but likely achievable in 6- to 10-year time horizon	Projected to be sustainable in less than 5 years	Currently sustainable
Potential for Scale	Output	Reaching <10,000; no growth or falling output; one of many players at regional level	Reaching >10,000 people; no significant growth in scale from before; small player	Reaching >100,000 people; 5x prior output and small player at regional level	Reaching >1 million people; 10x prior output and leading player in solving regional or national problem

Potential for Social Impact	Impact of product on quality of life of the poor	Product/service has little potential to improve the quality of life of the poor; serious potential for unintended consequences	Product/service has some potential to improve the quality of life of the poor	Product/service has significant potential to improve the quality of life of the poor	Compelling evidence outlining the product's/service's significant impact on quality of life of the poor
	Systems change	No identifiable systems change or potential unclear	Identifiable potential for minor systems change	Product/service demonstrates potential for significant systems change	Observable systems change resulting from the product, service, or investment process
Management Capacity	CEO/entrepreneurs	First-time entrepreneur with little or no business building experience; compelling but muddled vision and little capacity to lead	Entrepreneur with some experience in building a growing enterprise; clear vision	Entrepreneur with either compelling vision or strong capabilities and experience in managing growing enterprise (but not both)	Seasoned entrepreneur with numerous successful ventures; clear and compelling visionary with management experience and skills
	Management team	No management team beyond founder	Incomplete management team in key positions; several low-quality team players	Building team with most key positions filled with strong people; plausible successor on team	High-quality people in all major functional leadership positions; strong number 2 identified

Source: Acumen internal documents.

A screen provides criteria for a match between an investor and investee. One type of screen helps clarify the investor's objectives, identifying not only what the funder will support but also what it will not support. Such screens need not be complicated. For example, in the early days of building its portfolio, Acumen identified five key criteria for screening potential investments, along with operational measures for each on a scale of 1 to 4 (see Table 7.2). Over time, as the organization gained more experience, these criteria evolved and were incorporated into a more elaborate screening and diligence process. The key point is that the process of establishing and using such criteria serve as an internal disciplining mechanism that helps the funder clarify its own investment thesis—and thus in anticipating the basis on which individual investments will be measured.

Another type of a screen is offered by MCC, which makes grants to national governments in the developing world for large-scale poverty reduction projects. One of its core principles is to work only with countries that already have "good policies and governance" in comparison to their peers, on the premise that these initial conditions increase aid effectiveness. Such selection criteria constitute what the capacity building literature calls "readiness" assessments (Blumenthal 2001, 2003; Light 2004; McKinsey & Company 2001). In order to screen for good policies and governance, the organization developed a series of selection criteria taken from independent sources. The indicators were summarized on a scorecard, shown in Figure 7.1 for the country of Ghana. The indicators are grouped into three main categories— economic freedom, ruling justly, and investing in people. The score for each indicator was compared to the median for a peer group of countries with a similar per capita income level. In order to satisfy an indicator, a country needed to score above the median. Notably, none of the indicators on the scorecard were developed in-house but were taken from reputable third-party sources, thus providing credibility to MCC's selection process. For example, under the category of ruling justly, the indicators on political rights, civil liberties, and freedom of information were taken from Freedom House, while the other three indicators were taken from the World Bank and Brookings Institution.

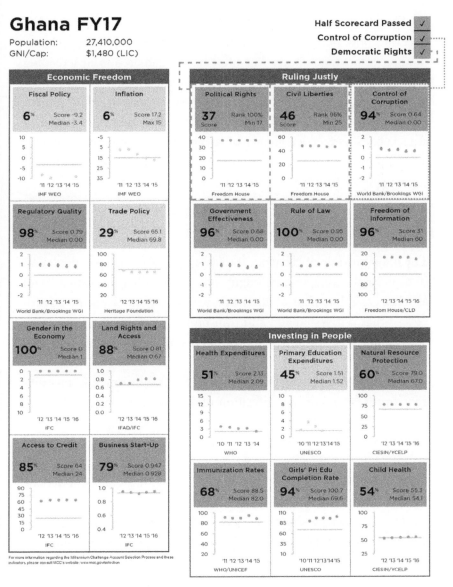

FIGURE 7.1 Selection Criteria Scorecard for Ghana, Millennium Challenge Corporation

Source: Millennium Challenge Corporation, US Government.

The use of explicit screening criteria by both Acumen and MCC illustrate how performance metrics can be useful even before any funding enters the picture. The information gathered from screening is useful not only for identifying potential matches but also for surfacing the readiness of investees for an influx of capital. MCC, for instance, offers funding to countries that have failed to meet its eligibility criteria but stand a good chance of doing so with some capacity-building support. Acumen similarly uses its screening process to identify capacity needs where it can add value to potential investees.

Diligence

The main purpose of diligence is to assess performance potential, that is, to estimate what success might look like for that investment, and at what cost. The central challenge is to codify the assessment process so that it is systematic and transparent, and can thus be consistently applied across potential investments, while also being improved over time.

To identify the potential performance of an investment, any diligence process requires clarification of an investee's model of social change, or the cause-effect hypotheses that underlie its work. Articulating a social change model typically involves developing a theory of change, logic models, system framing, and ensuring alignment with the organization's business model (see Chapter 1 for an overview of these concepts and tools).

The diligence process also requires establishing clarity on accountability. What would success look like in terms of performance metrics? As the cases in this book have shown, the key performance metrics for any enterprise are contingent on the organization's strategy—such that a *niche* strategy is best focused on accountability for outputs, an *integrated* strategy on accountability for outputs and individual outcomes, an *emergent* strategy on interim outcomes or "influence," and an *ecosystem* strategy on individual and societal outcomes. (For a summary see Chapter 6, and for detailed illustrations see chapters 2 to 5.)

In order to set accountability metrics that are based on evidence, any diligence process benefits from tapping existing scientific knowledge. Such knowledge is available in the form of studies in the scholarly literature, and through "systematic reviews" that synthesize the results of numerous studies. For example, the International Initiative on Impact Evaluation (3ie) and the Campbell Collaboration have developed online databases that synthesize available research for consumption by funders, evaluators, public agencies, and other social sector actors (see the Appendix for resources). Using scientific research to inform investment decisions, however, requires an internal capacity to both identify and use that research. For example, the Robin Hood Foundation found that its own program staff needed considerable support in tapping the scientific literature. It thus hired a full-time metrics manager, who was an expert in evaluation with a doctorate in education and a professional background in impact measurement, to provide such support. Acumen and MCC went even further, creating entire teams within their organizations devoted to supporting performance measurement.

Investee capacity is also best assessed at the diligence stage. Funders can support their investees not only by providing capital but also by helping them to build capacities for executing their social change models. MCC, for instance, offers funding to countries that have failed to meet its selection criteria but stand a good chance of doing so with some highly targeted capacity building. Acumen similarly uses its diligence process to identify capacity needs where it can add value to potential investees, such as in building out the enterprise's management team, its board, or its revenue model. A range of useful capacity assessment tools are widely available, including organizational self-assessments developed by nonprofit leaders, consulting firms, and NGO trainers, as well as assessments focused on particular types of interventions such as policy advocacy (see the Appendix for resources).

Finally, during the diligence process, all funders face the challenge of how best to allocate their limited resources. How can an investor compare one potential investee to another, when the metrics for social performance are so different among them? Over the past decade, there has been growing attention to methods for quantifying the expected return of a social investment in order to then compare and benchmark different investments (Kramer 2005; Tuan 2008). These methods of quantification—such as social return on investment (SROI), benefit-cost (BC) ratios, and economic rates of return (ERR)—are all variations of benefit-cost analysis. As I outline below, both the Robin Hood Foundation and MCC have been at the forefront of using such methods to estimate the expected social returns of their investments.

Comparing Cost-Effectiveness

One of the leading advocates of benefit-cost analysis in philanthropy has been the Robin Hood Foundation, a grant-making organization that calculates BC ratios for all two hundred of its grants every year. At face value, the method is deceptively simple: divide total benefits by total costs in order to get a BC ratio that can be compared across investments. The challenge lies in defining benefits and costs, setting boundaries around the analysis, and in making explicit any assumptions in the calculations so that they can be improved.

Robin Hood defines benefits as private gains that accrue to poor individuals over their lifetimes as a result of an intervention (i.e., individual outcomes). Benefits are typically operationalized as the expected "boost in lifetime earnings" experienced by beneficiaries; a *boost* refers to the difference in earnings with the intervention as compared to without it, and it is thus an attempt at a counterfactual calculation (i.e., what would have happened without the intervention). For a job training program, for example, this calculation typically relies on estimates of the pre- and post-training incomes of participants, and also draws on existing scientific research on the long-term and intergenerational effects of income gains. Calculating the benefits of education programs is more difficult and requires drawing on research that links educational attainment to earnings. For instance, the foundation's staff first identifies a set of results that can be immediately observed, such as school attendance, standardized test scores, and high school graduation. Then, they search for studies that link those measures to expected lifetime earnings or quality of life (outcomes). The benefits calculation is even more complex for healthcare programs where there is growing use of a nonmonetary measure, the quality adjusted life year (QALY), which assesses the number of extra months or years of life of a "reasonable quality" that a person might gain from an intervention (Drummond et al. 2009; Prieto and Sacristán 2003).

In order to compare the value of one investment to another, Robin Hood takes the quantified benefits (such expected lifetime earnings boost) and divides it by costs (typically the amount of the grant) in order to generate a BC ratio. The result is a list of BC rankings by portfolio. Table 7.3 provides such a list for the foundation's job training portfolio (with the names of organizations anonymized), enabling it to compare potential investments within a single portfolio over consecutive years. The substantial changes in some of the assessments over such a short period of time are due to new data or revisions in Robin Hood's own research and method about the benefits of the interventions.

The details of the methodology—such as the assumptions behind the benefit and cost calculations, and how they change over time—are controversial and have been subject to much criticism. The deeper insight, however, is that the foundation has an explicitly articulated method for comparing investments. It has shared the method publicly, along with 163 metrics equations, inviting comment and criticism in order to improve the method (Robin Hood Foundation 2014; Weinstein 2009; Weinstein and Bradburd 2013). This transparency is a critical component of its accountability to the public. Arguably, foundations that make resource allocation decisions without such transparency are essentially unaccountable.

MCC uses a similar approach in its due diligence process for grant making to national governments. It estimates an ERR for each investment, which serves as a forecast of the project's likely economic impact. Benefits assessments focus on long-term increases in farmer

TABLE 7.3 Job Training Benefit-Cost Rankings, Robin Hood Foundation

Rank	Type of Program	Demographics	B/C Rounded Year 1	B/C Rounded Year 2
1	Sector (trade)	Immigrants	70:1	15:1
2	Sector (transportation)	Some ex-offenders	60:1	20:1
3	Sector (technology)	Immigrants	60:1	10:1
4	Sector (health)	Immigrants, women	50:1	50:1
5	Placement-only	Ex-offenders, some youth	45:1	20:1
6	Sector (health)	Immigrants, women	40:1	30:1
7	Sector (health)	All	40:1	20:1
8	Sector (health)	Immigrants, women	40:1	10:1
9	Sector (health)	Immigrants, women	35:1	15:1
10	Sector (technology)	Some ex-offenders	35:1	10:1
11	Sector (health)	Immigrants, women	35:1	5:1
12	Sector (transportation)	All	35:1	10:1
13	Sector	Immigrants, women	30:1	10:1
14	Sector (trade)	Women	30:1	5:1
15	Placement-only	All	30:1	10:1
16	Sector (health)	Immigrants, women	30:1	10:1
17	Sector (health)	Immigrants, women	25:1	15:1
18	Sector (trade)	Some ex-offenders	25:1	5:1
19	Sector (health, technology)	Youth	25:1	5:1
20	Sector (health)	Immigrants, women	20:1	NA
21	General	Youth	20:1	10:1
22	Sector (technology)	Immigrants	20:1	5:1
23	Placement-only	Some ex-offenders	20:1	5:1
24	Placement-only	Immigrants	20:1	15:1
25	Sector (trade)	Women	20:1	5:1
26	Sector (health)	Immigrants, women	20:1	5:1

Source: Robin Hood Foundation documents.

incomes as a result of the investment. Costs include the expenses not only to MCC but also to other investing parties. In comparing potential investments, MCC generally seeks those with an ERR hurdle rate of 10 percent at a twenty-year time horizon (MCC 2017). All of these assessments are publicly available on its website.

MCC's process of assessment is more complex than Robin Hood's, given both the size of its grants and the scale of its projects. For example, in considering a major commitment of $547 million for agriculture and transportation infrastructure in Ghana, MCC conducted an analysis of the constraints to growth in the country and the sectors most likely to yield poverty reduction through economic growth. An MCC team worked with its counterparts in Ghana to collect baseline data on existing road infrastructure, agricultural crops and yields, irrigation infrastructure, ferry services, rural credit and financial services, land tenure constraints, and so on. This intensive diligence process took approximately two years to complete. As MCC gained more experience in making such large public sector investments, it increased the time allocated to diligence to approximately three years.

A common challenge in monetizing benefits lies in the fact that the research linking interventions to quantifiable benefits remains sparse and highly context specific. In practice, benefit-cost assessment methods appear to be most useful for interventions where cause-effect knowledge is relatively well established, such as for the delivery of basic goods and services. But such methods are less likely to be useful for assessing interventions with high causal uncertainty, such as in policy advocacy or human rights work. It is perhaps for this reason that neither Robin Hood nor MCC have successfully applied their assessment method to policy work and have hesitated to support it. The impact investing community more generally has shied away from supporting complex interventions in policy advocacy, human rights, and democratization because of the difficulties in establishing cause-effect models and in monetizing benefits.

Proponents of benefits quantification acknowledge these problems, arguing instead that it is the discipline of assessment that matters more than the actual numbers, pressing one to clarify goals, to be explicit about assumptions, and to consider risks and limitations. They argue that all funders necessarily rank-order potential grants or investments anyway, and that quantitative methodologies provide some transparency in the decision process, without which the basis for grant allocation "remains opaque and, therefore, largely beyond effective challenge" (Weinstein 2009, 23).

Recognizing both the controversial nature of such comparisons and the limitations of doing so, both Robin Hood and MCC use their assessments with caution, employing them as one input among many in their diligence process, and revisiting their assessments at the end of a grant period. For instance, MCC's own analysis comparing estimated to actual ERRs upon project closeout found that approximately three-fourths of projects had ERRs that declined over the period of a grant, and that more than one-third failed to meet the agency's threshold of a 10 percent rate of return (Ospina and Block 2017). In short, both funders recognize the limitations of the method but find it valuable as a vehicle for disciplining their own thinking and for providing a common language for comparing one potential investment to another.

The key point is that all funders must somehow allocate their resources, and they are best served by developing a transparent and systematic diligence process. Philanthropic foundations have often been criticized for being accountable to no one; this perception is fed by how their resource allocation decisions are made—often without transparent criteria or deliberation with stakeholders, and with weak measures of their own effectiveness—despite aiming to serve the public good (Eisenberg 2004; Hall 2004; Schambra 2013). Regardless of the methodology a funder adopts for assessing the social performance of its investees, making that method explicit provides a basis for accountability, both internally to its own staff and externally to its investees and the public.

Improvement

Once an organization receives an investment, the funder's measurement role shifts to one of supporting improvement in investee performance, while also gathering evidence of interim progress. This role involves three distinct functions: (1) tracking whether work is proceeding according to plan (monitoring), (2) helping to build appropriate performance measurement and management systems within the investee (impact management), and (3) gathering insights directly from customers or beneficiaries in order to improve operations, programs, and downward accountability (feedback). These functions are summarized in the fourth column of Table 7.1.

The first of these functions, monitoring, typically involves (a) baseline data collection on conditions prior to the intervention (such as the poverty and income levels in a region, access to basic goods or services, and so on); (b) project work plans that establish measurable targets based on logic models; and (c) periodic reporting on progress, with reports or scorecards based on key performance indicators and usually conducted on a quarterly or semiannual basis. For example, in Chapter 3 we examined the case of the Aga Khan Rural Support Programme in India, which received extensive funding over a period of nearly two decades from the European Commission. Each grant was accompanied by clear annual targets and indicators that were developed by the NGO in collaboration with a monitoring team sent by the funder, thus providing an evidence base for midcourse corrections.

Second, the execution of any monitoring mechanism requires a capacity for impact management within the organization. A significant role for funders lies in working with their investees to build their internal performance systems and capabilities. As the cases in this book have shown, the type of performance system best suited to an investee's needs is contingent on its social change strategy. An organization with a niche strategy, like Ziqitza Health Care (Chapter 2), needs a system of standardization designed to produce outputs of consistent quality. On the other hand an integrated strategy, like the Aga Khan Rural Support Programme's natural resource management work (Chapter 3), requires a coordination system to prioritize and sequence multiple interventions. In contrast, an emergent strategy, like WIEGO's advocacy work with the ILO (Chapter 4), is best served by an adaptation system that enables it to quickly adjust its actions in response to changes in its environment. And finally an ecosystem strategy, such as Miriam's Kitchen's for tackling chronic homelessness (Chapter 5), requires orchestration capabilities that align the work of diverse actors in order to generate system-level outcomes. In short, an organization's performance systems must be matched to its improvement needs. An important role for funders lies in supporting their investees in identifying and building the right performance systems.

Moreover, any system for improving performance requires direct feedback from clients or constituents. The use of monitoring frameworks in international development have long been criticized as "distort[ing] accountability by overemphasizing short-term quantitative targets and favoring hierarchical management structures—a tendency to 'accountancy' rather than 'accountability'" (Edwards and Hulme 1996a, 968; see also Lindenberg and Bryant 2001; Najam 1996a). What has been missing from many funder-driven monitoring processes is a commitment to *downward accountability*—strengthening the voices of beneficiaries or customers through systematic data collection on their needs, preferences, and perceptions—in order to learn how best to improve their lives (Ebrahim, Battilana, and Mair 2014). As I outline below, a number of organizations discussed in this book have been at the forefront of developing methods for gathering such feedback and using it for improving social performance. I devote particular attention to a method developed by Acumen in which I have been directly involved.

Feedback Mechanisms for Downward Accountability

One of the earliest approaches to improving downward accountability, participatory rural appraisal (PRA), was developed in the 1980s to incorporate local knowledge into the prioritization, design, and planning of development interventions (Chambers 1994; Roche 1999). One of the pioneers in testing and systematizing this method was the Aga Khan Rural Support Programme (discussed in Chapter 3), which used interactive methods to gather information on the community and its resources—such as mapping exercises and walks through villages and fields with community members to collect data on local forest or water resources and community wealth and social rankings, and to identify local priorities and concerns—while simultaneously building rapport between program staff and community members (AKRSP n.d.). A series of other advances built on this early experience, including a set of participatory poverty and social assessment methods, as well as complaint and response mechanisms, promoted by the World Bank (Ebrahim and Herz 2011; Rietbergen-McCracken and Narayan 1998; Robb 2002; Woods 2001).

A limitation of these early methods was that while they solicited beneficiary input at key planning moments, such as during project design and midproject reviews, they often did not systematically incorporate beneficiary feedback as a part of ongoing operations. More recently, a suite of tools has begun to address this shortfall by drawing on customer feedback methods. Among the most developed of these approaches is a "Constituent Voice" methodology that not only systematically gathers feedback from customers or beneficiaries but also uses the process to build engaged relationships with them (Bonbright, Campbell, and Nguyen 2009; McKinsey & Company 2010).[5] A similar set of methods is available to help funders gather feedback on their own performance based on the perceptions of their grantees (Center for Effective Philanthropy 2004; Buteau and Glickman 2018). Both are part of a growing tool chest of feedback methods and crowd-sourced feedback platforms (Scott and Orlikowski 2012; Twersky, Buchanan, and Threlfall 2013; Whittle 2013). Other related approaches include "developmental evaluation" that aims to provide real-time feedback to support innovation in complex environments (Patton 2011).

In the impact investing world, Acumen has been at the forefront of developing a customer feedback approach—what it calls Lean Data[SM]—that focuses on listening to customers in order to serve them better. Such enterprises confront a number of challenges related to performance: a dynamic environment in which entrepreneurs must iterate and refine their social change models; severe financial constraints, such that any data collection must be relatively inexpensive; and limited human capital that is focused on running a business. Lean Data attempts to address these constraints by combining principles of customer feedback with lean experimentation (Murray and Ma 2015) in order to generate useful information for improving business and social change models (Dichter, Adams, and Ebrahim 2016).[6]

In early 2014, Acumen undertook a number of pilot experiments, several of which are summarized in Table 7.4. One of these pilots was with Ziqitza Health Care Limited, the ambulance service in India that we examined in Chapter 2, in which Acumen was an equity investor. For the first ten years of its history, Ziqitza lacked reliable data on its customer demographics and needs. Acumen, in partnership with the Grameen Foundation, began to train Ziqitza's call center employees in two Indian states to pose a set of ten questions to its clients. The questions—such as "How many members does your household have?" or "What is the main source of lighting fuel for your household?"—were borrowed from the Poverty Probability Index (PPI), a survey developed by the Grameen Foundation that measured ten statistically validated predictors of poverty (Choudhury 2014). Within a month of that initial training, Ziqitza surveyed one thousand of its customers, and found that three-quarters of its customers were living below the World Bank poverty line of $2.50 per day, and that it was serving women, pregnant women in particular, at a disproportionately high level. The survey also revealed areas for improvement. In rural Orissa state, for example, ZHL's penetration among those below the poverty line fell short of the state average by 11 percentage points. The findings pointed to a clear need for ZHL to do a better job of improving access in hard-to-reach regions and to increase public awareness about its services.

These early experiments helped Acumen to articulate the core components of its Lean Data methodology:

- an *impact question* that provides relevant *learning* to the entrepreneur

- a *method* that combines an enabling instrument (e.g., a well-tested survey) with an enabling technology (e.g., text messaging, interactive voice response, or phone calls through call centers[7]) to allow for quick and cost-effective access to customers

- *quality assurance* mechanisms for gathering high-quality data from customers

- *actions* that can be taken quickly in order to improve the business or social change model

Between 2014 and 2017, Acumen carried out over eighty Lean Data projects—with the direct cost of each data collection effort averaging about $10,000 to $30,000, and taking two to eight weeks to collect, analyze, and feed into managerial decision making, depending on

TABLE 7.4 Lean Data Pilots, Acumen

Company	Impact Question	Learning	Method	Quality Assurance	Actions
Ziqitza Health Care Limited Ambulance services India	Does the Ziqitza ambulance service succeed in reaching low-income customers? How does usage vary between male and female customers?	Most customers (75 percent) are below the poverty line; pregnant women are a core market	Call center survey Cost: $14,000 over the course of four months	Working with Grameen Foundation to train call center staff on survey execution and in-person validation of subsample	Improving access in hard-to-reach regions; working with local governments in remote areas to increase public awareness of services
Burn Cookstove sales Kenya	Do buyers of Burn cookstoves reduce charcoal usage to the expected degree (by 60 percent) as a result of using the product?	Customers' use of charcoal decreases to the same degree as laboratory tests had predicted it would	SMS texting, call center surveys Cost: $3,000 over the course of four weeks	Using call center interviews to validate SMS data	Working to understand which distribution channels are most effective at reaching poor rural customers
Edubridge Vocational training India	Which factors account for the difference between "successful" and "unsuccessful" trainees?	Customers with better urban social networks are more likely to get and keep a job; poorer students are more likely to seek and keep jobs	Call center survey Cost: $1,500 over the course of four months	Using Acumen personnel to train call center staff	Using data to segment customers and working to improve the match between training services and trainee needs

(continued)

TABLE 7.4 *(continued)*

Company	Impact Question	Learning	Method	Quality Assurance	Actions
KZ Noir Coffee processing Rwanda	What is the poverty level of KZ Noir farmers? Do their earnings improve through participation in KZ Noir's premium-sharing program?	Preliminary results show that 59 percent of KZ Noir farmers are extremely poor; data on changes in farmers' income are forthcoming	SMS texting and in-person tablet-based surveys Cost: $15,000 over the course of two months	Enlisting researchers at a third-party firm (IDinsight) to implement survey	Using results (such as a high incidence of bank account usage among customers) to improve premium-sharing program
SolarNow Solar energy systems Uganda	Does in-house financing improve the ability of SolarNow to reach the poor? Does household expenditure on energy decline as a result of using a SolarNow product?	Reach among the poor is better than expected (49 percent of customers live on less that $2.50 per day); most customers show only a small savings in energy expenditure in the first three to four years after purchase	Call center survey Cost: $2,000 over the course of four weeks	Using a third-party call center as well as remote field staff; using SolarNow's call center for follow-up survey to test for consistency of responses	Starting to conduct surveys on a quarterly basis to track customer segmentation and customer satisfaction

Source: Adapted from Dichter, Adams, and Ebrahim in *Stanford Social Innovation Review* (2016). NB: Cost figures do not account for Acumen staff time. Reproduced with permission.

the degree of complexity and customization. By 2018 it had conducted over two hundred such data-gathering projects, demonstrating that meaningful data could be collected quickly, reliably, and cost-effectively. The advantages of cost and time stood in stark contrast to Acumen's experience with randomized control trials, which typically took years to conduct, often at a cost of hundreds of thousands of dollars.

More generally the experience of Lean Data, and other methods such as PRA and Constituent Voice, offers a number of general insights for designing useful feedback mechanisms. First, a key driver of meaningful measurement is relevance to the operations of the enterprise. Managers typically view impact measurement through the lens of monitoring and compliance, as an upward accountability obligation to their funders. Without an impact question that directly informs operations, it is difficult to get buy-in from managers in the enterprises. Second, meaningful measurement is instrumental to closing the gap between upward and downward accountability. Feedback methods open up a channel for listening to customers or beneficiaries, particularly if they can be done at a large scale and systematically incorporated into decision making. And third, meaningful measurement requires the building of capacity both in the investor and investee, but it does not have to be costly. It is unrealistic to expect most social sector organizations, especially early-stage enterprises, to develop useful performance measurement practices on their own. The responsibility falls on funders to support the development of usable and cost-effective tools of measurement. In short, funders have a central role to play in breaking the "metrics myth"—the wide gap between the rhetoric of social impact measurement and the actual state of practice in the field (Emerson 2015).

Evaluation

Finally, during the fourth stage of investment decision making, the focus of performance measurement shifts to taking stock of the results that were achieved. The boundary between the improvement and evaluation stages is porous (see Table 7.1), in that data and insights gathered during improvement feed into an evaluation of outcomes.

An analogous relationship exists in the assessment of financial performance in accounting, where management accounting involves gathering data on an ongoing basis to inform current decisions in an enterprise (improvement), while financial accounting provides a retrospective picture of performance over a specified period of time (evaluation).[8]

Any evaluation must address two basic questions: Were the intended results of an intervention achieved? How important was the intervention to producing those results? The answers to these questions provide a basis for the funder to decide whether to reinvest in or to exit from an investment, while also drawing lessons for future investments in its portfolio. The first question is typically addressed through cumulative performance data over a fixed period of time—often called *summative evaluation*—for example, by measuring increases in farmer incomes or declines in chronic homelessness rates over a multiyear period. It provides an opportunity to revisit the expected returns calculated during the diligence phase in order to compare those estimates to actual returns. Data for such assessments can sometimes be gathered independently of the investee. For instance, information on farmer poverty levels can be collected using the Poverty Probability Index by a third-party contractor. Or data on urban poverty and homelessness rates are often already gathered by city governments.

The second question, on whether the intervention actually caused those results, is more difficult to address. This is the so-called counterfactual challenge, of comparing the results to what would have happened in the absence of the intervention. There are a number of different evaluation approaches to answering this question. I group them into two broad categories:

- *Attribution-based methods* that seek to establish a statistical correlation between an intervention and a set of results. Rigor is established through experimental or quasi-experimental designs involving a control or comparison group. Such methods are best suited to contexts where it is possible to: (a) isolate cause-effect mechanisms for testing, (b) minimize nonlinear or interacting effects, and (c) establish separate treatment and control groups.

- *Contribution-based methods* that seek to establish a testable association between an intervention and a set of results. Rigor is established by using multiple sources of evidence to support or challenge an intervention's theory of change against alternative explanations. Such methods are best suited to contexts where (a) the intervention is complex, with multiple or interacting cause-effect mechanisms that cannot be readily isolated; and (b) the setting is complex, such that a control group or other observable counterfactual cannot be established.

The purpose of attribution- and contribution-based methods is to make credible causal inferences. In other words, both test claims about causality. There is a common misperception among many social sector organizations and their funders that attribution-based methods provide greater rigor than contribution-based methods. Randomized control trials (RCTs) in particular are often described as being the gold standard for assessing impact (Asian Development Bank 2006; European Evaluation Society 2007; Jones 2009), with advocates claiming that they yield unambiguous findings that can help funders allocate scarce resources to programs that are proven to work (Banerjee 2007; Center for Global Development 2006). However, such claims only hold true when the conditions for an experimental design can be met. A more pragmatic approach is to understand what type of method is appropriate under what circumstances, and then to apply that method with rigor.

The RCT methodology is best known for its use in clinical field trials of new medications, where it is fairly straightforward to separate those receiving treatment from those that do not, and where the interventions are discrete and homogenous (White 2009). Where random selection of program beneficiaries is not possible, quasi-experimental methods are preferred, for example, by comparison to a group that is very similar but just falls below the threshold for receiving the intervention (known as *regression discontinuity design*), or which received a more established version of the treatment (known as a *difference in differences comparison*) (So and Staskevicius 2015, 41). Such attribution-based methods appear to be best suited to activities where the intervention, its effects, and its target population can be readily isolated and observed—for example, in the provision of vaccines, conditional cash transfers to the poor, or the distribution of new seed varieties to farmers. But even when these conditions can be satisfied, actually carrying out an experimental design can be constrained by cost or ethical considerations. Moreover, experimental designs are less appropriate for activities where a comparison group is hard to isolate, such as in policy advocacy, macroeconomic reform, and even some investments in infrastructure where a comparable counterfactual is hard to establish (Jones et al. 2009; Prowse 2007).

A primary critique of attribution-based methods is that their positivist underpinnings lead them to oversimplify causality and fail to account adequately for political, social, and institutional context (Chambers et al. 2009; Khagram et al. 2009; Pawson 2013; Virtanen and Uusikylä 2004). Moreover, the claims of many empirical economic studies, including randomized control trials applied to social problems, have recently been called into question due to failures to replicate them (Economist 2018). For example, an examination of 6,700 empirical studies in the economics literature found that over 90 percent were underpowered, meaning that their samples were too small to adequately judge effects. And even among the studies that avoided this problem, about 80 percent exaggerated their results (Ioannidis, Stanley, and Doucouliagos 2017). Another study that sought to replicate eighteen economics experiments from two top-tier economics journals failed to replicate seven of them (Camerer et al. 2016). The implication of these analyses is that even studies that meet the so-called gold standard must be interpreted with care and perhaps a grain of salt.

Contribution-based methodologies are more appropriate where either the intervention or the context is sufficiently complex that it is not feasible to create an experiment with a control group (Lemire, Nielsen, and Dybdal 2012; Mayne 2011; Rogers 2007, 2009). For example, in policy advocacy work such as WIEGO's efforts to influence the International Labor Organization (Chapter 4), the very notion of a control group does not make sense. But it is nonetheless possible to trace the process through which WIEGO sought to influence the ILO and to triangulate and challenge WIEGO's internal narrative of that process against rival explanations offered by other stakeholders.

In terms of rigor, contribution-based methods require systematic attention to specifying the key interventions, observable outcomes, counterfactuals, and the possible pathways for achieving those outcomes. Methodological rigor lies in hypothesizing how an outcome was achieved (by explicitly laying out its nonlinear and interactive pathways), gathering evidence from multiple sources to support or challenge those causal claims, and in considering alternative explanations for the same outcomes. A range of methods is available for systematically undertaking such assessments, particularly process tracing and contribution analysis, and their derivatives such as outcome harvesting and outcome mapping (Beach and Pedersen 2013; Befani and Mayne 2014; Bennett 2010; Bennett and Checkel 2015; Davies and Dart 2005; Earl, Carden, and Smutylo 2001; Wilson-Grau and Britt 2012). Many of these methods draw on advances in comparative case study designs from the field of political science, which enable cautious causal inferences to be drawn while also uncovering the processes through which outcomes were likely achieved (Bennett and Checkel 2015; Brady and Collier 2004; George and Bennett 2005; Gerring 2007; Khagram et al. 2009).

Regardless of the methodology adopted, both attribution- and contribution-based methods require substantial research expertise, commitment to longitudinal study, and allocation of resources. Such investments are typically beyond the capabilities of front-line enterprises and require adequate funder support to be done well. It is thus crucial for funders to work with their investees in identifying when it makes sense to invest in evaluation, what methods are most appropriate, and how the findings might feed into learning across a series of interventions.

The experience of MCC is instructive in this regard. It is perhaps the only global aid agency that conducts postcompletion evaluations for at least 85 percent of its investments or "compacts" with partner countries (Center for Global Development 2017). The terms of the evaluations are developed in close partnership with those country governments and, due to the level of expertise required, are typically carried out by independent evaluators where possible. Moreover, in a departure from the practices of many funders, MCC makes the findings of these evaluations publicly available on its website, whether or not the projects are deemed successful. For example, the agency funded a series of independent evaluations of farmer training activities in five countries, using a quasi-experimental design to compare income changes experienced by farmers that had received training to a control group that was to receive training at a later date. The evaluation turned up mixed findings:

> While MCC was successful in meeting or exceeding its output and outcome targets and saw increases in farm incomes in [three of five] countries, **none of the evaluations were able to detect changes in household income**. This raises interesting questions about the "theories of change" embedded in the program logic for these and other farmer training programs, traditional assumptions of how program interventions lead to increased household income (as opposed to farm income) and the challenges associated with producing *and* measuring changes in household income. (MCC 2012, 2, emphases in the original)

While many funders advocate for evaluation, a funder's commitment to learning from evaluation findings is only truly tested in the face of negative results. The findings of the farmer training evaluations prompted a number of changes within MCC, such as greater attention at the diligence stage to articulating a theory of change and its causal chains, as well as deeper consideration of how one intervention such as farmer training might interact with other agricultural interventions in affecting outcomes such as household income. To better uncover these interactive effects, MCC might benefit from supplementing its current quasi-experimental evaluation method (attribution-based) with an analysis based on process tracing (contribution-based).

More broadly, the purpose of the MCC's evaluations is not only for internal learning, but also to build knowledge within the development industry more broadly. Prior to the release of these studies of farmer training, there had been very few impact evaluations worldwide on agricultural training using experimental designs (Independent Evaluation Group 2011). The agency's staff and leadership were cognizant of the fact that its evaluations would be closely followed and scrutinized by the international development community, particularly by think tanks and NGO watchdog groups that tracked foreign assistance, as well as by the US Congress. For example, the Center for Global Development, a prominent Washington think tank, published a series of briefs taking stock of the agency's progress following its ten-year anniversary (Center for Global Development 2015; Rose and Wiebe 2015). MCC's response to such scrutiny has generally been to increase its transparency; no wonder it is ranked as one of the most transparent donor agencies worldwide (Publish What You Fund 2017).

In summary, the four stages illustrated in Table 7.1 show that funders require different types of performance measurement toolkits at various points in their investment decision making—with search and diligence during preinvestment requiring a different set of tools and capacities than the postinvestment stages of improvement and evaluation. The three funders profiled in this chapter, all considered leaders in measurement, generally understand these distinctions. Moreover, they are realistic about their own roles and capacity constraints. Acumen understands that if its Lean Data approach is to be truly helpful to early-stage enterprises, customer feedback must be collected quickly, inexpensively, and reliably. And as a funder, Acumen recognizes that it is much better positioned than its investees to build sophisticated internal capacity for performance measurement. The Robin Hood Foundation similarly understands that its grantees do not have the capacity to adequately assess their own outcomes. Even Robin Hood itself does not, for the most part, actually measure outcomes for each investment. Instead it estimates outcomes based on the best available research that links outputs to outcomes. MCC is the only funder among the three that has the capacity to carry out multiyear evaluations using experimental methods that measure long-term outcomes. Its investments are of a sufficiently large scale to justify the expense, yielding valuable insights not only for its own learning but also for other international development agencies.[9]

Performance Measurement at a Portfolio Level

So far, our discussion on the roles of funders has focused primarily on assessing the performance of investees. But there is a larger question: *How might a funder assess its own performance at an aggregate or portfolio level?* In the world of for-profit investing, the reputation of an investor rests on the performance of its portfolio—how a collection of investments performs over time. In contrast, traditional grant makers such as philanthropic foundations that have their own endowments face little pressure to demonstrate portfolio performance because they do not depend on their external environment for resources. A handful of impact investors, however, are beginning to tackle this challenge by analyzing investment performance not only at an enterprise level but also at a portfolio, system, or market level (Bannick and Goldman 2012; Bannick et al. 2017; McCreless 2017; So and Staskevicius 2015).[10]

Portfolio performance assessment in the social sector is more complex than in the private sector. A private sector investor is able to calculate an average return on investment (ROI) because of a common monetary basis of measurement. A measure of average portfolio return is possible in the social sector using the benefit-cost methods discussed above—BC ratios, SROI, and ERR—but it falls short of addressing system-level impacts. The Robin Hood Foundation, for example, assesses its portfolio performance by calculating an average benefit-cost ratio for all of its investments, estimating that for every dollar it spends on grants it improves income and quality of life of its target beneficiaries by $12 (Robin Hood Foundation 2017), a return that was down from an estimate of $18 in 2010 (Ebrahim and Ross 2010).

This is certainly one way to assess the performance of a portfolio, and it has value in attracting investors or donors to the foundation.

But it tells us little about whether the portfolio as a whole is moving the needle on a complex social problem. Has poverty in New York City actually fallen as a result of Robin Hood's work? Are there synergies across investments, where a combination of investments stands a greater chance of addressing a social problem than each investment in isolation? For what results should the funder hold itself to account?

Therein lie two distinct opportunities for funders. The first lies in *designing their portfolios as an integrated strategy*. Because they support and oversee hundreds of nonprofits and social enterprises that typically act independently of one another, funders are uniquely positioned to connect that work in order to generate outcomes that are greater than the sum of the parts. What might such an "integrated strategy" for a portfolio look like? As we saw in Chapter 3, organizations like AKRSP, BRAC, and the Harlem Children's Zone implement a pipeline of interventions that, in combination, seek to produce long-term outcomes for individuals. But such vertically integrated offerings are rare; most investees offer niche services that are isolated from one another. Funders thus have an opportunity to construct their portfolios to enable such integration, for example by funding a pipeline of interventions in agriculture or youth development, or job training and placement that few investees can do on their own.

In fact, an assessment by Acumen of twenty enterprises in its energy portfolio noted a need for precisely such integration—for better upstream financing for households, deeper integration of various products and services, and collaborative funding with other investors, philanthropists, and governments in later-stage energy companies—in order to better scale impact (Acumen 2018). This way of thinking about a social portfolio—as a collection of interconnected assets that have greater value together—stands in contrast to conventional wisdom on for-profit portfolios where uncorrelated assets are valued over correlated ones because they reduce the overall risk to the investor.

The second related opportunity for funders lies in *coordinating their portfolios as an ecosystem strategy*. Many funders have specific issues that they support, and to which they bring a particular lens or expertise.

For example, both the Robin Hood Foundation and Acumen are heavily focused on supporting the delivery of basic goods and services to low-income populations. But neither organization has particular expertise in addressing public policies that contribute to poverty. What if they could collaborate with funders who do have policy advocacy expertise? As we have seen throughout this book, achieving long-term societal outcomes requires orchestrated action across an entire ecosystem. This does not mean that Robin Hood or Acumen should expand their portfolios to include advocacy, but that there may be benefits to coordinating their work with those who do. Just as organizations like Miriam's Kitchen and WIEGO (chapters 4 and 5) position and coordinate their work with other actors in their ecosystems, funders too can increase their effectiveness by deliberately planning their portfolios with an ecosystem outlook.

In summary, a portfolio approach to performance measurement adds a new set of considerations to the four stages of investment decision making (see the bottom row of Table 7.1).

Search

With a portfolio as the unit of analysis, the search for investments is guided by a broader "system framing" that involves identifying key actors engaged with a particular social problem (including other funders and government agencies), the interactions among them, and the institutions or structures that shape those interactions. For example, a funder interested in addressing chronic homelessness may search for key players, gaps, and opportunities in that ecosystem. This would include searching not only for cost-effective service providers but also for actors engaged in policy advocacy and in providing backbone support to the ecosystem (see Chapter 5 for an example of such an ecosystem for addressing homelessness).

Diligence

The process of due diligence for a portfolio requires two steps: understanding each investee's social change model, and positioning that investment within a *correlated* pool of investments. In other words, funders need a theory of change at a portfolio level—as a set of investments that can collectively produce social outcomes. The United Way of America, for example, has developed a "community impact" approach to its funding, in which each United Way chapter targets a specific local problem and then funds the work of multiple organizations towards solving it (see the conclusion of Chapter 5 for an example).

Improvement

In addition to tracking and improving the performance of each investment separately, the funder identifies portfolio performance targets in collaboration with its investees, and possibly with other funders. It seeks opportunities to better coordinate the work of investees in order to produce those outcomes. Doing so may require the funder to develop in-house capacity for convening and coordination—serving as type of connective tissue or orchestrator—or to fund such work by other backbone organizations. For example, the Bill and Melinda Gates Foundation convenes key players (service providers, funders, policy makers) working on major infectious diseases such as polio in order to jointly find ways of eradicating them. It is also a major supporter of a partnership network, the Global Fund to Fight AIDS, Tuberculosis and Malaria.

Evaluation

The purpose of evaluation at a portfolio level is to assess (a) whether system level outcomes or impacts were achieved and (b) the contribution of each investment to those results. This dual purpose suggests a role for both attribution- and contribution-based methods for assessing performance. The former can be useful for assessing whether a collection of interventions moved the needle on a social problem; the latter can be used for mapping the sequencing and interactions among those interventions. This combination of methods holds promise for helping a portfolio to test and revise its theory of change. For instance,

Millennium Challenge Corporation's evaluations of farmer training found that it needed to revisit its own theory of change about how farmer training affects household income—suggesting a need to better understand the complex interactions between training, irrigation, credit, and other interventions in contributing to household incomes.

The last row of Table 7.1 provides a general rubric of performance questions and methods for funders to consider at different stages of investment decision making, both at the level of individual investments and as a portfolio. It also offers a number of general insights. The first is an emphasis on contingency—that the most appropriate methods for performance measurement depend not only on organizational strategy but also on the stage of investment decision making. Second, performance measurement requires substantial capacity in both investees and investors. It is unrealistic for funders to expect their investees to have sophisticated measurement capabilities when they themselves do not. A key role for funders lies in building those capacities.

In sum, the opportunity for funders lies in taking advantage of their distinct structural position in the organizational ecosystem— higher up in the food chain than their investees, with the ability to see and connect various niches in the ecosystem—to orchestrate the production of societal impacts that no single investee or funder could achieve alone. Such an approach to portfolio design and coordination is necessarily strategic, requiring funders to have a theory of change for their portfolios (Brest and Harvey 2008; Frumkin 2006). Moreover, for the design process to be legitimate, it is best developed jointly with clients, investees, other funders, and policy makers rather than in a top-down fashion (Harvey 2016; Kania, Kramer, and Russell 2014).

Conclusion: Towards an Intelligent Accountability

In the opening chapter to this book, I drew upon Onora O'Neill's call for "intelligent forms of accountability" to enable effective social change. All too often, performance systems in the social sector are built in response to the demands of the external funding environment. A core aim of this book has been to demonstrate how performance systems can instead be designed in the service of social purpose, driven internally by an organization's strategy rather than by compliance with external demands. I have sought to be cognizant of the constraints facing social sector leaders working on complex social problems. Theirs is a world of realistic measurement, not of perfect measurement.

Three main questions have motivated this book. The first is simply "What to measure?" Framed in terms of accountability, this is the question of "for what" an organization should hold its feet to the fire. The normative response, common in the social sector, is that all organizations should be held to account for outcomes. But as the cases in this book have shown, this doesn't make sense for all organizations, and can even be counterproductive. Funders have an important role to play in working with their investees to develop realistic and feasible metrics that are aligned with the investee's strategy. That strategy, in turn, is shaped by the twin contingencies of uncertainty about cause-effect, and control over outcomes (as introduced in Chapter 1, Figure 1.3). This means that organizations with a niche strategy should be held to account for their outputs, those with an emergent strategy for interim outcomes of influence, and those with integrated and eco-systems strategies for long-term outcomes. This is a contingency approach to performance measurement, reflective of the pragmatic constraints facing social sector organizations.

The question that naturally follows is "to whom" does an organization owe accountability? Any social sector organization, whether a nonprofit or a business, is confronted with expectations from its diverse stakeholders—clients such as beneficiaries or customers, funders such as investors or donors, as well as regulators and partners. The core challenge lies in aligning upward accountability towards funders with downward accountability towards clients. Mechanisms of upward accountability are fairly well developed in the sector, and include quarterly or annual reporting to funders as well as external evaluations.

The real opportunity lies in developing downward mechanisms that give clients voice and influence in the decisions of the organizations that exist to serve them. Methodologies such as Lean Data and Constituent Voice are particularly important in closing this accountability gap. Here too, funders can play a pivotal role by supporting the development and use of such methodologies, and in making their own upward requirements subservient to downward accountability. Performance measures that are useful for funders but overburden their investees will be of little use for improving performance.

Relatedly, the third key question concerns "how" an organization can design and build its performance systems. The central thread of this book has been that the types of performance systems and capacities most appropriate for an organization's needs are contingent on its strategy—a niche strategy is best served by a system of standardization and quality control, an integrated strategy by a coordination system, an emergent strategy by an adaptation system, and an ecosystem strategy by an orchestration system (for a synthesis see Chapter 6, Figure 6.2). Funders have a crucial role to play in working with their investees to identify and strengthen the right performance systems so that they stand a greater chance of success. In each instance, the funder bears some responsibility for the success or failure of its investees, not only for taking credit when they succeed. And like their investees, funders require systems for assessing and improving the performance of their own portfolios. The deeper implication for designing intelligent accountability is that the relationship between a funder and an investee can be seen as mutually constitutive, driven by common goals and a shared stake in success.

Looking forward, there are many reasons for optimism. Social sector leaders and their funders are embracing performance measurement as critical to helping them achieve their missions. They are shifting from a focus on evaluating impact towards real-time feedback for improving their work. This is true of large, established organizations as well as new entrants to the field. And there is a growing recognition that while there is no one-size-fits-all approach to social performance measurement, one can develop useful contingency-based approaches.

Perhaps the most promising developments are emerging at an industry level. In impact investing, an industry that is barely a decade old, there are signs of convergence towards a series of shared fundamentals for measuring and managing social impacts. For instance, at the time of this writing, an initiative known as the Impact Management Project had launched a measurement convention based on the insights of over two thousand leading practitioners and organizations in the field. Another effort, the Performance Imperative campaign, was galvanizing hundreds of senior nonprofit leaders and grant makers to advocate among their peers for more systematic attention to performance management. It is this group's definition of high performance that I used in the opening chapter to this book. And prominent ratings agencies such as Charity Navigator were shifting away from using only financial efficiency ratios for assessing nonprofit performance and towards metrics on governance, transparency, and potentially on results reporting and constituent voice. In the private sector too, there is a growing appetite for environmental, social, and governance indicators to provide more comprehensive assessments of business performance in both public and private markets. And the United Nations' Sustainable Development Goals are galvanizing joint action by governments, businesses, and civil society to confront global social problems and to measure progress towards addressing them.

In other words, we are in the midst of a normative shift in society. Across the globe, creativity and commitment to social performance are growing, and we observe a steady convergence on how to assess and improve social impact. Yet in today's world of rapidly rising inequality—where social sector services are unable to keep up with societal need, where governments are stretched beyond their means, and where businesses still largely ignore their impacts on society—much work remains to be done. We owe it to the next generation to create a future where measuring social change will be the norm, embedded in how we value performance—not only of social enterprises and nonprofits, but of all organizations in our society.

APPENDIX: PRACTICAL RESOURCES

An electronic version of this appendix can be downloaded at https://fletcher.tufts.edu/people/alnoor-ebrahim.

Methods	Description	Innovators and Users	Sample Resources
		Better Evaluation	BetterEvaluation.org https://www.betterevaluation.org/en/approaches
		Global Impact Investing Network	https://iris.thegiin.org/guidance https://navigatingimpact.thegiin.org
		Impact Management Project	http://www.impactmanagementproject.com
		Innovations for Poverty Action–Goldilocks Resources	https://www.poverty-action.org/goldilocks/resources https://www.poverty-action.org/goldilocks/toolkit
	Web resources that include a wide range of performance measurement and management materials	International Initiative for Impact Evaluation (3ie)	http://www.3ieimpact.org
General Resources		The Organization for Economic Co-operation and Development–Development Assistance Committee	http://www.oecd.org/dac/evaluation/
		Overseas Development Institute (ODI) Methods Lab Evaluation Toolkit	https://www.odi.org/publications/10378-methods-lab-evaluation-toolkit
		Performance Imperative	http://leapambassadors.org/products/performance-imperative/
		World Bank	http://ieg.worldbankgroup.org/evaluators-networks http://siteresources.worldbank.org/EXTEVACAPDEV/Resources/4585672-1251481378590/MandE_tools_methods_approaches.pdf
		Annie E. Casey Foundation	http://www.aecf.org/m/resourcedoc/aecf-theoryofchange-2004.pdf
		Better Evaluation–Theory of Change	https://www.betterevaluation.org/en/resources/guides/creating_program_logic_models
Theory of Change and Logic Models	Guides for identifying and linking the key results expected from an intervention: inputs, activities, outputs and outcomes.	Center for Evaluation Innovation	http://www.evaluationinnovation.org/publications/pathways-change-10-theories-inform-advocacy-and-policy-change-efforts
		Center for Theory of Change	http://www.theoryofchange.org/what-is-theory-of-change/
		Innovation Network	https://www.innonet.org/media/logic_model_workbook_0.pdf
		Leap of Reason	https://leapofreason.org/get-the-books/
		W. K. Kellogg Foundation	https://www.wkkf.org/resource-directory/resource/2006/02/wk-kellogg-foundation-logic-model-development-guide

Category	Item	URL
System Framing Emergent set of ideas and approaches for understanding complex, nonlinear, and adaptive systems that cannot be readily predicted	Cognitive Edge–Cynefin framework	http://cognitive-edge.com/videos/cynefin-framework-introduction/
	Democracy Fund	http://www.democracyfund.org/systems
	FSG	https://www.fsg.org/tools-and-resources/systems-thinking-toolkit-0
	Institute of Development Studies (IDS)	https://opendocs.ids.ac.uk/opendocs/handle/123456789/4387
	Full Frame Initiative	http://fullframeinitiative.org/resources/about-the-full-frame-approach-and-five-domains/
	Kumu–data visualization platform	https://kumu.io/
	New England Complex Systems Institute	http://www.necsi.edu/research/social/
	New Philanthropy Capital	http://www.thinknpc.org/publications/systems-change/
	Oxfam	https://policy-practice.oxfam.org.uk/publications/systems-thinking-an-introduction-for-oxfam-programme-staff-579896
	Schwab Foundation for Social Entrepreneurship	http://reports.weforum.org/schwab-foundation-beyond-organizational-scale/
	Future-Fit Business Benchmark	http://futurefitbusiness.org/resources/downloads/
Systematic Reviews of Scientific Literature Summaries of the best available research on an issue or question; syntheses of results of numerous studies	Campbell Collaboration	https://campbellcollaboration.org
	Innovations for Poverty Action (IPA)	https://www.poverty-action.org/publication/resources-finding-and-using-evidence-reviews-and-evaluations
	International Initiative for Impact Evaluation	http://www.3ieimpact.org/en/evidence/systematic-reviews/
	Mathematica–What Works Clearinghouse	https://www.mathematica-mpr.com/our-capabilities/systematic-research-reviews https://www.mathematica-mpr.com/our-publications-and-findings/projects/what-works-clearinghouse
Cost-Effectiveness Comparisons Methods for assessing the social value of investments by quantifying benefits and costs, thus enabling comparison across potential investments	Abdul Latif Jameel Poverty Action Lab, MIT (CEA)	https://www.povertyactionlab.org/research-resources/cost-effectiveness
	Millennium Challenge Corporation—Economic Rate of Return (ERR)	https://www.mcc.gov/resources/story/story-cdg-guidelines-for-economic-and-beneficiary-analysis
	REDF–Social Return on Investment	http://redf.org/learn-category/sroi/
	Robin Hood Foundation–Benefit Cost Ratios (BCR)	https://www.robinhood.org/what-we-do/metrics/
	Social Value UK–Guide to Social Return on Investment (SROI)	http://www.socialvalueuk.org/resources/sroi-guide/

(continued)

Methods	Description	Innovators and Users	Sample Resources
Monitoring	Ongoing assessment of key indicators or targets to manage and improve performance	Blue Avocado, Dashboards	http://bluea.wpengine.com/wp-content/uploads/attachments/non-profit_dashboard_article_from_blue_avocado.pdf
		Bridgespan Group	https://www.bridgespan.org/insights/blog/measuring-to-improve
		Innovations for Poverty Action	https://www.poverty-action.org/publication/goldilocks-toolkit-monitoring-learning-and-accountability https://www.poverty-action.org/publication/resources-monitoring
		International NGO Training and Research Center (INTRAC)	https://www.intrac.org/wpcms/wp-content/uploads/2016/06/Monitoring-and-Evaluation-Series-Baselines-10.pdf
		McKinsey & Company–Social Impact Assessment	http://mckinseyonsociety.com/social-impact-assessment/
		Poverty Probability Index (PPI)	https://www.povertyindex.org/about-ppi
		Society for Nonprofits–Balanced Scorecard	https://www.snpo.org/publications/sendpdf.php?id=1645
		Health Compass	http://www.thehealthcompass.org/how-to-guides/how-develop-monitoring-and-evaluation-plan
Feedback	Use of participant feedback to be more responsive to the people the program aims to serve	Acumen–Lean Data	https://acumen.org/lean-data/ https://acumen.org/wp-content/uploads/2015/11/Lean-Data-Field-Guide.pdf
		Business for Social Responsibility–Participatory Learning and Action Toolkit	https://herproject.org/files/toolkits/HERproject-Participatory-Learning.pdf
		Feedback Labs	http://feedbacklabs.org/toolkit/
		Keystone Accountability–Constituent Voice	http://keystoneaccountability.org http://keystoneaccountability.org/wp-content/uploads/2009/08/Technical-Note.pdf
		Institute of Development Studies (IDS)–Participatory Methods	http://www.participatorymethods.org/method/participatory-poverty-assessments

	Approaches to assessing organizational capacity, and conducting formative and developmental evaluation	Better Evaluation—Developmental Evaluation	http://www.betterevaluation.org/en/plan/approach/developmental_evaluation
		Bolder Advocacy—Advocacy Capacity Tool (ACT!)	http://bolderadvocacy.org/tools-for-effective-advocacy https://bolderadvocacy.org/resource-library/tools-for-effective-advocacy/evaluating-advocacy/advocacy-capacity-tool-act/
Capacity Assessment for Organizations		FSG—Developmental Evaluation	https://www.fsg.org/blog/case-developmental-evaluation
		Performance Imperative—Performance Practice	https://leapambassadors.org/products/performance-practice/
		McKinsey & Company—Organizational Capacity Assessment Tool (OCAT)	https://www.mckinsey.com/industries/social-sector/how-we-help-clients/organizational-capacity-assessment-tool
		The National Council of Nonprofits	https://www.councilofnonprofits.org/tools-resources/organizational-self-assessments
	Methods for assessing the impact of an intervention by comparing outcomes in a group that receives a treatment to a control or comparison group	Abdul Latif Jameel Poverty Action Lab (J-PAL), MIT	https://www.povertyactionlab.org/research-resources/introduction-evaluations
		Better Evaluation	https://www.betterevaluation.org/resources/guide/unicef_impact_evaluation_series http://www.betterevaluation.org/en/resources/guide/quasi-experimental_design_and_methods
		Innovations for Poverty Action	https://www.poverty-action.org/publication/resources-and-tools-impact-evaluation
Attribution-Based Evaluation		International Initiative for Impact Evaluation	http://www.tandfonline.com/doi/abs/10.1080/19439342.2013.764652 http://www.3ieimpact.org/en/evaluation/resources/impact-evaluation-resources/
		UNICEF Office of Research	https://www.unicef-irc.org/KM/IE/impact_7.php
		World Bank Group and Inter-American Development Bank	http://www.worldbank.org/en/research/dime http://www.worldbank.org/en/programs/sief-trust-fund/publication/impact-evaluation-in-practice

(continued)

Methods	Description	Innovators and Users	Sample Resources
	Methods for assessing impact when the intervention or setting is complex, such that causal pathways cannot be isolated and a control group cannot be established	Better Evaluation–Outcome Harvesting, Process Tracing, and Contribution Analysis	http://www.betterevaluation.org/en/plan/approach/outcome_harvesting http://www.betterevaluation.org/evaluation-options/processtracing https://www.betterevaluation.org/en/plan/approach/contribution_analysis
		Center for Evaluation Innovation–Contribution Analysis, Advocacy Strategy Framework	http://www.evaluationinnovation.org/sites/default/files/Contribution%20Analysis_0.pdf http://www.evaluationinnovation.org/sites/default/files/Adocacy%20Strategy%20Framework.pdf
Contribution-Based Evaluation		Centre for Development Studies–Qualitative Impact Assessment Protocol	https://www.gov.uk/dfid-research-outputs/the-qualitative-impact-assessment-protocol-quip http://www.bath.ac.uk/cds/documents/quip-briefing-paper-march-2015.pdf
		International Initiative for Impact Evaluation–Evaluating Advocacy	http://www.3ieimpact.org/en/publications/working-papers/working-paper-29/
		Most Significant Changes	http://mande.co.uk/special-issues/most-significant-change-msc/
		Outcome Harvesting	http://outcomeharvesting.net/resources/
		Outcome Mapping Learning Community	https://www.outcomemapping.ca/

NOTES

Introduction

1. See McKeever (2016).

2. In 2017, about $228 billion in impact investing assets were under management by 226 organizations that were members of the GIIN (Global Impact Investing Network 2018). Some projections estimated a $500 billion market within the decade (Monitor Institute 2009; O'Donohoe et al. 2010), while more cautious estimates put it at eventually reaching "hundreds of billions of dollars" (Clark, Emerson, and Thornley 2015).

3. See, for example, Barman (2016); Ebrahim and Weisband (2007); Ferguson (1990); Lamont (2012).

Chapter 1

1. I am grateful to Paul Brest for highlighting the tension in these different uses of the term, and for making a case that *impact* be used to indicate the difference made by an intervention.

2. For an overview of cause-effect relationships as discussed in the accounting and organization theory literatures, see: Chenhall 2003; Galbraith 1973; Ittner 2014; Koonce, Seybert, and Smith 2011; Lukka 2014; Merchant and Otley 2007; Thompson 1967.

3. Thank you to Gerhard Speckbacher for pointing out the limitations of the balanced scorecard in measuring social outcomes and impacts, as the method is largely silent about how to link organization-level measures to complex social impacts occurring outside the organization. In a paper on the application of the balanced scorecard to nonprofits, Kaplan (2010, 23) proposes replacing financial results as the ultimate outcome with an "objective related to their *social impact* and *mission*," cautioning that this "social impact objective may take years to become noticeable, which is why the measures in the other perspectives provide the short- to intermediate-term targets and feedback necessary for year-to-year control and accountability."

4. For a detailed examination of several different mechanisms see Chamberlin (2018). For example, some of the other mechanisms she identifies include social impact guarantees (SIGs), in which government provides the upfront capital but is reimbursed by private guarantors if outcome targets are *not* met; as well as social success notes (SSNs) and social impact incentives (SIIs), in which service providers receive loans from investors but with repayment of principal and/or interest made by a separate outcome payer contingent on meeting performance benchmarks.

5. The Paris Declaration on Aid Effectiveness aimed to improve the quality of aid and its impact on international development. First, it emphasizes country ownership as fundamental to improving the impact of aid on the basis that aid is more effective when partner countries take leadership over their development policies and strategies. Second, the declaration focuses on results by identifying twelve indicators of aid effectiveness. These indicators measure the developing country's ability to use aid (e.g., clear strategic priorities for poverty reduction, reliable systems for procurement and public financial management) as well as the efforts by donor agencies to help build country capacity, for example, by using the partner country's procurement and financial management systems rather than the donor's own systems, by disbursing aid on a more predictable schedule, and by reducing requirements that aid be "tied" to the purchases of goods and services from the donor country (OECD 2008).

6. My definition of strategy is inspired by Michael Porter's work on competitive strategy with its emphasis on integrating an organization's value proposition with its value chain (Magretta 2011; Porter 1980). The analog to the value chain in the social sector is an organization's social change model, particularly its theory of change and logic model. However, it is important to note that competition is not at the heart of my definition of strategy because many social sector actors operate in settings of market failure, seeking to deliver goods or services to communities that markets (and government) have failed to provide. Moreover, a growing number of social sector actors are looking to scale their impact through collaboration rather than competition. For more on this topic, see Hansmann (1996), Weisbrod (1988), and Moore (1997).

7. The analogous concept in the business literature is the value chain. But the task of articulating a value chain is more complicated in social sector organizations due to the fact that value creation does not stop at outputs but extends beyond the organizational boundary to outcome and impacts.

8. Implementing a social change model requires resources. A perennial strategic challenge facing social sector organizations is how to sustainably fund change. While it is not the purpose of this book to explore how to build revenue streams, it is important to note that sustainable revenue generation remains a major obstacle in the sector to delivering social results. For example, one study found that of

over 200,000 nonprofit organizations established in the United States from 1975 to 2008 (excluding hospitals and universities), only 201 succeeded in growing their annual revenues to over $50 million—or only one-tenth of 1 percent (Kim and Bradach 2012)! Moreover, it has been widely documented that a central barrier to improving the capacity of social sector organizations to deliver social change is the lack of funding for overhead or general operating costs (Eckhart-Queenan, Allen, and Tuomala 2013; Eckhart-Queenan, Etzel, and Prasad 2016; Keating 2003).

9. As the management scholar James D. Thompson (1967) noted a half century ago, complex organizations are often expected to be accountable for different things, with yardsticks of performance varying across different stakeholder groups. This complex agency problem is especially pronounced in the social sector, where demands for accountability from funders can be at odds with the expectations of different beneficiary or client groups.

10. For more on how to manage the many demands of accountability from diverse stakeholders, see Ebrahim (2016).

11. There is some evidence that success in immunization efforts may not follow as linear a logic as anticipated by many funders and global health organizations. Efforts to eradicate polio, for example, through a "vertical" strategy of immunization campaigns have been set back by the reemergence of polio cases in countries thought to have eliminated it. Global actors, such as the Bill and Melinda Gates Foundation, have thus increasingly considered combining immunization campaigns with "horizontal" strategies that include strengthening basic health systems and services in poor countries. The causal logic of such a combined vertical-horizontal strategy is less well understood, but it is driven by a concern that without a broader system of functioning health, hygiene, and sanitation services for the poor, many diseases will return or be difficult to contain (Guth 2010). The Ebola outbreak in West Africa in 2014 highlighted the need for basic health infrastructure.

12. A related framework developed by David Snowden adds a fourth context of cause and effect—chaotic—where causal relationships are "impossible to determine because they shift constantly and no manageable patterns exist—only turbulence" (Snowden and Boone 2007; Snowden and Kurtz 2003). For a video introduction to this framework and its implications for leadership, see: http://cognitive-edge.com/videos/cynefin-framework-introduction/.

13. Prior scholarship on performance measurement in the business literature has used variations of these two factors to describe the limitations on individuals or organizations in influencing performance outcomes (for reviews, see Choudhury 1986; Demski 1976; Giraud, Langevin, and Mendoza 2008; Merchant 1989; Merchant and Otley 2007).

14. Interdependence may be characterized as pooled, sequential, or reciprocal depending on the mechanisms of coordination required (Thompson 1967, 54–56),

and it is a feature not only of complex organizations but also of interorganizational relationships such as alliances, joint ventures, networks (Gulati and Singh 1998; Oster 1995) and cross-sector social partnerships (Bryson, Crosby, and Stone 2006; Stone, Crosby, and Bryson 2010; Vurro, Dacin, and Perrini 2010). Drawing on these literatures, causal interdependence in the creation of social value can be defined as the degree to which the activities in a results chain are interrelated such that achieving social impacts depends on their coordination.

15. For an extensive scholarly treatment of causality, especially on the role of assignment mechanisms for making causal inferences, see Imbens and Rubin (2015).

16. Even with randomized control trials, scientists don't always agree on the findings. The research on deworming has been a subject of substantial controversy among development evaluators and economists, earning it the moniker of the "worm wars." For a summary of the worm wars and extensive links to the research and debates, see a post by the economist David Evans on the World Bank's blog: http://blogs.worldbank.org/impactevaluations/worm-wars-anthology (accessed April 29, 2016).

Chapter 2

1. Oxford Dictionaries (2018).

2. As quoted in *Business Standard* (Deoras 2014)

3. Disclosure: Shaffi Mather studied in the midcareer program at Harvard Kennedy School in 2006–7, at which time he enrolled in my graduate course on "Accountability and Policy." He was developing ZHL's business model at the time, and employed ideas from the course on accountability and audit processes.

4. Approximately USD 75–150 using a 2015 exchange rate of USD 1 = INR 65.

5. In 2015, the founding team held an 85 percent stake in ZHL, with the remaining equity held by several external investors including Acumen and Global Medical Response India (ZHL 2015).

6. There was also a third model focused on corporate partnerships, which I do not discuss here due to its modest size, about $5,500 in revenue in 2015. Under this model, ZHL managed ambulance services for private hospitals and manufacturing firms that needed an emergency medical response team on site.

7. The organization provided two types of ambulances: basic life support (BLS) and advanced life support (ALS). A BLS ambulance was typically used to provide prehospital care to patients who did not require extensive support or cardiac monitoring during transport. These vehicles were equipped to control bleeding, perform cardiopulmonary resuscitation, administer oxygen, and handle splint treatment. An ALS ambulance provided a higher level of care and included a de-

fibrillator, ECG machine, cardiac monitor, portable ventilator, suction machine, resuscitation kit, emergency medicines, and pulse oximeter. Both the BLS and ALS ambulances had equipment for rescuing and carrying patients including a collapsible stretcher, a scoop stretcher and spine board, a wheelchair that could also be used as a stair-chair, and rescue tools. They also stocked medicines and other general items. They were staffed with a driver, helper, and trained paramedic. In 2015, a BLS ambulance was estimated to cost between Indian Rupees (INR) 1.5 to 1.8 million (USD 23,000–27,000), and an ALS ambulance was estimated to cost between INR 1.8 to 2.2 million (USD 27,000–34,000).

8. While it appears that response time matters for patient survival in cardiac cases, it is less clear for other types of medical conditions (Blackwell and Kaufman 2002; Blackwell et al. 2009; Pons and Markovchick 2002). In cases that require fire and rescue services, there is evidence to show that shorter response time positively affects patient survival (Mattsson and Juas 1997; Sund et al. 2011).

9. PPI was a poverty measurement tool developed by the Grameen Foundation. It was a country-specific tool that was composed of ten questions to capture household characteristics and asset ownership. Responses to these questions were used to compute the likelihood of a household living below the poverty line. For more details see http://www.povertyindex.org (accessed April 3, 2018). Also see Chapter 7.

10. Total Quality Management approaches were widely adopted by industry in the United States and Europe in the 1980s and 1990s as a response to the rise of Japanese manufacturing (Deming 1986; Feigenbaum 1983; Ishikawa 1985). The US government adopted TQM practices in the Department of Defense and the armed forces, and more broadly advocated its diffusion through the Malcolm Baldridge National Quality Award. More recent manifestations of TQM ideas can be found in quality certification processes such as ISO 9000, Six Sigma, and Lean Manufacturing.

11. Numerous efforts are underway to gather and synthesize the findings of research to be useful to social sector organizations. See, for example, the International Initiative on Impact Evaluation (3ie), the Campbell Collaboration, and Giving Evidence, among others. See Chapter 7 and the Appendix for resources.

Chapter 3

1. Oxford English Dictionary (2018).

2. The formal acronym for the organization is AKRSP(I), which differentiates it from its larger sister organization in Pakistan, AKRSP(P). For simplicity, I use AKRSP in this chapter except when citing a source or quotation.

3. Disclosures: I was part of a group of young professionals placed with development NGOs by the Canadian International Development Agency and the Aga

Khan Foundation Canada in 1991; I was placed with AKRSP. Some of my subsequent doctoral work was funded by a scholarship from the Aga Khan Foundation in Geneva. I have since provided occasional charitable contributions to the foundation. The current research was funded by the Harvard Business School.

4. This endowment of INR 25.9 million (approximately USD 2 million at the time; exchange rate for conversion used USD 1 = INR 12.53) was unusual for an Indian NGO at the time. The AKF is part of the larger Aga Khan Development Network (AKDN), a collection of nondenominational development agencies that work in poor regions of Asia and Africa, founded by His Highness the Aga Khan (see www.akdn.org).

5. AKRSP also carried out activities in a number of other areas such as animal husbandry, drinking water provision, alternative energy development, agroforestry, and even youth training and education. I focus here only on the interventions that have remained at the core of AKRSP's work over its thirty-year history.

6. The Philippine experience with participatory irrigation management was documented in a book that was widely read by AKRSP's senior managers (Korten and Siy 1988).

7. A particularly influential book by Robert Chambers, published around the time of AKRSP's founding, was titled *Rural Development: Putting the Last First* (Chambers 1983).

8. The CMNR grant from the EC, in the amount of EUR 14.4 million, was channeled through the Aga Khan Foundation. It was to be distributed among two organizations in Gujarat: AKRSP and the N. M. Sadguru Water and Development Foundation (Sadguru). Sadguru was a large rural development NGO operating in the region, and had been one of the pioneers in lift irrigation and agroforestry prior to AKRSP. For a more detailed examination of AKRSP, Sadguru, and their relationships with a global network of funders in the 1990s, see Ebrahim (2003b).

9. This kind of "mutual adjustment" is common in early stage organizations of modest size, where it is still possible to coordinate effectively through personal interaction (Mintzberg 1983).

10. It is noteworthy that AKRSP was one of the early adopters of the LFA in international development, and that bilateral aid agencies like the EC were its strongest advocates in the 1990s. This was well before the widespread adoption of logic models in the United States, advanced by national organizations such as the United Way and the Urban Institute.

11. A critique of the LFA, and of logic models more broadly, is that they are overly technocratic, thereby reducing complex social and political realities into simplified and discrete components of a project, and relegating risks and uncertainties to a column of "assumptions" (Ebrahim 2002).

12. This grant totaled EUR 25.5 million (approximately USD 24 million in 2002; exchange rate for conversion EUR 1= USD 0.94). Both the CMNR and SCALE grants were channeled through the Aga Khan Foundation.

13. The evaluation relied on a 2011 study by AKRSP and a think tank, the Indian Natural Resource Economics and Management Foundation, for this assessment.

14. The SCALE project also identified other results related to increasing the asset base of poor households and partnering with other NGOs to develop replicable solutions to rural livelihood development. I focus here only on the results related to community institutions, as these were the heart of the project.

15. The final review of the CMNR project referenced studies conducted by the Gujarat Institute for Development Research, Institute of Rural Management at Anand, Indian Institute for Forest Management, and the Tata Energy Research Institute (European Commission 2001: 39).

16. AKRSP's final report for the SCALE project, and the final external evaluation commissioned by the EC, referenced several studies to back up their claims of outcomes (COWI and Atkins 2013; AKRSP 2012). Baseline data were not available at AKRSP headquarters during my visit in 2015, nor were many of the cited studies. As a result, it was not possible to independently assess the quality of those studies.

17. Every company with a minimum net worth of INR 5 billion (USD 83 million), or minimum revenue of INR 10 billion (USD 166 million), or minimum net profit of INR 50 million (USD 830,000) had to spend 2 percent of three-year average annual profits towards corporate social responsibility. However, the act only regulated expenditure outlays, resulting in varied outputs and outcomes. See Government of India's Ministry of Corporate Affairs website, http://www .mca.gov.in/MinistryV2/companiesact2013.html and http://www.mca.gov.in/ SearchableActs/Section135.htm (accessed April 15, 2018).

18. For a visual depiction of the HCZ's pipeline, see its website: http://hcz .org/about-us/ (accessed June 3, 2016).

Chapter 4

1. Merriam-Webster Dictionary 2018; Oxford Dictionaries 2018.

2. See International Labour Organization (ILO), International Labour Conference, http://www.ilo.org/global/about-the-ilo/how-the-ilo-works/international -labour-conference/lang--en/index.htm (accessed May 23, 2017).

3. At the time of this writing, London's transportation agency had declared Uber, the ride-hailing service, to be insufficiently "fit and proper" to operate in the city. At the same time, the European Commission was considering a proposal to de-

velop protections for workers in the gig economy, estimated to be about one-third of Europe's workforce (Alderman 2017).

4. The founding participants came from a diverse set of actors: membership-based organizations of informal workers such as the Self-Employed Women's Association, and HomeNet (an alliance of home-based workers); international organizations such as the United Nations Statistical Division, United Nations Development Fund for Women (UNIFEM), the International Labour Organization, and the World Bank; and an academic from Harvard University.

5. WIEGO's statistics program was initially codirected with Jacques Charmes, an economist and statistician, who was a cofounder of WIEGO and later became research director at the French Scientific Research Institute.

6. For more on the ICLS and its standard-setting process, see: http://ilo.org/global/statistics-and-databases/meetings-and-events/international-conference-of-labour-statisticians/lang--en/index.htm (accessed June 6, 2017).

7. The World Health Organization (WHO), the International Labour Organization (ILO), and the United Nations Children's Emergency Fund (UNICEF) are all United Nations agencies.

8. WIEGO commissioned three papers for this Delhi Group meeting: Charmes (1998); Ferran (1998); Pedrero (1998).

9. The meeting was the International Labour Conference of 2002. To prepare its members for a discussion on the informal economy, the ILO produced a report, *Decent Work and the Informal Economy* (ILO 2002a). WIEGO's background papers prepared for this report included Carr and Chen (2001) and Chen, Jhabvala, and Lund (2001).

10. The ILOSTAT database can be found at www.ilo.org/ilostat (accessed April 13, 2018). Some of the best data, according to Vanek, are collected by Mexico, which produces quarterly reports on its informal economy including assessments of its contribution to GDP.

11. There are seventeen Sustainable Development Goals. The metric on informal employment (8.3.1) is part of Goal 8: "Promote sustained, inclusive and sustainable economic growth, full and productive employment and decent work for all." For the final list of indicators see: https://unstats.un.org/sdgs/indicators/indicators-list/ (accessed June 6, 2017).

12. This was the International Classification of Status in Employment. See: http://www.ilo.org/global/statistics-and-databases/statistics-overview-and-topics/status-in-employment/current-guidelines/lang--en/index.htm (accessed January 19, 2018).

13. There is a long tradition of theory in the social sciences on conceptualizing social systems and the relationship between structures of power and agency. See, for example, work on structuration (Bourdieu 1977; Giddens 1984), discourse

and genealogy (Foucault 1980, 1984), and liberation theology (Fals-Borda 1988; Freire 1970).

14. There are many practical tools available online for conducting systems framing and mapping. For a very useful set of guides and mapping visualization tools, see the Democracy Fund's resources at http://www.democracyfund.org/systems (accessed September 29, 2017). See also FSG's guides "Actor Mapping" and "Trend Mapping" available at http://fsg.org/tools-and-resources/guide-actor-mapping and http://fsg.org/tools-and-resources/guide-trend-mapping, and New Philanthropy Capital's "Systems Change: A Guide to What It Is and How to Do It" available at http://www.thinknpc.org/publications/systems-change/ (all accessed June 7, 2017).

15. For examples of system maps for complex democracy projects, see the Democracy Fund: http://www.democracyfund.org/systems. Many of these maps were created using Kumu, an interactive data visualization platform: https://kumu.io/markets/system-mapping.

16. A total of thirty-four MBOs are part of WIEGO's core network. Examples include the Self-Employed Women's Association (SEWA) in India with over two million members, the Trades Union Congress in Ghana with a membership of about half a million, and the Red Latinoamericana de Recicladores, a network of waste pickers in seventeen Latin American countries.

17. The developers of outcome harvesting call their maps "outcome chains." I prefer to call them "influence maps" as they rarely point to actual outcomes, but instead illuminate how the organization seeks to influence parts of a system. For resources on outcome harvesting, see: http://outcomeharvesting.net/resources/ and http://www.betterevaluation.org/en/plan/approach/outcome_harvesting (accessed June 7, 2017)

18. My description of WIEGO's theory of change is adapted from two sources: an evaluation conducted for SIDA (Klugman 2014b), and the organization's five-year strategy for 2013–2018 (WIEGO 2013).

19. In both of these examples, WIEGO partnered with local membership-based organizations. In Bogotá, it worked with the Asociación Cooperativa de Recicladores de Bogotá (ARB), which was itself a membership organization of several thousand waste pickers. In Accra, it worked with the Makola Market Traders Union and the Ga East Traders Union.

20. I further elaborate the distinction between attribution-based and contribution-based methods in Chapter 7.

21. For a highly accessible step-by-step overview of contribution analysis, as applied to several policy examples, see Kane et al. (2017). They divide the process into seven main steps, and provide useful insights on how to conduct each step. There is also a growing and related literature on approaches to evaluating complexity (Patton 2011; Preskill and Gopal 2014).

22. This theory of change and background are drawn from a teaching case on the National Campaign written three years after its founding (Sawhill and Harmeling 2000).

23. This description of the BLTP is based on an evaluation by Campbell and Uvin (2015).

Chapter 5

1. Merriam Webster Dictionary (2018).

2. The sources for these data vary, with most taken from the Continuum of Care (CoC) in each city or county, a program set up and funded by the US Department of Housing and Urban Development to address homelessness in a comprehensive manner with other federal agencies. For reports specific to each CoC, see https://www.hudexchange.info/programs/coc/ (accessed April 15, 2018).

3. The PSH model was pioneered by Sam Tsemberis, a professor of psychiatry at Columbia University Medical Center, and piloted through a nonprofit organization he founded in 1992, Pathways to Housing. See: https://www.pathwayshousingfirst.org (accessed April 15, 2018). It is important to note the boundaries of the PSH model. PSH interventions target people who are already chronically homeless; they do not aim to address the factors that led to homelessness in the first place.

4. USICH is comprised of nineteen federal agencies and departments, of which several manage or fund programs to assist the homeless, including the departments of Housing and Urban Development, Health and Human Services, Homeland Security, Veterans Affairs, Labor, and Education.

5. It is important to note that while Miriam's Kitchen focused its efforts on the most difficult clients (the chronically homeless), the largest and fastest growing homeless segment was homeless families. In addition, these numbers are not entirely reliable and should be treated as approximations. As Figure 5.2 shows, data on the number of homeless veterans has been consistently collected only since 2011. However, these point-in-time numbers may substantially underestimate the numbers of homeless veterans. A dashboard set up by Community Solutions to track veterans on a monthly basis in DC suggests that although forty-five veterans were housed per month in 2016 on average, the numbers of homeless veterans did not decline due to an increasing inflow of veterans into the city.

6. For more on the 25 Cities Initiative, see https://www.va.gov/HOMELESS/25cities.asp (accessed April 15, 2018)

7. For more on the Built for Zero campaign, organized by Community Solutions, see: https://www.cmtysolutions.org/what-we-do/built-for-zero and http://builtforzero.weebly.com/ (accessed April 15, 2018)

8. The VI-SPDAT is a combination of two instruments. The Vulnerability Index (VI) is a tool based on medical research to assess individuals for elevated risk of death on the streets. It was developed by Jim O'Connell of Boston's Health Care for the Homeless. The Service Prioritization Decision Assistance Tool (SPDAT) was developed by Iain DeJong of OrgCode Consulting to assist case managers and front-line workers in systematically collecting intake data and triaging services. A partnership between OrgCode and Community Solutions resulted in creating a hybrid instrument, VI-SPDAT, to provide information for prioritizing a homeless person's housing and support needs. To access this tool, among others, see: http://www.orgcode.com/products, and for a training video, see: https://vimeo.com/86520820. For background on the development of the instrument, see: http://ceslosangeles.weebly.com/uploads/1/2/2/1/1221685/spdat_vi-spdat_evidence_brief_final.pdf (all accessed April 15, 2018). For an illustration of its implementation in New Orleans, see (Cels, De Jong, and Nauta 2012).

9. Monthly updates are publicly posted on a website: http://www.coordinatedentry.com/successes.html (accessed October 29, 2017)

10. The ICH was established by DC's Homeless Service Reform Act of 2005 to facilitate interagency, cabinet-level leadership in planning, policy making, and budgeting for homeless services (see ich.dc.gov). Similarly, at the federal level, the United States Interagency Council on Homelessness (USICH) was tasked with coordinating the efforts of nineteen federal agencies. The USICH was established by the Stewart B. McKinney Homeless Assistance Act of 1987 and reauthorized by Homeless Emergency Assistance and Rapid Transition to Housing (HEARTH) Act of 2009 (see www.usich.gov).

11. This view is consistent with a view of civil society as a space for civil discourse among diverse interests, as articulated by the political theorist Antonio Gramsci (1971), and is also resonant with a freedoms-based perspective on development advanced by the economist Amartya Sen (1999).

12. The Advocacy Capacity Tool for Organizational Assessment is available at: http://bolderadvocacy.org/tools-for-effective-advocacy (accessed July 11, 2016). Other capacity assessment tools include: Organizational Capacity Assessment Tool developed by McKinsey & Company and Venture Philanthropy Partners: https://mckinseyonsociety.com/ocat/; Participatory Self Assessment of NGO Capacity developed by the International NGO Training and Research Centre (INTRAC): http://www.intrac.org/data/files/resources/131/OPS-10-Participatory-Self-Assessment-of-NGO-Capacity.pdf; The National Council of Nonprofits also lists a series of tools: https://www.councilofnonprofits.org/tools-resources/organizational-self-assessments (all accessed July 31, 2016). For advocacy evaluation, see Coffman (2009). See also the Appendix to this book.

13. For a review of the scholarly literature on the challenges of designing and governing such cross-sector collaborations, see Bryson et al. (2006) and Stone et al. (2010).

14. A HUD report identifies five key elements of permanent supported housing programs (Culhane and Byrne 2010): (1) housing that is affordable for those on SSI incomes (i.e., persons spend no more than 30 percent of their incomes); (2) clients have choice and control over housing; (3) housing is permanent, which most often means that a lease agreement is in a client's name, and maintenance of housing is not contingent on participating in services; (4) housing is functionally separate from, though still linked to services; and (5) supportive services are not delivered according to a set program but rather are flexible and tailored to the needs of individual clients. All of these elements are based on the central principles of integration of services, personal control, personal choice.

15. Even the business research literature on joint synergistic production in teams and organizational coordination systems has shown that an adequate isolation of the work of individual team members towards a goal is typically not possible or appropriate when their work is highly interdependent (e.g., Alchian and Demsetz 1972; Mintzberg, 1983; Srikanth and Puranam 2014).

16. This example draws primarily from Grossman and Ross (2012).

Chapter 7

1. I focus here on funders with direct links to the organizations they support, not those that operate at an arm's length through intermediaries. For simplicity, I use the term *investment* broadly to include support in the form of grants, loans, and equity, and I similarly use the term *investees* as a broad umbrella that includes *grantees*. My focus is in the social returns from these investments rather than their financial returns.

2. For examples of funder efforts to support performance measurement in their investees, see a report by the Center for Effective Philanthropy (Buteau and Glickman 2018), as well as profiles of several funders such as the Blagrave Trust, Einhorn Family Charitable Trust, Impetus-PEF, Mulago Foundation, and the Weingart Foundation, all available at: https://leapambassadors.org/products/building-case-funders/ (accessed November 8, 2018).

3. My discussion of these three organizations draws upon and updates my teaching cases, available through Harvard Business Publishing (see Cole et al. 2018; Ebrahim and Rangan 2010, 2011; Ebrahim and Ross 2010).

4. This table builds on the work of two former students who conducted a study under my supervision on the measurement practices of over twenty impact investors (So and Capanyola 2016; So and Staskevicius 2015), and my prior work

on categorizing measurement methods in nonprofit organizations (Ebrahim and Rangan 2014).

5. I briefly served as an advisor to Keystone Accountability in the early 2000s, in a voluntary capacity, when it was in the early stages of developing its constituent voice methodology.

6. This discussion on Lean Data is based on an article that first appeared in the *Stanford Social Innovation Review*, coauthored with Acumen's chief innovation officer and its director of impact (Dichter, Adams, and Ebrahim 2016). I continue to engage with Acumen, serving in a voluntary capacity on its Lean Data Advisory Council.

7. While ZHL used its own call centers for reaching its customers, several of the other pilots demonstrated that technological advances—such as cheap text messaging and interactive voice response—could substantially improve the efficiency and speed of data collection from customers or beneficiaries while retaining quality.

8. I am grateful to Tom Adams, chief impact officer at Acumen, for this analogy.

9. MCC's entire monitoring and evaluation process is laid out in considerable detail on its website. Its process overview (section 7.1.3) aligns closely with the four-stage process outlined in this chapter. See: https://www.mcc.gov/resources/doc/policy-for-monitoring-and-evaluation (accessed July 20, 2017). The monitoring and evaluation plans for each country are publicly available, as are the actual evaluations (https://www.mcc.gov/our-impact/independent-evaluations).

10. Although I do not discuss it here, there is a related debate in impact investing on the "additionality" of an investment or its "investment impact," that is, how much it increases the social benefits produced by an enterprise beyond what would have occurred without that investment (Brest and Born 2013). Some investors like Root Capital have laid out an explicit basis for making that counterfactual assessment (McCreless 2017), relying primarily on assessments of whether the enterprise would be able to access other comparable sources of funding.

REFERENCES

Abizaid, O. 2015. *ARB: Fighting for an Inclusive Model for Recycling in Bogotá*. Women in Informal Employment: Globalizing and Organizing (WIEGO), http://wiego.org/resources/arb-fighting-inclusive-model-recycling-bogota.

Acumen (Producer). 2013. 2013 Investor Gathering: Committed to Care. https://www.youtube.com/watch?v=P8MautuiZjQ (accessed April 13, 2017).

Acumen. 2015. *The Lean Data Field Guide*. New York: Acumen. http://acumen.org/wp-content/uploads/2015/11/Lean-Data-Field-Guide.pdf.

Acumen. 2018. *Energy Impact Report*. New York: Acumen. https://acumen.org/wp-content/uploads/2018/02/Acumen-Energy-Impact-Report.pdf (accessed November 9, 2018).

Advisory Board Company. 2015. *Uncovering the Health Care and Police Costs of Chronic Homelessness in the District: Advisory Board Analysis for Miriam's Kitchen*.

Aga Khan Foundation. 1994. *Community Management of Natural Resources, Gujarat, India: Overall Work Plan (1994–2001)*. New Delhi: Aga Khan Foundation.

Aga Khan Foundation. 2001. *Sustainable Community-Based Approaches for Livelihoods Enhancement (SCALE)* Aga Khan Foundation.

Aga Khan Rural Support Programme (India) (AKRSP). n.d. *PRA—The AKRSP(I) Way*. Ahmedabad, India: Aga Khan Rural Support Programme (India).

Aga Khan Rural Support Programme (India) (AKRSP). 1990. *Annual Progress Report 1989*. Ahmedabad, India: Aga Khan Rural Support Programme (India).

Aga Khan Rural Support Programme (India) (AKRSP). 1999. *Strategies to Position AKRSP(I) in the Year 2010: A Concept Paper*. Ahmedabad, India: Aga Khan Rural Support Programme (India).

Aga Khan Rural Support Programme (India) (AKRSP). 2000. *Logical Framework for Institutional Development (LOGFID)*. Ahmedabad, India: Aga Khan Rural Support Programme (India).

Aga Khan Rural Support Programme (India) (AKRSP). 2002. *Community Management of Natural Resources (CMNR), India (ALA/93/33): Completion Report of CMNR Project*. Ahmedabad: Aga Khan Rural Support Programme (India).

Aga Khan Rural Support Programme (India) (AKRSP). 2008. *Institutional Approach to Natural Resource Management and Improving Quality of Life: Experiences from Junagadh.* Gadu, India: Aga Khan Rural Support Programme (India).

Aga Khan Rural Support Programme (India) (AKRSP). 2011a. *Annual Report 2010.* Ahmedabad, India: Aga Khan Rural Support Programme (India).

Aga Khan Rural Support Programme (India) (AKRSP). 2011b. *A River Is Born Again: Case Study on Meghal River Basin Revival.* Ahmedabad, India: Aga Khan Rural Support Programme (India) and Aga Khan Foundation (India).

Aga Khan Rural Support Programme (India) (AKRSP). 2012. *Sustainable Community-Based Approaches for Livelihood Enhancement (SCALE): Annual Narrative Progress Report 2012 (ALA/01/83, IND/AIDCO/2001/0083-01).* Ahmedabad, India: Aga Khan Rural Support Programme (India).

Aga Khan Rural Support Programme (India) (AKRSP). 2013. *Annual Report 2012.* Ahmedabad, India: Aga Khan Rural Support Programme (India).

Aga Khan Rural Support Programme (India) (AKRSP). 2015. *Annual Report 2014.* Ahmedabad, India: Aga Khan Rural Support Programme (India).

Alchian, A. A., and H. Demsetz. 1972. "Production, Information Costs, and Economic Organization." *American Economic Review* 62: 777–95.

Alderman, L. 2017. "Europe Surveys the Gig Economy and Wants Worker Safeguards." *New York Times*, October 2.

Anthony, R. N., and D. W. Young. 2004. "Financial Accounting and Financial Management." In *The Jossey-Bass Handbook of Nonprofit Leadership and Management, 2nd Edition*, edited by R. D. Herman & Associates. San Francisco: Jossey-Bass/Wiley.

Asian Development Bank. 2006. *Impact Evaluation: Methodological and Operational Issues.* Manila: ADB.

AusAID. 2005. *The Logical Framework Approach* Australian Agency for International Development (AusAID), Commonwealth of Australia.

Baird, S., J. H. Hicks, M. Kremer, and E. Miguel. 2011. "Worms at Work: Long-Run Impacts of Child Health Gains." Working Paper. https://www.cgdev.org/doc/events/KLPS-Labor_2011-05-16-Circulate.pdf.

Balch, O. 2014. "Pay for Your Ambulance? How India's Poorest Are Gaining Access to Healthcare." *The Guardian.* http://www.theguardian.com/sustainable-business/2014/oct/24/ambulance-india-poor-access-to-healthcare.

Banerjee, A., E. Duflo, N. Goldberg, D. Karlan, R. Osei, W. Parienté, J. Shapiro, B. Thuysbaert, and C. Udry. 2015. ""A Multifaceted Program Causes Lasting Progress for the Very Poor: Evidence from Six Countries. *Science* 348 (6236): 1260799. doi:10.1126/science.1260799.

Banerjee, A. V. 2007. *Making Aid Work.* Cambridge, MA: MIT Press.

Banerjee, A. V., and E. Duflo. 2009. "The Experimental Approach to Development Economics." *Annual Review of Economics* 1: 151–78.

Bannick, M., and P. Goldman. 2012. *Priming the Pump: The Case for a Sector Based Approach to Impact Investing*. Omidyar Network. https://www.omidyar.com/insights/priming-pump-case-sector-based-approach-impact-investing.

Bannick, M., P. Goldman, M. Kubzansky, and Y. Saltuk. 2017. "Across the Returns Continuum." *Stanford Social Innovation Review* (Winter).

Barbaro, M., and J. Gillis. 2005. "Wal-Mart at Forefront of Hurricane Relief." *Washington Post*, September 6.

Barman, E. 2016. *Caring Capitalism: The Meaning and Measure of Social Value in the Market*. New York: Cambridge University Press.

Battilana, J., and M. Kimsey. 2017. "Should You Agitate, Innovate, or Orchestrate? A Framework for Understanding the Roles You Can Play in a Movement for Social Change." *Stanford Social Innovation Review* (September 18).

Beach, D., and R. Pedersen. 2013. *Process-Tracing Methods: Foundations and Guidelines*. Ann Arbor: University of Michigan Press.

Beer, T., and J. Coffman. 2015. *Four Tools for Assessing Grantee Contribution to Advocacy Efforts*. Center for Evaluation Innovation. http://www.evaluationinnovation.org/publications/advocacy-strategy-framework.

Befani, B., and J. Mayne. 2014. "Process Tracing and Contribution Analysis: A Combined Approach to Generative Causal Inference for Impact Evaluation." *IDS Bulletin* 45 (6): 17–36.

Behn, R. D. 2001. *Rethinking Democratic Accountability*. Washington, DC: Brookings Institution.

Bellman, E. 2008. "A Traumatized Mumbai Seeks to Protect Itself." *Wall Street Journal*, December 18. http://www.wsj.com/articles/SB122955279595415689.

Benjamin, L. M. 2008. "Account Space: How Accountability Requirements Shape Nonprofit Practice." *Nonprofit and Voluntary Sector Quarterly* 37 (2): 201–23.

Benjamin, L. M. 2012. "Nonprofit Organizations and Outcome Measurement." *American Journal of Evaluation* 33 (3): 431–47. doi:10.1177/1098214012440496.

Bennett, A. 2010. "Process Tracing and Causal Inference." In *Rethinking Social Inquiry: Diverse Tools, Shared Standards*, edited by H. Brady and D. Collier. New York: Rowman and Littlefield.

Bennett, A., and J. T. Checkel, J. T., eds. 2015. *Process Tracing: From Metaphor to Analytical Tool*. Cambridge: Cambridge University Press.

Berlin, G. 2016. *Learning from Experience: A Guide to Social Impact Bond Investing*. New York: MDRC. http://www.mdrc.org/sites/default/files/Learning_from_Experience_SIB.pdf.

Bernstein, H. 1992. "Agrarian Structures and Change: India." In *Rural Livelihoods: Crises and Responses*, edited by H. Bernstein, B. Crow, and H. Johnson. Oxford: Oxford University Press.

Bickman, L. 1987. "The Functions of Program Theory." In *Using Program Theory in Evaluation, New Directions for Program Evaluation*, edited by L. Bickman. San Francisco: Jossey-Bass.

Blackwell, T. H., and J. S. Kaufman. 2002. "Response Time Effectiveness: Comparison of Response Time and Survival in an Urban Emergency Medical Services System." *Academic Emergency Medicine* 9 (4): 288–95.

Blackwell, T. H., J. A. Kline, J. Willis, and G. M. Hicks. 2009. "Lack of Association Between Prehospital Response Times and Patient Outcomes." *Prehospital Emergency Care* 13 (4): 444–50.

Blalock, A. B. 1999. "Evaluation Research and the Performance Management Movement." *Evaluation* 5 (2): 117–49.

Blumenthal, B. 2001. "Improving the Impact of Nonprofit Consulting." *Journal of Nonprofit Management* (Summer): 1–17.

Blumenthal, B. 2003. *Investing in Capacity Building: A Guide to High-Impact Approaches*. New York: The Foundation Center.

Bonbright, D., D. Campbell, and L. Nguyen. 2009. *The 21st Century Potential of Constituency Voice: Opportunities for Reform in the United States Human Services Sector*. Alliance for Children & Families, United Neighborhood Centers of America, and Keystone Accountability.

Bourdieu, P. 1977. *Outline of a Theory of Practice*. Translated by R. Nice. Cambridge: Cambridge University Press.

Bradach, J., and A. Grindle. 2014. *Transformative Scale: The Future of Growing What Works*. The Bridgespan Group and Stanford Social Innovation Review. https:// www.bridgespan.org/insights/library/transformative-scale/transformative -scale-nine-pathways.

Brady, H. E., and D. Collier, eds. 2004. *Rethinking Social Inquiry: Diverse Tools, Shared Standards*. Lanham, MD: Rowman and Littlefield.

Breman, J. 1985. *Of Peasants, Migrants and Paupers: Rural Labour Circulation and Capitalist Production in West India*. Delhi: Oxford University Press.

Brest, P. 2012. "A Decade of Outcome-Oriented Philanthropy." *Stanford Social Innovation Review* (Spring): 42–47.

Brest, P., and K. Born. 2013. "When Can Impact Investing Create Real Impact?" *Stanford Social Innovation Review* (Fall).

Brest, P., and H. Harvey. 2008. *Money Well Spent: A Strategic Plan for Smart Philanthropy*. New York: Bloomberg.

Brest, P., and H. Harvey. 2018. *Money Well Spent: A Strategic Plan for Smart Philanthropy, Second Edition*. Stanford, CA: Stanford University Press.

Brest, P., H. Harvey, and K. Low. 2009. Calculated Impact. *Stanford Social Innovation Review* (Winter): 50–56.

Bromley, P., and J. W. Meyer. 2014. "'They Are All Organizations': The Cultural Roots of Blurring between the Nonprofit, Business, and Government Sectors." *Administration and Society*. doi:10.1177/0095399714548268.

Brown, D. L. 2009. "At Miriam's Kitchen, Michelle Obama Feeds and Mingles with the Homeless." *Washington Post*, March 5. http://voices.washingtonpost .com/44/2009/03/05/at_miriams_kitchen_michelle_ob.html.

Brown, L. D., A. Ebrahim, and S. Batliwala. 2012. "Governing International Advocacy NGOs." *World Development* 40 (6): 1098–108.

Bryson, J. M., B. C. Crosby, and M. M. Stone. 2006. "The Design and Implementation of Cross-Sector Collaborations: Propositions from the Literature." *Public Administration Review* 66 (s1): 44–55.

Burns, D. 2012. "Participatory Systemic Inquiry." *IDS Bulletin* 43 (3): 88–100.

Burns, D., and S. Worsley. 2015. *Navigating Complexity in International Development: Facilitating Sustainable Change at Scale*. Rugby, UK: Practical Action Publishing.

Burt, M. R. 2003. "Chronic Homelessness: Emergence of a Public Policy." *Fordham Urban Law Journal* 30: 1267–79.

Buteau, E., and J. Glickman. 2018. *Understanding and Sharing What Works: The State of Foundation Practice.* Center for Effective Philanthropy. https://cep.org/portfolio/ understanding-sharing-what-works-the-state-of-foundation-practice/ (accessed November 8, 2018).

Camerer, C. F., A. Dreber, E. Forsell, T.-H. Ho, J. Huber, M. Johannesson, M. Kirchler, et al. 2016. "Evaluating Replicability of Laboratory Experiments in Economics." *Science* 351 (6280): 1433–36.

Campbell, D. 2002. "Outcomes Assessment and the Paradox of Nonprofit Accountability." *Nonprofit Management and Leadership* 12 (3): 243–59.

Campbell, S., and P. Uvin. 2015. "The Burundi Leadership Training Program." In *Across the Lines of Conflict: Facilitating Cooperation to Build Peace*, edited by M. Lund and S. McDonald, 281–312. New York: Columbia University Press.

Cardinali, D. 2015. "When Scale Means Contraction: Putting Quality Considerations First." *Nonprofit Quarterly* (November 11).

Carr, M., and M. A. Chen. 2001. *Globalization and the Informal Economy: How Global Trade and Investment Impact on the Working Poor*. Geneva: International Labour Office, Employment Sector. https://www.ilo.org/wcmsp5/groups/public/---ed _emp/documents/publication/wcms_122053.pdf.

Cels, S., J. De Jong, and F. Nauta. 2012. "Just a Tool? Implementing the Vulnerability Index in New Orleans." In *Agents of Change: Strategy and Tactics for Social Innovation*, 95–114. Washington, DC: Brookings Institution.

Center for Effective Philanthropy. 2004. *Listening to Grantees: What Nonprofits Value in Their Foundation Funders*. Cambridge, MA: Center for Effective Philanthropy

(CEP). http://www.effectivephilanthropy.org/wp-content/uploads/2014/01/ListeningtoGrantees.pdf .

Center for Global Development. 2006. *When Will We Ever Learn? Improving Lives through Impact Evaluation.* Washington, DC: Evaluation Gap Working Group, Center for Global Development.

Center for Global Development. 2015. *MCC at Ten: Papers and Briefs.* Washington, DC: Center for Global Development. https://www.cgdev.org/page/mcc-ten.

Center for Global Development. 2017. *Foreign Assistance Agency Brief: Millennium Challenge Corporation.* Washington, DC: Center for Global Development.

Center for Theory of Change. 2014. Theory of Change. http://www.theoryofchange.org.

Chamberlin, A. 2018. "The Role of Pay-for-Success Mechanisms within Capital Markets for Social Change in France and the US." MA thesis, Tufts University, Medford, MA. https://dl.tufts.edu/catalog/tufts:sd.0000785.

Chambers, R. 1983. *Rural Development: Putting the Last First.* London: Routledge.

Chambers, R. 1994. "Participatory Rural Appraisal (PRA): Analysis of Experience." *World Development* 22 (10): 1253–68.

Chambers, R., D. Karlan, M. Ravallion, and P. Rogers. 2009. *Designing Impact Evaluations: Different Perspectives* (Working Paper 4). International Initiative for Impact Evaluation.

Chambers, R., N. C. Saxena, and T. Shah. 1989. *To the Hands of the Poor: Water and Trees.* New Delhi: Oxford and IBH Publishing.

Chapman, C. S. 1997. "Reflections on a Contingent View of Accounting." *Accounting, Organizations and Society* 22 (2): 189–205.

Charmes, J. 1998. *Women Working in the Informal Sector in Africa: New Methods and New Data.* United Nations Statistics Division; Gender and Development Programme of the United Nations Development Programme (UNDP); and Women in Informal Employment: Globalizing and Organizing (WIEGO).

Chen, H. T. 1990. *Theory-driven Evaluation.* Thousand Oaks, CA: Sage.

Chen, M. A. 2012. *The Informal Economy: Definitions, Theories and Policies.* WIEGO Working Paper No. 1.

Chen, M. A., R. Jhabvala, and F. Lund. 2001. *Supporting Workers in the Informal Economy: A Policy Framework.* Geneva: International Labour Office, Employment Sector. http://www.ilo.org/wcmsp5/groups/public/---ed_emp/documents/publication/wcms_122055.pdf.

Chenhall, R. H. 2003. "Management Control Systems Design within Its Organizational Context: Findings from Contingency-Based Research and Directions for the Future." *Accounting, Organizations and Society* 28: 127–68.

Chenhall, R. H. 2006. "The Contingent Design of Performance Measures." In *Contemporary Issues in Management Accounting*, edited by A. Bhimani, 92–116. Oxford: Oxford University Press.

Chertavian, G. 2012. *A Year Up: How a Pioneering Program Teaches Young Adults Real Skills for Real Jobs-With Real Success.* New York: Viking.

Choudhury, D. 2014. *Poverty Profile of Ziqitza's Clients.* Grameen Foundation India. http://acumen.org/content/uploads/2014/09/ZHL-PPI-study-final.pdf.

Choudhury, N. 1986. "Responsibility Accounting and Controllability." *Accounting and Business Research* 16 (63): 189–98.

Clark, C., J. Emerson, and B. Thornley. 2015. *The Impact Investor: Lessons in Leadership and Strategy for Collaborative Capitalism.* San Francisco: Wiley.

Coffman, J. 2009. *A User's Guide to Advocacy Evaluation Planning.* Cambridge, MA: Harvard Family Research Project. http://www.hfrp.org.

Coffman, J., and T. Beer. 2015. *The Advocacy Strategy Framework: A Tool for Articulating an Advocacy Theory of Change.* Center for Evaluation Innovation. http://www.evaluationinnovation.org/publications/advocacy-strategy-framework.

Cole, S., V. K. Rangan, A. Ebrahim, and C. R. Brumme. 2018. *Acumen Fund: Managing Towards Impact* (Case Number 218-086). Boston: Harvard Business School Publishing.

Commission of the European Communities. 1993. *Project Cycle Management: Integrated Approach and Logical Framework.* Brussels: Commission of the European Communities.

Commission of the European Communities, International Monetary Fund, Organisation for Economic Co-operation and Development, United Nations, and World Bank. 2008. *System of National Accounts, 2008.* New York: United Nations.

Coordinated Entry. 2016. District of Columbia Coordinated Assessment and Housing Placement October 2016 Update. http://www.coordinatedentry.com/uploads/2/9/8/5/29850959/coordinated_entry_october_2016_update.pdf.

COWI and Atkins. 2013. *Sustainable Community-Based Approaches to Livelihoods Enhancement (SCALE)—Final End Term Evaluation.* Brussels, Belgium, and Peterborough, UK: COWI Belgium and WS Atkins International Ltd.

Crutchfield, L. R., and H. M. Grant. 2008. *Forces for Good: The Six Practices of High-Impact Nonprofits.* San Francisco: Jossey-Bass.

Culhane, D. P., and T. Byrne. 2010. *Ending Chronic Homelessness: Cost-Effective Opportunities for Interagency Collaboration.* White Paper commissioned by the New York State Office of Mental Health and New York City Department of Homeless Services.

Culhane, D. P., S. Metraux, and T. Hadley. 2002. "Public Service Reductions Associated with Placement of Homeless Persons with Severe Mental Illness in Supportive Housing." *Housing Policy Debate* 13 (1): 107–63.

Davies, R., and J. Dart. 2005. *The 'Most Significant Change' (MSC) Technique: A Guide to Its Use.* BetterEvaluation. http://www.mande.co.uk/wp-content/uploads/2005/MSCGuide.pdf.

Dear, A., A. Helbitz, R. Khare, R. Lotan, J. Newman, G. C. Sims, and A. Zaroulis. 2016. *Social Impact Bonds: The Early Years.* Social Finance. http://socialfinance

.org/content/uploads/2016/07/SIBs-Early-Years_Social-Finance_2016 _Final.pdf.

Deming, W. E. 1986. *Out of the Crisis*. Cambridge, MA: MIT Press.

Democracy Fund. 2016. Systems Mapping Terms. http://www.democracyfund .org/media/uploaded/SystemsMapping_Glossary_2016june21.pdf.

Demski, J. S. 1976. "Uncertainty and Evaluation Based on Controllable Performance." *Journal of Accounting Research* 14 (2): 230–45.

Deoras, N. P. 2014. "An Ambulance in Need Is Noble Business Indeed." *Business Standard*, May 3. http://www.business-standard.com/article/companies/an -ambulance-in-need-is-noble-business-indeed-114050300919_1.html.

Department of Housing and Urban Development. 2015. *Homeless Emergency Assistance and Rapid Transition to Housing: Defining "Chronically Homeless."* https://www .hudexchange.info/resources/documents/Defining-Chronically-Homeless -Final-Rule.pdf.

Department of Housing and Urban Development. 2016. *2016 Annual Homeless Assessment Report (AHAR) to Congress*. https://www.hudexchange.info/resource/ 3031/pit-and-hic-data-since-2007/.

Dichter, S., T. Adams, and A. Ebrahim. 2016. "The Power of Lean Data." *Stanford Social Innovation Review* (Winter).

District of Columbia Interagency Council on Homelessness (DCICH). 2015. *Homeward DC: Strategic Plan 2015–2020*. Washington, DC: District of Columbia Interagency Council on Homelessness.

Dobbie, W., and R. G. Fryer. 2009. *Are High Quality Schools Enough to Close the Achievement Gap? Evidence from a Social Experiment in Harlem* (NBER Working Paper No. 15473). Cambridge, MA: National Bureau of Economic Research. http:// www.nber.org/papers/w15473.

Dogbe, T. D., and S. Annan. 2015. *Addressing the Occupational Health and Safety (OHS) Needs of Informal Workers: Market Traders and Street Vendors in Accra, Ghana*. Unpublished report, Women in Informal Employment: Globalizing and Organizing.

Drummond, M., D. Brixner, M. Gold, P. Kind, A. McGuire, E. Nord, and Consensus Development. 2009. "Toward a Consensus on the QALY." *Value in Health* 12: S31–S35. doi:10.1111/j.1524-4733.2009.00522.x.

Earl, S., F. Carden, and T. Smutylo. 2001. *Outcome Mapping: Building Learning and Reflection into Development*. Ottawa: International Development Research Centre.

Ebrahim, A. 2002. "Information Struggles: The Role of Information in the Reproduction of NGO-Funder Relations." *Nonprofit and Voluntary Sector Quarterly* 31 (1): 85–113.

Ebrahim, A. 2003a. "Making Sense of Accountability: Conceptual Perspectives for Northern and Southern Nonprofits." *Nonprofit Management and Leadership* 14 (2): 191–212.

Ebrahim, A. 2003b. *NGOs and Organizational Change: Discourse, Reporting and Learning.* Cambridge: Cambridge University Press.

Ebrahim, A. 2005. "Accountability Myopia: Losing Sight of Organizational Learning." *Nonprofit and Voluntary Sector Quarterly* 34 (1): 56–87.

Ebrahim, A. 2016. "The Many Faces of Nonprofit Accountability." In *The Jossey-Bass Handbook of Nonprofit Leadership and Management (4th Edition)*, edited by D. O. Renz, 102–124. San Francisco: Wiley.

Ebrahim, A., J. Battilana, and J. Mair. 2014. "The Governance of Social Enterprises: Mission Drift and Accountability Challenges in Hybrid Organizations." *Research in Organizational Behavior* 34: 81–100.

Ebrahim, A., and S. Herz. 2011. "The World Bank and Democratic Accountability: The Role of Civil Society." In *Building Global Democracy? Civil Society and Accountable Global Governance*, edited by J. A. Scholte, 58–77. Cambridge: Cambridge University Press.

Ebrahim, A., and V. K. Rangan. 2010. *The Millennium Challenge Corporation and Ghana* (Case Number 310-025). Boston: Harvard Business School Publishing.

Ebrahim, A., and V. K. Rangan. 2011. *Acumen Fund: Measurement in Impact Investing (A)* (Case Number 310-011). Boston: Harvard Business School Publishing.

Ebrahim, A., and V. K. Rangan. 2014. "What Impact: A Framework for Measuring the Scale and Scope of Social Performance." *California Management Review* 56 (3): 118–41.

Ebrahim, A., and C. Ross. 2010. *The Robin Hood Foundation* (Case Number 310-031). Boston: Harvard Business School Publishing.

Ebrahim, A., and E. Weisband, E., eds. 2007. *Global Accountabilities: Participation, Pluralism, and Public Ethics.* Cambridge: Cambridge University Press.

Eckhart-Queenan, J., J. Allen, and J. Tuomala. 2013. *Stop Starving Scale: Unlocking the Potential of Global NGOs.* Boston: Bridgespan Group.

Eckhart-Queenan, J., M. Etzel, and S. Prasad. 2016. "Pay-What-It-Takes Philanthropy." *Stanford Social Innovation Review* (Summer): 37–41.

Economic Roundtable. 2009. *Where We Sleep: Costs When Homeless and Housed in Los Angeles.* Los Angeles: Economic Roundtable. http://shnny.org/uploads/Where_We_Sleep.pdf.

Economist. 2018. "Free Exchange: Many Microeconomic Results Are Shaky." *The Economist.* economist.com/micro2018.

Edwards, M., and D. Hulme. 1996a. "Too Close for Comfort? The Impact of Official Aid on Nongovernmental Organizations." *World Development* 24 (6): 961–73.

Edwards, M., and D. Hulme, eds. 1996b. *Beyond the Magic Bullet: NGO Performance and Accountability in the Post-Cold War World.* West Hartford, CT: Kumarian.

Eikenberry, A. M., and J. D. Kluver. 2004. "The Marketization of the Nonprofit Sector: Civil Society at Risk?" *Public Administration Review* 64: 132–40.

Eisenberg, P. 2004. *Challenges for Nonprofits and Philanthropy: The Courage to Change: Three Decades of Reflections by Pablo Eisenberg.* Edited by Stacy Palmer. Lebanon, NH: University Press of New England for Tufts University Press.

Emerson, J. 2015. "The Metrics Myth." http://www.blendedvalue.org/the-metrics-myth.

Espeland, W. N., and M. L. Stevens. 2008. "A Sociology of Quantification." *European Journal of Sociology* 49 (3): 401–36.

European Commission. 2001. *CMNR Final Review and Appraisal Mission Report.* Brussels: Commission of the European Communities.

European Evaluation Society. 2007. *EES Statement: The Importance of a Methodologically Diverse Approach to Impact Evaluation—Specifically with Respect to Development Aid and Development Interventions.* Nijnerk, The Netherlands: EES Secretariat.

Fals-Borda, O. 1988. *Knowledge and People's Power.* New Delhi: Indian Social Institute.

Fals-Borda, O., and A. Rahman, eds. 1991. *Action and Knowledge: Breaking the Monopoly with PAR.* New York: Apex.

Faust, D. G. 2013. Letter to the Editor. *New York Times,* February 22.

Feigenbaum, A. V. 1983. *Total Quality Control (Third ed.).* New York: McGraw-Hill.

Ferguson, J. 1990. *The Anti-Politics Machine: "Development," Depoliticization, and Bureaucratic Power in Lesotho.* Cambridge: Cambridge University Press.

Ferran, L. 1998. *Note on Concepts and Techniques for Estimating the Contribution of Women in the Informal Sector.* United Nations Statistics Division; Gender and Development Programme of the United Nations Development Programme (UNDP); and Women in Informal Employment: Globalizing and Organizing (WIEGO). http://www.wiego.org/sites/wiego.org/files/publications/files/Ferran_Contribution_Women_Workers_1998.pdf.

Foucault, M. 1980. "Two Lectures: 7 January 1976, 14 January 1976." Translated by A. Fontana and P. Pasquino. In *Power/Knowledge: Selected Interviews and Other Writings 1972–1977,* edited by C. Gordon, 78–108. New York: Pantheon.

Foucault, M. 1984. "Nietzsche, Genealogy, History." Translated by D. F. Bouchard and S. Simon. In *The Foucault Reader,* edited by P. Rabinow, 76–100. New York: Pantheon.

Foucault, M. 1991. "Governmentality." In *The Foucault Effect: Studies in Governmentality,* edited by G. Burchell, C. Gordon, and P. Miller. Chicago: University of Chicago.

Fowler, A. 2000. "NGDOs as a Moment in History: Beyond Aid to Social Entrepreneurship or Civic Innovation?" *Third World Quarterly* 21 (4): 637–54.

Freire, P. 1970. *Pedagogy of the Oppressed.* New York: Herder and Herder.

Freire, P. 1973. *Education for Critical Consciousness.* New York: Seabury.

Frumkin, P. 2002. *On Being Nonprofit: A Conceptual and Policy Primer.* Cambridge, MA: Harvard University Press.

Frumkin, P. 2006. *Strategic Giving: The Art and Science of Philanthropy.* Chicago: University of Chicago.

Funnell, S. 1997. "Program Logic: An Adaptable Tool for Designing and Evaluating Programs." *Evaluation News and Comment* 6 (1): 5–7.

Galbraith, J. R. 1973. *Designing Complex Organizations*. New York: Addison-Wesley.

George, A., and A. Bennett. 2005. *Case Studies and Theory Development in the Social Sciences*. Cambridge, MA: MIT Press.

Gerring, J. 2007. *Case Study Research: Principles and Practices*. Cambridge: Cambridge University Press.

Ghosh, J., and K. Bharadwaj. 1992. "Poverty and Employment in India." In *Rural Livelihoods: Crises and Responses*, edited by H. Bernstein, B. Crow, and H. Johnson. Oxford: Oxford University Press.

Giddens, A. 1984. *The Constitution of Society: Outline of a Theory of Structuration*. Berkeley: University of California Press.

Giraud, F., P. Langevin, and C. Mendoza. 2008. "Justice as a Rationale for the Controllability Principle: A Study of Managers' Opinions." *Management Accounting Research* 19 (1): 32–44.

Gladwell, M. 2006. "Million-Dollar Murray: Why Problems Like Homelessness May Be Easier to Solve Than to Manage." *New Yorker*, February 13.

Glasrud, B. 2001. "The Muddle of Outcome Measurement: Be Careful How You Measure Programs." *Nonprofit World* 19 (6): 35–37.

Global Impact Investing Network. 2018. *Annual Impact Investor Survey 2018*. New York: GIIN. https://thegiin.org/research/publication/annualsurvey2018.

Glouberman, S., and B. Zimmerman. 2002. *Complicated and Complex Systems: What Would Successful Reform of Medicare Look Like?* Commission on the Future of Health Care in Canada. http://publications.gc.ca/collections/Collection/CP32-79-8-2002E.pdf.

Gonzales, R. P., G. R. Cummings, H. A. Phelan, M. S. Mulekar, and C. B. Rodning. 2009. "Does Increased Emergency Medical Services Prehospital Time Affect Patient Mortality in Rural Motor Vehicle Crashes? A Statewide Analysis." *American Journal of Surgery* 197: 30–34.

Goodman, P. S., and J. M. Pennings, eds. 1977. *New Perspectives on Organizational Effectiveness*. San Francisco: Jossey-Bass.

Gramsci, A. 1971. *Selections from the Prison Notebooks*. New York: International Publishers.

Greene, J. 1999. "The Inequality of Performance Measurements." *Evaluation* 5 (2): 160–72.

Grossman, A., and C. Ross. 2012. *United Way* (Case No. 9-310-014). Boston: Harvard Business Publishing.

Gugerty, M. K., and D. Karlan. 2014. "Measuring Impact Isn't for Everyone." *Stanford Social Innovation Review* (April 2).

Gulati, R., P. Puranam, and M. Tushman. 2012. "Meta-Organization Design: Rethinking Design in Interorganizational and Community Contexts." *Strategic Management Journal* 33: 571–86.

Gulati, R., and H. Singh. 1998. "The Architecture of Cooperation: Managing Coordination Costs and Appropriation Concerns in Strategic Alliances." *Administrative Science Quarterly* 43 (4): 781–814.

Gustafsson-Wright, E., I. Boggild-Jones, D. Segell, and J. Durland. 2017. *Impact Bonds in Developing Countries: Early Learnings from the Field.* Center for Universal Education, Brookings Institution. https://www.brookings.edu/wp-content/uploads/2017/09/impact-bonds-in-developing-countries_web.pdf.

Guth, R. A. 2010. "Gates Rethinks His War on Polio." *Wall Street Journal*, April 23.

Hall, P. D. 2004. A Historical Perspective on Evaluation in Foundations. In *Foundations and Evaluation: Contexts and Practices for Effective Philanthropy*, edited by M. T. Braverman, N. A. Constantine, and J. K. Slater. San Francisco: Jossey-Bass.

Hall, P. D. 2005. *A Solution is a Product in Search of a Problem: A History of Foundations and Evaluation Research.* http://www.hks.harvard.edu/fs/phall/EVALUATION .pdf.

Hampshire, J. 1991. *Aga Khan Rural Support Programme India: Review of Programme Planning, Budgeting and Monitoring Systems.* West Sussex, UK: Information Technology and Agricultural Development Ltd.

Hanleybrown, F., J. Kania, and M. Kramer. 2012. "Channeling Change: Making Collective Impact Work." *Stanford Social Innovation Review* (January).

Hansmann, H. 1996. *The Ownership of Enterprise.* Cambridge, MA: Belknap.

Harlem Children's Zone. 2011. *2010–2011 Biennial Report.* New York: Harlem Children's Zone.

Harvey, H. 2016. "Why I Regret Pushing Strategic Philanthropy." *Chronicle of Philanthropy*, April 4. https://philanthropy-com.ezp-prod1.hul.harvard.edu/article/Opinion-Why-I-Regret-Pushing/235924.

Homeless Emergency Assistance and Rapid Transition to Housing Act (S. 896 HEARTH Act) of 2009. https://www.hudexchange.info/resource/1717/s -896-hearth-act/ (accessed November 6, 2019).

Hirschman, A. O. 1970. *Exit, Voice, and Loyalty: Responses to Decline in Firms, Organizations, and States.* Cambridge, MA: Harvard University Press.

Hopwood, A. G. 1980. "The Organizational and Behavioral Aspects of Budgeting and Control." In *Topics in Management Accounting*, edited by J. Arnold, B. Carsberg, and R. Scapens, 221–40). Oxford: Philip Allen.

Hussmanns, R. 2001. "Informal Sector and Informal Employment: Elements of a Conceptual Framework." Paper presented at the Fifth Meeting of the Expert Group on Informal Sector Statistics (Delhi Group), New Delhi, September 19–21, 2001.

Hwang, H., and W. W. Powell. 2009. "The Rationalization of Charity: The Influences of Professionalism in the Nonprofit Sector." *Administrative Science Quarterly* 54: 268–98.

ICF International. 2010. *Communities in Schools National Evaluation: Five Year Summary Report*. Fairfax, VA: ICF International.

ILO. 2002a. *Decent Work and the Informal Economy, International Labour Conference 90th Session 2002, Report VI*. Geneva: International Labour Organization.

ILO. 2002b. *Women and Men in the Informal Economy: A Statistical Picture*. Geneva: International Labour Office, International Labour Organization.

ILO. 2013a. *Measuring Informality: A Statistical Manual on the Informal Sector and Informal Employment*. Geneva: International Labour Office, International Labour Organization.

ILO. 2013b. *Transitioning from the Informal to the Formal Economy, International Labour Conference, 103rd Session 2014, Report V(1)*. Geneva: International Labour Organization. https://www.ilo.org/wcmsp5/groups/public/---ed_norm/---relconf/documents/meetingdocument/wcms_218128.pdf.

ILO. 2013c. *Women and Men in the Informal Economy: A Statistical Picture (second edition)*. Geneva: International Labour Office, International Labour Organization.

ILO. 2015. *Recommendation 204: Recommendation Concerning the Transition form the Informal to the Formal Economy, Adopted by the Conference at its One Hundred and Fourth Session, Geneva, 12 June 2015*. Geneva: International Labour Organization. https://www.ilo.org/wcmsp5/groups/public/---ed_norm/---relconf/documents/meetingdocument/wcms_377774.pdf.

Imbens, G. W., and D. B. Rubin. 2015. *Causal Inference for Statistics, Social, and Biomedical Sciences: An Introduction*. New York: Cambridge University Press.

Inclusive Business Action Network. 2014. "Finding Out about Clients—Groundbreaking Work by ZHL Ambulance Service, Acumen and Grameen." http://www.inclusivebusinesshub.org/editor-s-choice-october-finding-out-about-clients-groundbreaking/.

Independent Evaluation Group. 2011. *Impact Evaluations in Agriculture: An Assessment of the Evidence*. Washington, DC: World Bank.

Ioannidis, J. P. A., T. D. Stanley, and H. Doucouliagos. 2017. "The Power of Bias in Economics Research." *Economic Journal* 127 (605): F236–F265.

IPA. 2016. *Impact Measurement with the CART Principles*. Innovations for Poverty Action (IPA). http://www.poverty-action.org/goldilocks.

Ishikawa, K. 1985. *What Is Total Quality Control? The Japanese Way*. Englewood Cliffs, NJ: Prentice-Hall.

Ittner, C. D. 2014. "Strengthening Causal Inferences in Positivist Field Studies." *Accounting, Organizations and Society* 39: 545–49.

J. P. Morgan and GIIN. 2015. *Eyes on the Horizon: The Impact Investor Survey*. New York: J. P. Morgan and the Global Impact Investing Network.

Jaeger, D. A., T. J. Joyce, and R. Kaestner. 2016. "Does Reality TV Induce Real Effects? On the Questionable Association Between 16 and Pregnant and Teenage

Childbearing." IZA Discussion Paper No. 10317. http://ftp.iza.org/dp10317.pdf.

Jones, H. 2009. *The "Gold Standard" Is Not a Silver Bullet for Evaluation* (ODI Opinions 127). London: Overseas Development Institute.

Jones, M. B. 2007. "The Multiple Sources of Mission Drift." *Nonprofit and Voluntary Sector Quarterly* 36 (2): 299–307.

Jones, N., H. Jones, L. Steer, and A. Datta. 2009. *Improving Impact Evaluation Production and Use* (Working Paper 300). London: Overseas Development Institute.

Kane, R., C. Levine, C. Orians, and C. Reinelt. 2017. *Contribution Analysis in Policy Work: Assessing Advocacy's Influence.* Center for Evaluation Innovation. http://www.evaluationinnovation.org/sites/default/files/Contribution Analysis_0.pdf.

Kania, J., and M. Kramer. 2011. "Collective Impact." *Stanford Social Innovation Review* (Winter): 36–41.

Kania, J., M. Kramer, and P. Russell. 2014. "Strategic Philanthropy for a Complex World." *Stanford Social Innovation Review* (Summer).

Kaplan, R. S. 2001. "Strategic Performance Measurement and Management in Nonprofit Organizations." *Nonprofit Management and Leadership* 11 (3): 353–70.

Kaplan, R. S. 2010. "Conceptual Foundations of the Balanced Scorecard." *Harvard Business School Working Paper 10–074.*

Kaplan, R. S., and D. P. Norton. 1996. *The Balanced Scorecard: Measures that Drive Performance.* Boston: Harvard Business School Publishing.

Kaplan, R. S., and D. P. Norton. 2004. *Strategy Maps: Converting Intangible Assets into Tangible Outcomes.* Boston: Harvard Business School Publishing.

Kearney, M. S., and P. B. Levine. 2014. *Media Influences on Social Outcomes: The Impact of MTV's 16 and Pregnant on Teen Childbearing.* Cambridge, MA: National Bureau of Economic Research.

Kearns, K. P. 1996. *Managing for Accountability: Preserving the Public Trust in Nonprofit Organizations.* San Francisco: Jossey-Bass.

Keating, E. 2003. "Is There Enough Overhead in This Grant?" *Nonprofit Quarterly* (March).

Keystone. 2009. *Developing a Theory of Change* (Impact Planning and Learning Guide 2). London: Keystone: Accountability for Social Change. http://www.keystoneaccountability.org/sites/default/files/2 Developing a theory of change.pdf.

Khagram, S., C. Thomas, C. Lucero, and S. Mathes. 2009. "Evidence for Development Effectiveness." *Journal of Development Effectiveness* 1 (3): 247–70.

Kim, P., and J. Bradach. 2012. "Why More Nonprofits are Getting Bigger." *Stanford Social Innovation Review* (2).

Klugman, B. 2014a. *Summary of External Evaluation of WIEGO for SIDA 2011–2014.* Swedish International Development Agency (SIDA) and Women in Informal Employment: Globalizing and Organizing (WIEGO).

Klugman, B. 2014b. *WIEGO Outcomes Evaluation 2011—Mid-2014, Report to SIDA*. Swedish International Development Agency (SIDA) and Women in Informal Employment: Globalizing and Organizing (WIEGO).

Knight, V. A., and P. R. Harper. 2012. "Modelling Emergency Medical Services with Phase-Type Distributions." *Health Systems* 1 (1): 58–68.

Knowlton, L. W., and C. C. Phillips. 2013. "Creating Program Logic Models." In *The Logic Model Guidebook: Better Strategies for Great Results (Second edition)*, 35–48. Thousand Oaks, CA: Sage.

Knutsen, W. L., and R. S. Brower. 2010. "Managing Expressive and Instrumental Accountabilities in Nonprofit and Voluntary Organizations: A Qualitative Investigation." *Nonprofit and Voluntary Sector Quarterly* 39 (4): 588–610.

Koonce, L., N. Seybert, and J. Smith. 2011. "Causal Reasoning in Financial Reporting and Voluntary Disclosure." *Accounting, Organizations and Society* 36: 209–25.

Koppell, J. G. S. 2005. "Pathologies of Accountability: ICANN and the Challenge of "Multiple Accountabilities Disorder." *Public Administration Review* 65 (1): 94–108.

Korten, F. F., and R. Y. Siy, eds. 1988. *Transforming a Bureaucracy: The Experience of the Philippine National Irrigation Administration*. West Hartford, CT: Kumarian.

Kramer, M., R. Graves, J. Hirschhorn, and L. Fiske. 2007. *From Insight to Action: New Directions in Foundation Evaluation*. FSG Social Impact Advisors. https://www.issuelab.org/resources/1391/1391.pdf.

Kramer, M. R. 2005. *Measuring Innovation: Evaluation in the Field of Social Entrepreneurship*. Skoll Foundation and FSG Social Impact Advisors. https://www.issuelab.org/resources/10220/10220.pdf.

Krauskopf, J., and B. Chen. 2010. "Administering Services and Managing Contracts: The Dual Role of Government Human Services Officials." *Journal of Policy Analysis and Management* 29 (3): 5–8.

Lamont, M. 2012. "Toward a Comparative Sociology of Valuation and Evaluation." *Annual Review of Sociology* 38 (21): 1–21.

Leeuw, F., and J. Vaessen. 2009. *Impact Evaluations and Development: NONIE Guidance on Impact Evaluation*. Washington, DC: Network of Networks on Impact Evaluation (NONIE). http://documents.worldbank.org/curated/en/411821468313779505/Impact-evaluations-and-development-NONIE-guidance-on-impact-evaluation.

Lemire, S. T., S. B. Nielsen, and L. Dybdal. 2012. "Making Contribution Analysis Work: A Practical Framework for Handling Influencing Factors and Alternative Explanations." *Evaluation* 18 (3): 294–309.

Lepoutre, J., R. Justo, S. Terjesen, and N. Bosma. 2013. "Designing a Global Standardized Methodology for Measuring Social Entrepreneurial Activity: The Global Entrepreneurship Monitor Social Entrepreneurship Study." *Small Business Economics* 40: 693–714.

Lerner, J. S., and P. E. Tetlock. 1999. Accounting for the Effects of Accountability. *Psychological Bulletin* 125 (2): 255–75.

Lewis, D., and S. Madon. 2003. "Information Systems and Non-governmental Development Organizations (NGOs): Advocacy, Organizational Learning and Accountability in a Southern NGO." *Information Society* 20 (2): 117–26.

Light, P. C. 2004. *Sustaining Nonprofit Performance: The Case for Capacity Building and the Evidence to Support It.* Washington, DC: Brookings Institution.

Lindenberg, M., and C. Bryant. 2001. *Going Global: Transforming Relief and Development NGOs.* Bloomfield, CT: Kumarian.

Lindgren, L. 2001. "The Nonprofit Sector Meets the Performance-Management Movement: A Programme-Theory Approach." *Evaluation* 7 (3): 285–303.

Lukka, K. 2014. "Exploring the Possibilities for Causal Explanation in Interpretive Research." *Accounting, Organizations and Society* 39: 559–66.

Magretta, J. 2011. *Understanding Michael Porter.* Boston: Harvard Business Publishing.

Mair, J., and L. Hehenberger. 2014. "Front Stage and Back Stage Convening: The Transition from Opposition to Mutualistic Co-Existence in Organizational Philanthropy." *Academy of Management Journal* 57 (4): 1174–200.

March, J. G. 1991. "Exploration and Exploitation in Organizational Learning." *Organization Science* 2 (1): 71–87.

Mares, A. S., and R. A. Rosenheck. 2010. "Twelve-Month Client Outcomes and Service Use in a Multisite Project for Chronically Homelessness Adults." *Journal of Behavioral Health Services & Research* 37 (2): 167–83.

Mason, D. E. 1996. *Leading and Managing the Expressive Dimension: Harnessing the Hidden Power Sources of the Nonprofit Sector.* San Francisco: Jossey-Bass.

Mattsson, B., and B. Juas. 1997. "The Importance of the Time Factor in Fire and Rescue Service Operations in Sweden." *Accident Analysis and Prevention* 29 (6): 849–57.

Mayne, J. 2001. "Addressing Attribution through Contribution Analysis: Using Performance Measures Sensibly." *Canadian Journal of Program Evaluation* 16 (1): 1–24.

Mayne, J. 2008. *Contribution Analysis: An Approach to Exploring Cause And effect.* Rome: Institutional Learning and Change Initiative.

Mayne, J. 2011. "Contribution Analysis: Addressing Cause and Effect." In *Evaluating the Complex: Attribution, Contribution and Beyond*, edited by K. Forss, M. Marra, and R. Schwartz, 53–96. New Brunswick, NJ: Transaction Publishers.

Mayne, J. 2012. "Contribution Analysis: Coming of Age?" *Evaluation* 18 (3): 270–80.

McCreless, M. 2015. *A Client-Centric Approach: Impact Evaluation that Creates Value for Participants.* Cambridge, MA: Root Capital.

McCreless, M. 2017. "Toward the Efficient Impact Frontier." *Stanford Social Innovation Review* (Winter).

McKeever, B. S. 2016. *The Nonprofit Sector in Brief 2015: Public Charities, Giving, and Volunteering.* Washington, DC: Urban Institute. https://www.urban.org/sites/default/files/publication/72536/2000497-The-Nonprofit-Sector-in-Brief-2015-Public-Charities-Giving-and-Volunteering.pdf.

McKinsey & Company. 2001. *Effective Capacity Building in Nonprofit Organizations.* Reston, VA: Venture Philanthropy Partners.

McKinsey & Company. 2010. *Learning for Social Impact: What Foundations Can Do.* Social Sector Office, McKinsey & Company. http://mckinseyonsociety.com/downloads/tools/LSI/McKinsey_Learning_for_Social_Impact_white_paper.pdf.

McLaughlin, J. A., and G. B. Jordan. 1999. "Logic Models: A Tool for Telling Your Program's Performance Story." *Evaluation and Program Planning* 22: 65–72.

Meadows, D. H. 2008. *Thinking in Systems: A Primer.* White River Junction, VT: Sustainability Insititute and Chelsea Green Publishing.

Meera, S. 2013. "A Business Model around Private Ambulance Service." *The Smart CEO*, October 1.

Mehran, F. 2009. *WIEGO Impact Evaluation—Evaluator's Assessment Report: Mainstreaming the Measurement of the Informal Economy In Labour Force and Economic Statistics.* WIEGO. http://www.wiego.org/sites/default/files/publications/files/Mehran-WIEGO-Impact-Evaluation-Report-Stat.pdf.

Merchant, K. A. 1989. *Rewarding Results: Motivating Profit Center Managers.* Boston: Harvard Business School Publishing.

Merchant, K. A., and D. T. Otley. 2007. "A Review of the Literature on Control and Accountability." In *Handbook of Management Accounting Research*, edited by C. S. Chapman, A. G. Hopwood, and M. D. Shields, 785–802. Kidlington, UK: Elsevier.

Merriam-Webster Dictionary. 2018. https://www.merriam-webster.com/dictionary/emergent; https://www.merriam-webster.com/dictionary/ecosystem (all accessed November 2, 2018)

Meyer, M. W. 2002. *Rethinking Performance Measurement: Beyond the Balanced Scorecard.* Cambridge: Cambridge University Press.

Meyer, M. W., and V. Gupta. 1994. "The Performance Paradox." *Research in Organizational Behavior* 16: 306–69.

Miguel, E., and M. Kremer. 2004. "Worms: Identifying Impacts on Education and Health in the Presence of Treatment Externalities." *Econometrica* 72 (1): 159–217.

Millennium Challenge Corporation (MCC). 2012. *MCC's First Impact Evaluations: Farmer Training Activities in Five Countries.* Washington, DC: Millennium Challenge Corporation. https://assets.mcc.gov/content/uploads/2017/05/issuebrief-2012002119501-ag-impact-evals.pdf.

Millennium Challenge Corporation. 2017. Economic Rates of Return (ERR). https://www.mcc.gov/our-impact/err.

Mintzberg, H. 1978. "Patterns in Strategy Formation." *Management Science* 24 (9): 934–48.

Mintzberg, H. 1983. *Structure in Fives: Designing Effective Organizations.* Upper Saddle River, NJ: Prentice-Hall.

Miriam's Kitchen. 2016. *Performance Management Report: October 1, 2015–March 31, 2016, Quarter Two.* https://miriamskitchen.org/wp-content/uploads/2016/05/FY-16-Q2-Performance-Management-Report.pdf.

Monitor Institute. 2009. *Investing for Social and Environmental Impact: A Design for Catalyzing an Emerging Industry.* Monitor Institute. https://www.issuelab.org/resources/5744/5744.pdf.

Montesquiou, A. de, T. Sheldon, F. F. DeGiovanni, and S. M. Hashemi. 2014. *From Extreme Poverty to Sustainable Livelihoods: A Technical Guide to the Graduation Approach.* CGAP and Ford Foundation. http://www.cgap.org/sites/default/files/graduation_guide_final.pdf.

Montgomery, A. W., P. A. Dacin, and M. T. Dacin. 2012. "Collective Social Entrepreneurship: Collaboratively Shaping Social Good." *Journal of Business Ethics* 111 (3): 375–88.

Moore, M. H. 1997. *Creating Public Value: Strategic Management in Government.* Cambridge, MA: Harvard University Press.

Moore, M. H. 2000. "Managing for Value: Organizational Strategy in For-Profit, Nonprofit, and Governmental Organizations." *Nonprofit and Voluntary Sector Quarterly* 29 (1): 183–204.

Morgan, P., and A. Qualman. 1996. *Institutional and Capacity Development, Results-Based Management and Organizational Performance.* Ottawa: Prepared for the Political and Social Policies Division, Policy Branch, Canadian International Development Agency

Morino, M. 2011. *Leap of Reason: Managing to Outcomes in an Era of Scarcity.* Washington, DC: Venture Philanthropy Partners.

Mudaliar, A., A. Pineiro, R. Bass, and H. Dithrich. 2017. *The State of Impact Measurement and Management Practice, First Edition.* New York: Global Impact Investing Network. https://thegiin.org/research/publication/imm-survey.

Mulgan, R. 2000. "'Accountability': An Ever-Expanding Concept?" *Public Administration* 78 (3), 555–73.

Murray, P., and S. Ma. 2015. "The Promise of Lean Experimentation." *Stanford Social Innovation Review* (Summer).

Najam, A. 1996a. "NGO Accountability: A Conceptual Framework." *Development Policy Review* 14: 339–53.

Najam, A. 1996b. "Understanding the Third Sector: Revisiting the Prince, the Merchant, and the Citizen." *Nonprofit Management and Leadership* 7 (2): 203–21.

National Alliance to End Homelessness. 2006. *What Is Housing First? Solutions Brief.* Washington, DC: Author.

Nørreklit, H. S. O. 2000. "The Balance on the Balanced Scorecard—A Critical Analysis of Some of Its Assumptions." *Management Accounting Research* 11 (1): 65–88.

Nørreklit, H. S. O. 2003. "The Balanced Scorecard: What Is the Score? A Rhetorical Analysis of the Balanced Scorecard." *Accounting, Organizations and Society* 28 (6): 591–619.

O'Donohoe, N., C. Leijonhufvud, Y. Saltuk, A. Bugg-Levine, and M. Brandenburg. 2010. *Impact Investments: An Emerging Asset Class.* J.P. Morgan, Rockefeller Foundation, Global Impact Investing Network. https://thegiin.org/knowledge/publication/impact-investments-an-emerging-asset-class.

O'Neill, O. 2002. *A Question of Trust: The BBC Reith Lectures 2002.* Cambridge: Cambridge University Press.

O'Connell, J. 2016. "DC Mayor Targets Another $106 Million for Affordable Housing." *Washington Post*, October 10.

O'Keeffe, C., J. Nicholl, J. Turner, and S. Goodacre. 2011. "Role of Ambulance Response Times in the Survival of Patients with Out-of-Hospital Cardiac Arrest." *Emergency Medical Journal* 28: 703–6.

Organisation for Economic Co-operation and Development (OECD). 2008. *Paris Declaration on Aid Effectiveness and the Accra Agenda for Action.* Paris: Organisation for Economic Co-operation and Development. http://www.oecd.org/dataoecd/30/63/43911948.pdf.

Organisation for Economic Co-operation and Development (OECD). 2015. *Social Impact Investment: Building the Evidence Base.* Paris: Organisation for Economic Co-operation and Development.

Ospina, S., and M. Block. 2017. *2016 Report on Closeout ERRs* Millennium Challenge Corporation. https://www.mcc.gov/resources/doc/report-2016-report-closeout-errs.

Oster, S. M. 1995. *Strategic Management of Nonprofits.* Oxford: Oxford University Press.

Ostrom, E. 2010. "Beyond Markets and States: Polycentric Governance of Complex Economic Systems." *American Economic Review* 100 (3): 641–72.

Oxford Dictionaries. 2018. https://en.oxforddictionaries.com/definition/niche; https://en.oxforddictionaries.com/definition/emergent (all accessed October 28, 2018).

Oxford English Dictionary. 2018. http://www.oed.com (accessed October 28, 2018)

Padgett, D. K., B. F. Henwood, and V. Stanhope. 2007. "Housing First Services for People Who Are Homeless with Co-occurring Serious Mental Illness and Substance Abuse." *Research on Social Work Practice* 16: 74–83.

Panel on the Nonprofit Sector. (2005). *Strengthening Transparency, Governance, Accountability of Charitable Organizations: A Final Report to Congress and the Nonprofit*

Sector. Washington, DC: Independent Sector. http://www.nonprofitpanel.org/Report/final/Panel_Final_Report.pdf.

Patton, M. Q. 2011. *Developmental Evaluation: Applying Complexity Concepts to Enhance Innovation and Use*. New York: Guilford.

Pawson, R. 2013. *The Science of Evaluation: A Realist Manifesto*: London: Sage.

Pedrero, M. 1998. *Homeworkers and Homebased Work*. New York: United Nations Statistics Division.

Pell, J., J. Sirel, A. Marsden, I. Ford, and S. Cobbe. 2001. "Effect of Reducing Ambulance Response Times on Deaths from Out of Hospital Cardiac Arrest: Cohort Study." *British Medical Journal* June (322): 1385–88.

Performance Imperative. 2015. *The Performance Imperative: A Framework for Social-Sector Excellence*. Leap of Reason Ambassadors Community. http://leapofreason.org/performance-imperative/.

Pfeffer, J., and G. R. Salancik. 1978. *The External Control of Organizations: A Resource Dependence Perspective*. New York: Harper and Row.

Philanthropy Action. 2009. The Worst (and Best) Way to Pick A Charity This Year [Press release]. http://www.philanthropyaction.com/documents/Worst_Way_to_Pick_A_Charity_Dec_1_2009.pdf.

Poate, D. 1989. *AKRSP(I): Monitoring, Reporting and Impact Assessment*. West Sussex, UK: Information Technology & Agricultural Development Ltd.

Poister, T. H. 2003. *Measuring Performance in Public and Nonprofit Organizations*. San Francisco: Jossey-Bass.

Pons, P. T., J. S. Haukoos, W. Bludworth, T. Cribley, K. A. Pons, and V. J. Markovchick. 2005. "Paramedic Response Time: Does It Affect Patient Survival?" *Academic Emergency Medicine* 12 (7): 594–600.

Pons, P. T., and V. J. Markovchick. 2002. "Eight Minutes or Less: Does the Ambulance Response Time Guideline Impact Trauma Patient Outcome?" *Journal of Emergency Medicine* 23 (1): 43–48.

Porter, M. 1980. *Competitive Strategy*. New York: Free Press.

Porter, M. E., and M. R. Kramer. 1999. "Philanthropy's New Agenda: Creating Value." *Harvard Business Review* (November–December): 121–30.

Powell, W. W., D. L. Gammal, and C. Simard. 2005. "Close Encounters: The Circulation and Reception of Managerial Practices in the San Francisco Bay Area Nonprofit Community." In *Global Ideas: How Ideas, objects and Practices Travel in the Global Economy*, edited by B. Czarniawska and G. Sevón, 233–58. Copenhagen: Liber & Copenhagen Business School Press.

Power, M. 1999. *The Audit Society: Rituals of Verification*. Oxford: Oxford University Press.

Preskill, H., and S. Gopal. 2014. *Evaluating Complexity: Propositions for Improving Practice*. FSG. https://www.fsg.org/publications/evaluating-complexity.

Prieto, L., and J. A. Sacristán. 2003. "Problems and Solutions in Calculating Quality-Adjusted Life Years (QALYs)." *Health and Quality of Life Outcomes* 1 (80). doi:10.1186/1477-7525-1-80.

Prowse, M. 2007. *Aid Effectiveness: The Role of Qualitative Research in Impact Evaluation* (ODI Background Note). London: Overseas Development Institute.

Publish What You Fund. 2017. *Aid Transparency Index: 2016 Index*. Publish What You Fund, The Global Campaign for Aid Transparency. http://ati .publishwhatyoufund.org/wp-content/uploads/2016/02/ATI-2016_Report _Proof_DIGITAL.pdf.

Rahnema, M. 1997. "Participation." In *The Development Dictionary: A Guide to Knowledge as Power*, edited by W. Sachs. Hyderabad, India: Orient Longman.

Rangan, V. K. 2004. "Lofty Missions, Down-to-Earth Plans." *Harvard Business Review* 82 (3).

Rangan, V. K., and L. A. Chase. 2015. "The Payoff of Pay-for-Success." *Stanford Social Innovation Review* (Fall): 28–36.

Rietbergen-McCracken, J., and D. Narayan. 1998. *Participation and Social Assessment: Tools and Techniques*. Washington, DC: World Bank. http://documents .worldbank.org/curated/en/673361468742834292/Participation-and-social -assessment-tools-and-techniques.

Robb, C. M. 2002. *Can the Poor Influence Policy? Participatory Poverty Assessments in the Developing World*. Washington, DC: International Monetary Fund, World Bank.

Robin Hood Foundation. 2014. *Metrics Equations*. https://robinhoodorg-production .s3.amazonaws.com/uploads/2017/04/Metrics-Equations-for-Website_Sept -2014.pdf.

Robin Hood Foundation. 2017. Homepage.

Roche, C. 1999. *Impact Assessment for Development Agencies: Learning to Value Change*. Oxford: Oxfam GB.

Roduner, D., W. Schläppi, and W. Egli. 2008. *Logical Framework Approach and Outcome Mapping: A Constructive Attempt of Synthesis*. Zurich: AGRIDEA and NADEL.

Rogers, P. J. 2007. "Theory-Based Evaluation: Reflections Ten Years On." *New Directions for Evaluation* 2007 (114): 63–67.

Rogers, P. J. 2008. "Using Programme Theory to Evaluate Complicated and Complex Aspects of Interventions." *Evaluation* 14 (1): 29–48.

Rogers, P. J. 2009. "Matching Impact Evaluation Design to the Nature of the Intervention and the Purpose of the Evaluation." In *Designing Impact Evaluations: Different Perspectives, Working Paper 4*, edited by R. Chambers, D. Karlan, M. Ravallion, and P. Rogers. New Delhi: International Initiative for Impact Evaluation. http://www.3ieimpact.org/media/filer/2012/05/07/Working_Paper_4.pdf.

Rogers, P. J., A. J. Petrosino, T. Hacsi, and T. A. Huebner. 2000. "Program Theory Evaluation: Practice, Promise and Problems." In *Program Theory Evaluation:*

Challenges and Opportunities, edited by P. J. Rogers, A. J. Petrosino, T. Hacsi, and T. A. Huebner, 5–13. San Francisco: Jossey-Bass.

Rose, S., and F. Wiebe. 2015. *Focus on Results: MCC's Model inPractice (brief)*. Washington, DC: Center for Global Development. https://www.cgdev.org/publication/ft/focus-results-mccs-model-practice-brief.

Rosenheck, R., W. Kasprow, L. Frisman, and W. Liu-Mares. 2003. "Cost-Effectiveness of Supported Housing for Homeless Persons with Mental Illness." *Arch Gen Psychiatry* 60 (9): 940–51.

Rosenman, M. 2013. "Obama's College Scorecard Is a Bad Idea for All Nonprofits." *Chronicle of Philanthropy*, February 19.

Sawhill, J., and S. Harmeling. 2000. *National Campaign to Prevent Teen Pregnancy* (Case Number 9-300-105). Boston: Harvard Business School Publishing.

Sawhill, J. C., and D. Williamson. 2001. "Mission Impossible? Measuring Success in Nonprofit Organizations." *Nonprofit Management and Leadership* 11 (3): 371–86.

Schambra, W. 2013. "The Problem with Strategic Philanthropy (According to Bill Schambra)." *Nonprofit Quarterly* (August 12).

Scott, S. V., and W. J. Orlikowski. 2012. "Reconfiguring Relations of Accountability: Materialization of Social Media in the Travel Sector." *Accounting, Organizations and Society* 37 (1): 26–40.

Scott, W. R. 1977. "Effectiveness of Organizational Effectiveness Studies." In *New Perspectives on Organizational Effectiveness*, edited by P. S. Goodman and J. M. Pennings. San Francisco: Jossey-Bass.

Scott, W. R. 1992. *Organizations: Rational, Natural, and Open Systems* (3rd ed.). Englewood Cliffs, NJ: Prentice Hall.

Sen, A. 1999. *Development as Freedom*. New York: Alfred A. Knopf.

Shumway, J., J. Segal, and M. Etzel. 2018. "Pay for Systems Change: The Real Promise of Pay-for-Success Lies in Changing How Government Funds Social Services." *Stanford Social Innovation Review*.

Smith, S. R. 1999. "Government Financing of Nonprofit Activity." In *Nonprofits and Government: Collaboration and Conflict*, edited by E. T. Boris and C. E. Steuerle, 177–210. Washington, DC: Urban Institute.

Smith, S. R., and M. Lipsky. 1993. *Nonprofits for Hire: The Welfare State in the Age of Contracting*. Cambridge, MA: Harvard University Press.

Snowden, D. J., and M. E. Boone. 2007. "A Leader's Framework for Decision Making." *Harvard Business Review* (November).

Snowden, D. J., and C. F. Kurtz. 2003. "The New Dynamics of Strategy: Sense-Making in a Complex and Complicated World." *IBM Systems Journal* 42 (3): 462–83.

So, I., and A. S. Capanyola. 2016. "How Impact Investors Actually Measure Impact." *Stanford Social Innovation Review*, May 16.

So, I., and A. Staskevicius. 2015. *Measuring the "Impact" in Impact Investing.* Social Enterprise Initiative, Harard Business School. http://www.hbs.edu/socialenterprise/Documents/MeasuringImpact.pdf.

Social Impact Investment Taskforce. 2014. *Measuring Impact: Subject Paper of the Impact Measurement Working Group.* Social Impact Investment Taskforce. http://www.thegiin.org/cgi-bin/iowa/resources/research/625.html.

Speckbacher, G., J. Bischof, and T. Pfeiffer. 2003. "A Descriptive Analysis on the Implementation of Balanced Scorecards in German-Speaking Countries." *Management Accounting Research* 14: 361–87.

Srikanth, K., and P. Puranam. 2014. "The Firm as a Coordination System: Evidence from Software Services Offshoring." *Organization Science* 25 (4): 1253–71. http://dx.doi.org/10.1287/orsc.2013.0886.

Stachowiak, S. 2013. *Pathways for Change: 10 Theories to Inform Advocacy and Policy Change Efforts.* Center for Evaluation Innovation and ORS Impact. http://www.evaluationinnovation.org/publications/pathways-change-10-theories-inform-advocacy-and-policy-change-efforts.

Stone, M. M., B. C. Crosby, and J. M. Bryson. 2010. "Governing Public-Nonprofit Collaborations: Understanding Their Complexity and the Implications for Research." *Voluntary Sector Review* 1 (3): 309–34.

Stone, M. M., and S. Cutcher-Gershenfeld. 2001. "Challenges of Measuring Performance in Nonprofit Organizations." In *Measuring the Impact of the Nonprofit Sector*, edited by P. Flynn and V. A. Hodgkinson, 33–57. New York: Kluwer Academic/Plenum.

Suchman, E. A. 1967. *Evaluative Research: Principles and Practice in Public Service and Social Action Programs.* New York: Russell Sage Foundation.

Sund, B., L. Svensson, M. Rosenqvist, and J. Hollenberg. 2011. "Favorable Cost-Benefit in an Early Defibrillation Programme Using Dual Dispatch of Ambulance and Fire Services in Out-of-Hospital Cardiac Arrest." *European Journal of Health Economics* 13 (6): 811–18.

Táutiva, A. A., and R. O. Olaya. 2013. *Bogotá IEMS City Report: Waste Pickers in Bogotá.* Cooperative Association of Waste Pickers of Bogotá (ARB) and Women in Informal Employment Globalizing and Organizing (WIEGO). http://www.inclusivecities.org/es/emei/emei-bogota/.

Teles, D., and M. Schmitt. 2011. "The Elusive Craft of Evaluating Advocacy." *Stanford Social Innovation Review* 4 (Summer): 39–43.

Thompson, J. D. 1967. *Organizations in Action.* New York: McGraw-Hill.

Thompson, J. D., and A. Tuden. 1959. "Strategies, Structures, and Processes of Organizational Decision." In *Comparative Studies in Administration*, edited by J. D. Thompson, P. B. Hammond, R. W. Hawkes, B. H. Junker, and A. Tuden, 195–216. Pittsburgh: University of Pittsburgh Press.

Tierney, T. J., and J. L. Fleishman. 2011. *Give Smart: Philanthropy That Gets Results.* New York: Public Affairs.

Trelstad, B. 2008. "Simple Measures for Social Enterprise." *Innovations* 3 (3): 105–18.

Tsemberis, S., and R. F. Eisenberg. 2000. "Pathways to Housing: Supported Housing for Street-Dwelling Homeless Individuals with Psychiatric Disabilities." *Psychiatric Services* 51 (4): 487–93.

Tuan, M. T. 2008. *Measuring and/or Estimating Social Value Creation: Insights Into Eight Integrated Cost Approaches.* Impact Planning and Improvement, Bill and Melinda Gates Foundation. http://www.gatesfoundation.org/learning/Documents/WWL-report-measuring-estimating-social-value-creation.pdf.

Tuckman, H. T., and C. F. Chang. 2006. "Commercial Activity, Technological Change, and Nonprofit Mission." In *The Nonprofit Sector: A Research Handbook*, edited by W. W. Powell and R. Steinberg, 629–44. New Haven, CT: Yale University Press.

Tuertscher, P., R. Garud, and A. Kumaraswamy. 2014. "Justification and Interlaced Knowledge at ATLAS, CERN." *Organization Science* 25 (6): 1579–608.

Twersky, F., P. Buchanan, and V. Threlfall. 2013. "Listening to Those Who Matter Most, the Beneficiaries." *Stanford Social Innovation Review* (Spring).

United Nations. 1991. *The World's Women 1970–1990: Trends and Statistics.* (ST/ESA/STAT/SER.K/8). New York: United Nations.

United Nations. 1995. *The World's Women 1995: Trends and Statistics.* (ST/ESA/STAT/SER.K/12). New York: United Nations.

United Way of America. 1996. Outcome Measurement Resource Network. http://www.liveunited.org/Outcomes/Resources/What/why.cfm.

United Way of America. 2000. *Agency Experiences with Outcome Measurement: Survey Findings (Report 0196).* Alexandria, VA: United Way of America.

Urban Institute. 2006. *Building a Common Outcome Framework to Measure Nonprofit Performance.* Washington, DC, and Chicago, Illinois: Urban Institute and Center for What Works.

Urban Institute. 2016. Performance Measurement and Management. http://www.urban.org/policy-centers/cross-center-initiatives/performance-measurement-and-management/publications.

USICH. 2010. *Opening Doors: Federal Strategic Plan to Prevent and End Homelessness.* Washington, DC: United States Interagency Council on Homelessness.

Vakil, A. C. 1997. Confronting the Classification Problem: Toward a Taxonomy of NGOs. *World Development* 25 (12): 2057–70.

Vanek, J., M. A. Chen, F. Carré, J. Heintz, and R. Hussmanns. 2014. *Statistics on the Informal Economy: Definitions, Regional Estimates and Challenges.* WIEGO Working Paper (Statistics) No. 2. http://www.wiego.org/sites/default/files/publications/files/Vanek-Statistics-WIEGO-WP2.pdf.

Vanek, J., M. A., Chen, and G. Raveendran. 2015. *A Guide to Obtaining Data on Types of Informal Workers in Official Statistics: Domestic Workers, Home-Based Workers, Street Vendors and Waste Pickers.* WIEGO Statistical Brief No. 8. http://www.wiego.org/sites/default/files/publications/files/Vanek-Guide-Obtaining-Data-Informal-Workers-WIEGO-SB8.pdf.

Verma, S., S. Krishnan, and N. Joshi. 2011. *The Impact of AKRSP(I)'s Work in the Meghal River Basin, Junagadh: A Socio-Technical Analysis.* Ahmedabad, Gujarat: Aga Khan Rural Support Programme, India.

Victor, B., and R. S. Blackburn. 1987. "Interdependence: An Alternative Conceptualization." *Academy of Management Review* 12 (3): 486–98.

Virtanen, P., and P. Uusikylä. 2004. "Exploring the Missing Links between Cause and Effect: A Conceptual Framework for Understanding Micro-Macro Conversions in Programme Evaluation." *Evaluation* 10 (1): 77–91.

Vurro, C., M. T. Dacin, and F. Perrini. 2010. "Institutional Antecedents of Partnering for Social Change: How Institutional Logics Shape Cross-Sector Social Partnerships." *Journal of Business Ethics* 94: 39–53.

W. K. Kellogg Foundation. 2004. *Logic Model Development Guide.* Battle Creek, MI: W. K. Kellogg Foundation. https://www.wkkf.org/resource-directory/resource/2006/02/wk-kellogg-foundation-logic-model-development-guide.

Weber, E. P. 2003. *Bringing Society Back In: Grassroots Ecosystem Management, Accountability, and Sustainable Communities.* Cambridge, MA: MIT Press.

Wei-Skillern, J., and S. Marciano. 2008. "The Networked Nonprofit." *Stanford Social Innovation Review* (Spring): 38–43.

Weinstein, M. M. 2009. *Measuring Success: How Robin Hood Estimates the Impact of Grants (with C.E. Lamy).* New York: Robin Hood Foundation.

Weinstein, M. M., and R. M. Bradburd. 2013. *The Robin Hood Rules for Smart Giving.* New York: Columbia Business School Publishing.

Weir, A., D. Buddenberg, K. Bhatia, and N. Mountstephens. 1995. *Joint Monitoring Mission 1995: Draft Report, Community Management of Natural Resources (ALA/93/33).* New Delhi: Commission of the European Communities, Aga Khan Foundation.

Weir, A., and P. Shah. 1994. *Report of the Baseline Monitoring Mission: Community Management of Natural Resources (ALA/93/33).* New Delhi: Commission of the European Communities, Aga Khan Foundation.

Weisbrod, B. A. 1988. *The Nonprofit Economy.* Cambridge, MA: Harvard University Press.

Weisbrod, B. A. 2004. "The Pitfalls of Profits." *Stanford Social Innovation Review* 2 (3): 40–47.

Weiss, C. 1972. *Evaluation Research. Methods for Assessing Program Effectiveness.* Englewood Cliffs, NJ: Prentice-Hall.

Weiss, C. 1995. "Nothing as Practical as Good Theory: Exploring Theory-Based Evaluation for Comprehensive Community Initiatives for Children and Families." In *New Approaches to Evaluating Community Initiatives*, edited by J. Connell, A. Kubisch, L. Schorr, and C. Weiss. Washington, DC: Aspen Institute.

White, H. 2006. *Impact Evaluation: The Experience of the World Bank*. Washington, DC: World Bank.

White, H. 2009. "We All Agree We Need Better Evidence. But What Is It and Will It Be Used?" In *Better Evidence for a Better World*, Working Paper 2, edited by M. W. Lipsey and E. Noonan. New Delhi: International Initiative for Impact Evaluation. http://www.3ieimpact.org/media/filer/2012/05/07/Working _Paper_2.pdf.

Whitehurst, G. J., and M. Croft. 2010. *The Harlem Children's Zone, Promise Neighborhoods, and the Broader, Bolder Approach to Education*. Washington, DC: Brookings Institution, Brown Center on Education Policy.

Whittle, D. 2013. *How Feedback Loops Can Improve Aid (and Maybe Governance)*. Washington, DC: Center for Global Development. http://www.cgdev.org/ publication/how-feedback-loops-can-improve-aid.

WIEGO. 1997. *Women Workers in the Informal Sector: Report of a Strategic Planning Meeting, Rockefeller Study and Conference Centre, Bellagio, Italy, April 15–18th, 1997*. http://www.wiego.org/sites/wiego.org/files/reports/files/BELLAGIO %20REPORT%201997.pdf.

WIEGO. 2013. *WIEGO 5-Year Strategic Plan, April 2013–March 2018*.

WIEGO. 2015a. *Better OHS for Market Traders adn Street Vendors in Accra, Ghana*. http://www.wiego.org/sites/default/files/publications/files/WIEGO-Accra -Case-Study-Summary-2015.pdf.

WIEGO. 2015b. *Waste Pickers in Bogotá, Colombia; Informal Economy Monitoring Study, Executive Summary (English)*. http://www.inclusivecities.org/es/emei/emei -bogota/.

Wilson-Grau, R., and H. Britt. 2012. *Outcome Harvesting*. Cairo: Ford Foundation, MENA Office. http://outcomeharvesting.net/wp-content/uploads/2016/07/ Outcome-Harvesting-Brief-revised-Nov-2013.pdf?189db0.

Woods, N. 2001. "Making the IMF and the World Bank More Accountable." *International Affairs* (January).

Young, D. R., and L. M. Salamon. 2002. "Commercialization, Social Ventures, and For-Profit Competition." In *The State of Nonprofit America*, edited by L. M. Salamon. Washington, DC: Brookings Institution.

ZHL. 2015. *Annual Report 2014–15*. Mumbai, India: Ziqitza Health Care Limited. http://zhl.org.in/images/Annual Report_ 2014-2015.pdf.

ZHL. 2017. About 1298. http://1298.in/about_us.html.

ZHL. 2018. Ziqitza Health Care Limited, homepage. http://zhl.org.in.

INDEX

Page numbers followed by *f* or *t* indicate material in figures or tables.

www.ingramcontent.com/pod-product-compliance
Ingram Content Group UK Ltd.
Pitfield, Milton Keynes, MK11 3LW, UK
UKHW041855240225
455499UK00001B/10